Les Misérables

AN ADAPTED CLASSIC

Les Misérables

Victor Hugo

"… So long as ignorance and misery remain on earth, there shall be a need for books such as this."

GLOBE FEARON
Pearson Learning Group

Adaptor: Mary Ansaldo
Executive Editor: Virginia Seeley
Senior Editor: Jasper Jones
Art Director: Nancy Sharkey
Cover Design: Mike McIver Graphics
Cover Illustration and Interior Illustrations: Gershon Griffith
Production Manager: Winston Sukhnanand
Desk Top Specialist: Matthew Zuch
Marketing Manager: Margaret de Boer

ISBN 0-8359-0473-3
Printed in the United States of America

8 9 10 11 12 13   05 04 03 02

X 706388

1-800-321-3106
www.pearsonlearning.com

CONTENTS

Saint Denis and the Idyll of the Rue Plumet

Jean Valjean

ABOUT THE AUTHOR

Early Years and Writing

Victor Hugo is recognized as the most prominent writer in French literature of the 1800s. His works are important because of his greatness as a poet and prose writer. Also, his writings reflect the beliefs of the times.

Victor Hugo's father was an officer in the French Army during the age of Napoleon. He traveled with his father to Italy, Corsica, and Spain. In 1817, when he was fifteen years old, he won an award for poetry, which motivated him to become a writer. With his brothers, he began a magazine, but his father did not support his interest in writing. Still, he won awards for his work, and in 1822 King Louis XVIII granted him a small pension to do his work.

The same year that happened, he married his childhood sweetheart. Together they had four children, each born two years apart, from 1824 through 1830.

Hugo wrote many kinds of things, from lengthy novels to poetry and plays. One of his best-known novels, in addition to *Les Misérables*, is *The Hunchback of Notre Dame*, the story of Quasimodo, the bellringer at Notre Dame cathedral. Both novels have been made into movies several times. Now *Les Misérables* has won new fame as a musical stage show in cities around the world.

Politics and Exile

The years between 1841 and 1851 were important years in Victor Hugo's political education. He supported the monarchy of Louis Philippe (1830-1845).

During the Second Republic (1848-1851), he became committed to the democratic ideals he held for the rest of his life.

In 1851, it became clear to Hugo that Louis Napoleon, who had become president of the Republic, wanted to become emperor. As the nephew of Napoleon I, Louis Napoleon wanted to revive the splendor of the royal court and, along with it, dictatorial power. Strong in his democratic beliefs, Victor Hugo delivered an attack against the dictator in the National Assembly. Within several months, orders were issued for his arrest. Hugo fled to Belgium and finally settled on the British island of Guernsey in the English Channel. He was allowed to remain on Guernsey if he agreed to to stay out of England's foreign affairs.

Although his political activity was stopped, he wrote a great deal at that time. He had learned much about human nature, and he wrote about it, particularly in his poetry. He could have returned to France when Napoleon III (Louis) granted him amnesty. However, he vowed to be true to his conscience, and wrote "When Liberty returns, I shall return."

This decision gave him time to write *Les Misérables*, which was published in 1862. The original book, more than 1200 pages long, was immediately acclaimed as the novel of the century. His preface to the book (printed here on p. *x*) states his beliefs.

Return to France

In 1870, Hugo's predictions about Napoleon III came true. France was defeated in a war against Prussia, revolt broke out in Paris, and Louis Napoleon went into exile. Although Hugo returned in triumph, his nation in defeat saddened him. He tried to work for a just peace between France and Germany. Failing this, Hugo again left France and returned to Guernsey.

In 1873, Hugo again returned to France and was elected to the Senate three years later. He continued to publish, but these later works received less attention. When he died in 1883, his death was mourned by the nation. He left the following last testament:

I give 50,000 francs to the poor.

I wish to be carried to the cemetery
  in their hearse.

I refuse the prayers of all churches.

I believe in God.

PREFACE

So long as there shall exist, by reason of law and custom, a social condemnation which, in the face of civilization, artificially creates hells on earth, and complicates a destiny that is divine, with human fatality; so long as these three problems of the age—the degradation of man by poverty, the ruin of woman by starvation, and the dwarfing of childhood by physical and spiritual night—are not solved; so long as, in certain regions, social asphyxia shall be possible; in other words, and from a yet more extended point of view, so long as ignorance and misery remain on earth, there shall be a need for books such as this.

Hauteville House, 1862

ADAPTOR'S NOTE

In preparing this edition of *Les Misérables*, we have tried to include as much of Victor Hugo's great story as possible. We have modified some of Hugo's vocabulary and shortened and simplified many of his sentences and paragraphs. Certain French words, titles, and expressions have been retained to give the book a French flavor. They have been translated and explained in footnotes if an understanding of them is necessary to the story. The French names of the characters have been used, because most of them have no English equivalents.

HISTORICAL BACKGROUND
FOR THE NOVEL

Victor Hugo uses the history of France, from 1789 through the bloody uprisings in Paris in 1848, as a setting for *Les Misérables*. He describes the conflicts between the royalists and the revolutionaries, the bourgeoisie, or middle class, and the workers. In order to understand the setting of the novel better, some brief background may be helpful.

1789-1799: The French Revolution and After

On July 14, 1789, the people stormed and captured the Bastille, a fortress used a royal prison. This act symbolized the end of royal authority in France. King Louis XVI and his queen, Marie Antoinette, were executed in 1793. The people of France were bitterly divided between those who favored the former way (the Royalists) and those who believed in the ideals of the Revolution (the Republicans). The Republican ideals included freedom of expression, opinions, and religion, as well as equal treatment under the law. The French Republic was established in 1792.

From 1793 through 1795, the Convention governed France. During those years, France tried to export its political theories, and wars were waged against Germany and England. A terrible period called the Reign of Terror caused many people to abandon the Convention, so it gave over power to the Directory, which governed until 1799. France's wars of this time did have some success under Napoleon Bonaparte.

1800-1815: The Empire of Napoleon I

General Bonaparte overthrew the Directory in 1799, and his ambitions caused him to proclaim himself emperor in 1804. Under this First Empire, Napoleon conquered most of Europe. By 1810 about ten million people outside France were under French authority. However, in the winter of 1812, Napoleon led a disastrous expedition again Russia. Defeated, he left France in 1814 for the island of Elba. He returned the following year for "The Hundred Days," which ended when his army was defeated by the British on the battlefield of Waterloo in Belgium. This time Napoleon was exiled to the island of Saint Helena, in the Atlantic Ocean, where he died in 1821. Almost two million men had died in battle during the First Empire.

1815-1848: Restoration and July Monarchy

In reaction against the First Empire, the Bourbon royal family was restored to power. Louis XVIII, the brother of the executed Louis XVI, was a moderate king, who allowed some representation through a constitution. He reigned from 1815 through 1824. Charles X, succeeding Louis XVIII in 1824, tried to revoke the constitution and rule absolutely. A rebellion broke out in 1830, and at the end of three days, Charles abdicated. France began to face the Industrial Revolution.

Louis Philippe, a member of the royal family, was proclaimed king by the French Parliament. His greatest support came from the upper middle class, who had gained wealth and status from the industrialization of the country. Only those who could pay taxes were allowed to vote. Only about 200,000 of the thirty million French citizens were able to make their beliefs count.

Meanwhile the industrialization of France was creating a new class of working people. People began to flock to the cities seeking jobs and better living conditions. Their lives were hard, and riots and strikes broke out often. Victor Hugo describes the revolt of 1832 in this novel.

1848-1851: The Second Republic

Finally, after one street riot, Louis-Philippe left power, and the Second Republic came into being in February of 1848. Voting rights for all classes (of men) were declared, and reforms took place in working conditions. However, an economic depression occurred. Louis Napoleon Bonaparte was elected president of the Republic, promising order and stability. In June of 1848, the Paris workers revolted and were crushed by government troops. In December of 1851, Louis Napoleon dissolved the Assembly and named himself president for life. A year later, he named himself Napoleon III and proclaimed a Second Empire.

MAJOR CHARACTERS

Monseigneur Bienvenu ....the Bishop of Digne

Jean Valjean ....an escaped convict

Fantine ....an orphan girl

Felix Tholomyès...................Fantine's lover

Cosette.................the daughter of Fantine and Tholomyès

Monsieur Thénardier ....the keeper of an inn in Montfermeil

Madame Thénardier.......................his wife

Eponine and Azelma Thénardier ....their daughters

Monsieur Madeleine...............the mayor of Montreuil-sur-Mer

Javert...........................a police inspector in Montreuil-sur-Mer

Father Fauchelevant ....an old man

Father Champmathieu ....a petty thief

Boulatruelle...........................a road worker

Prioress of the Convent of the Petit Picpus

Madame Burgon ....the landlady of Gorbeau House

Gavroche ....an orphan of the streets

The Jondrettes ....a family of criminals

Monsieur Gillenormand...............a rich, conservative bourgeois

Marius Pontmercy ....his grandson

George Pontmercy............................Marius's father

Monsieur Mabeuf......................churchwarden at the Saint Sulpice church in Paris

Enjolas
Combeferre
Jean Prouvaire
Feuilly
Courfeyrac   } young
Bahorel   revolutionary
Lesgle (or Laigle) de Meaux,   intellectuals
    called Bossuet
Joly
Grantaire

Claquesous
Gueulemer   } four bandits
Babet   known as the
Monparnasse   Patron-Minette

Monsieur Leblanc ....Marius's name for
                              Jean Valjean

Fantine

1 *An Upright Man*

Monsieur Myriel—Monseigneur Bienvenu

In 1815 Monsieur Charles François-Bienvenu Myriel was the Bishop of Digne. Digne was a small town in which many tongues talked but few heads thought.

He lived with his unmarried sister, Mademoiselle Baptistine, and a servant, Madame Magloire. The sister was tall, thin, and "respectable." The housekeeper-maid was a plump, short, white-haired lady who bustled about, always out of breath.

The bishop was an extraordinarily unselfish man. When he saw the small size of the hospital next door as compared with his grand residence, he immediately switched living quarters. Of the allowance he received from the government and the town, he gave nearly all to the needy organizations, groups, and individuals in the community. Large sums of money passed through his hands. However, he did not change his way of life by adding the simplest luxury. He knew there was always more misery at the lower end than there was humanity at the top. So he gave away everything. He robbed himself to give to others. The poor in the community chose an affectionate name for him: Monseigneur Bienvenu. It pleased him: "I like the name," he said. "The 'welcome' of 'Bienvenu' balances the 'Monseigneur.'"

1

Good Bishop—Difficult Diocese

Although he had given up his carriage, the bishop still made his visits to the people. He traveled on foot in nearby neighborhoods. In the mountains, he rode a mule. To those who were shocked at his means of transportation, he said, "I know you think it shows pride for a poor priest to use the same conveyance used by Jesus Christ. But I have done it from necessity, I assure you, not from vanity."

On his visits, he was gentle and kind, and he preached much less than he talked. He made virtue accessible to everyone. He never used complicated examples to make a point. He would use the example of one region to explain something to another region. For example, if he saw that the needy were not being treated well, he would say, "Look at the people of Briançon. They have given the poor and widows the right to cut their meadow grasses three days before anyone else. When their houses are in ruins, they rebuild them free of charge. It is a countryside blessed by God. For a century they have had no murderers." In villages where there was no schoolmaster, he would cite the example of a nearby town: "Do you know what they do?" he would ask. "Since small districts cannot always afford a teacher, the salary is paid by the whole valley. Then the schoolmaster goes from place to place, teaching a week in one town—ten days in another. The teachers wear quills in their hat bands. Those who teach reading wear one. Those who teach reading and mathematics wear two; and those who teach reading, arithmetic, and Latin wear three. They are considered great scholars! But what a shame to be ignorant! Do what those people do."

Works to Match Words

He would talk like that, in a fatherly manner, using lots of images. His conversation was cheerful and pleasant. He adapted himself to the level of the two women who lived with him. But when he laughed, it was the laugh of a schoolboy. Madame Magloire sometimes called him "Your Highness." One day, getting up from his chair, he went to his library shelf for a book. It was on one of the upper shelves, and—since the bishop was rather short—he could not reach it. "Madame Magloire," he asked, "bring me a chair, please. My highness can't reach that shelf."

He called upon the rich to give alms to the poor if they wanted to escape the tortures of hell (which he described in fearful colors) and enter paradise (which he depicted as desirable and inviting).

He behaved the same with the rich as he did with the poor.

He condemned nothing hastily. He always considered the circumstances. He would say, "Let's see how the fault crept in." Being himself an ex-sinner, he believed in a philosophy which went something like this:

"We humans have a body which is both a burden and a temptation. We drag it along and give in to it. We ought to watch over it and keep it in bounds. To commit the least possible sin is the law for a human. To live entirely without sin is the dream of an angel. To be a saint is the exception. The rule is to be upright. Err, sin, falter—but always be upright.

"Teach the ignorant as much as you can. Society is guilty in not providing universal free education, and it must answer for the night it produces. If the soul is left in darkness, sins will be committed. The guilty one is not the person who commits the sin, but the one who causes the darkness."

He had his own strange way of judging things.

One day he heard the story of a criminal case to be tried. A poor man—out of love for a woman and their child—had been making counterfeit coins, his real money gone. (At that time, counterfeiting was punishable by death.) The woman was arrested for passing the first piece he made. She was held in prison, but there was no proof against her lover. She alone could testify against him and, if she did, would risk losing him. She denied his guilt and would not change her story. Frustrated, the king's prosecutor made a plan. He told her the man was unfaithful and produced pieces of some forged letters. Filled with jealousy, the woman denounced the man and confessed everything. Now he was to be tried along with her in a few days. The story was told and retold, and everyone was delighted by the prosecutor's clever trick. By bringing jealousy into play, he used anger to produce the truth. Justice had sprung from revenge. The bishop listened to the story in silence; then he asked, "Where are the man and woman to be tried?"

"At the Superior Court."

"And where is the king's prosecutor to be tried?"

Another time, the bishop went to pray with a man who had been condemned to death for murder. He spent all day with the poorly educated man—talking, encouraging, consoling. The next day, when they came for the man, the bishop was with him—side by side with the miserable creature bound with ropes. He climbed onto the cart with him and up onto the scaffold.

For the bishop, the sight of the guillotine[1] was a shock. The scaffold has a strange effect on one when it

---

1. **guillotine** machine for beheading people, used commonly during the French Revolution (1789) and the years following

is set up and ready. We may be indifferent to the death penalty or not declare an opinion—either way, so long as we have not seen a guillotine with our own eyes. But when we do, the shock is violent, and we choose sides, for or against. It is not a neutral thing. Whoever sees it is shaken to the core. It seems like some creature whose dark origins we cannot comprehend. The terrible sight of the scaffold mixes with the work it does. It becomes a kind of monster created by a carpenter and a judge. And the impression is both horrible and deep.

For days the bishop seemed overwhelmed by the experience. One evening his sister overheard him mutter, "I didn't believe it could be so monstrous. It's wrong to be so absorbed in divine laws that we do not see human laws. Death belongs to God alone. By what right do humans touch that unknown thing?"

With time, the impressions probably faded and disappeared. However, after that, the bishop always avoided passing the execution square.

What He Believed

Before such a soul as the Bishop of Digne, we are inclined to feel only respect. The conscience of an upright person should be taken for granted. Moreover, given his nature, we understand that all the beauties of human virtue can develop in a faith different from our own. The secrets of all of his innermost beliefs are not known to us. But it is sure that his beliefs never resulted in hypocrisy. He believed as much as he could. *Credo in Patrem,*[2] he often exclaimed: "Thou art with God."

It could be said, however, that the bishop had an excess of love. For that, he was considered vulnerable

---

2. ***Credo in Patrem*** Latin for "Believe in the Father"

by "serious men," "sober persons," "reasonable people."
What was this excess? His was a calm goodness, going
beyond humans, extending to lifeless things. He
indulged every creation of God. One morning in his garden, his sister saw him stop and look at something on
the ground. It was a large, black, hairy, horrible-looking
spider. He said, "Poor thing! It's not his fault!" Another
day, he sprained an ankle rather than crush an ant.

So lived this upright man. According to accounts of
his youth and early manhood, he had been a passionate, even violent, man. His universal tenderness was
the result of a strong conviction filtered through life
into his heart. A character, as well as a rock, may
have holes worn into it by drops of water. Such marks
are permanent, indestructible.

When the bishop talked with the childlike joy that
was one of his charms, everyone felt at ease in his
presence. Joy radiated from his whole being. His
ruddy complexion and white teeth, all of which were
well preserved for his seventy-five years—and which
showed when he laughed—gave him an open, easy air
that makes us say of someone: "He is a good fellow,"
and of an old man: "He is a good man." Respect for
him penetrated by degrees and made its way to your
heart. You felt you had before you one of those strong,
tested, forgiving souls where the thought is so great it
can only be gentle.

Sometimes late at night, if the two women who lived
with the bishop were awake, they could hear him walking the garden paths slowly. He would be there by himself: composed, tranquil, comparing the calmness of
his heart with the calmness of the skies. At such times
he felt something floating away from him and something else descending upon him. It was one of those
mysterious exchanges of the soul with the universe.

He would contemplate the grandeur and presence of God. He did not study Him; he was dazzled by Him. He reflected on the magnificent union of atoms which give visible forms to Nature. These unions form and dissolve continually, and from them come life and death.

What else did this old man need? This narrow enclosure with the sky for a backdrop was space enough for him to adore God in His most beautiful works. Is that not everything? A little garden to walk in and the universe to reflect on. At his feet something to gather; above his head something to study and meditate on. A few flowers on earth and all the stars in heaven.

What He Thought

Monseigneur Bienvenu was not a genius. He was not a prophet or a magician. He depended on the Gospels. He loved and he was a humble soul. That was enough. He was always busy finding for himself and inspiring in others the best ways of sympathizing and comforting. He saw the world as a permanent subject of sadness waiting to be consoled.

"Love one another." He declared that in order to feel complete. He desired nothing else. It was his whole doctrine. He shut himself up in it. He lived it. He was absolutely satisfied with it. He knew there were other mysteries of the universe—human destiny, good and evil, the conscience of man, death, the soul, nature, liberty, necessity, difficult problems, and others. Monseigneur Bienvenu was simply a man who accepted these mysteries without examining them or troubling his mind about them. He had in his soul a deep respect for the mystery that surrounded them.

2 *The Fall*

The Night after a Day's Walk

It was an hour before sunset on an October day in 1815. A man traveling on foot entered the little town of Digne. The few people who were at their windows or doors viewed the traveler with distrust. He was medium height, stout and hardy; he must have been about forty-six or -seven years old. A leather cap half hid his face, which was burned by the sun and wind and dripping with sweat. His chest showed through the coarse yellow shirt, and he wore a tie twisted like a rope, and rough blue trousers. They were worn and shabby, white on one knee and torn on the other. His gray jacket was ragged and patched on one side with a piece of green cloth sewn with string. On his back he carried a filled knapsack, tightly buckled and new. In his hand he carried an enormous gnarled stick. He wore no stockings in his hob-nailed shoes. His hair was cut short and his beard long.

The sweat, the heat, his long walk, and the dust added an unclean quality to his tattered appearance.

Nobody knew him; he was evidently a traveler. He must have been walking all day long, for he seemed very weary. He stopped to drink at the fountain at the end of the Boulevard Gassendi. He must have been very thirsty, because he stopped again two hundred steps farther on and drank again at the market-place fountain.

When he reached the corner of the Rue Poichevert, he turned left and went toward the mayor's office. He went in, and fifteen minutes later he emerged.

The traveler headed toward the inn, which was said to be the best for miles around, and he immediately went into the kitchen. All the stoves were burning, and there was a great fire in the fireplace. The host—who was also the cook—heard the door open and said without looking up, "What will Monsieur have?"

"Something to eat and a room."

"Nothing easier," said the host, but upon seeing the traveler he added, "for pay."

The man took a large leather purse from his pocket and answered, "I have money."

"Then," said the host, "I am at your service." But as he went back and forth he kept a careful eye on the traveler. When the man was warming himself with his back turned, the innkeeper took a pencil from his pocket and tore off a piece of newspaper that was lying nearby. He wrote a line or two, folded the paper, and handed the piece to a child who helped him in the kitchen. He whispered a word to the small boy, who ran off in the direction of the town hall.

The traveler, seeing none of this, inquired, "Is dinner almost ready?"

"Almost," the innkeeper replied.

The boy returned with the paper. The host, as someone who seemed to expect an answer, read the paper carefully; then he thought for a moment. Finally he stepped toward the traveler.

"Monsieur," he said, "I have no room for you."

"Why? Are you afraid I won't pay you? Do you want me to pay in advance? I have money, I tell you."

"It's not that. All the rooms are taken."

"Then put me in the stable," the man replied quietly.

"I cannot. The horses take up all the room."

"Well," the man answered, "a corner, with a bale of hay. We can see to that after dinner."

"I cannot give you any dinner."

This news was serious to the traveler. He got up.

"But I'm dying of hunger. I have been walking since sunrise. I have come thirty-five miles. I will pay, and I want something to eat."

"I have nothing," said the host.

"I am at an inn. I am hungry, and I will stay," declared the man. And he sat down again.

The innkeeper leaned over him and said, in a voice that made him tremble, "Go away!"

At these words, the traveler turned and opened his mouth as if to reply. The host, looking steadily at the traveler, added in the same low voice, "Stop. Enough of this. I know you are Jean Valjean. When I saw you come in, I suspected something. I sent to the mayor's office, and here is the reply."

Saying that, he held out the paper. The man glanced at it. After a minute, the innkeeper said, "It is my custom to be polite to everyone. Now go!"

The man bowed his head, picked up his knapsack, and went out.

He took the main street and walked without direction, slinking near the houses like a sad, humiliated animal. He did not turn around. If he had, he would have seen the innkeeper standing in his doorway with all his guests and the passersby gathered around him. They spoke excitedly and pointed at him. From the looks of fear and distrust that were exchanged, he would have known that before long his arrival would be the talk of the town.

He walked this way for some time, forgetting his fatigue, as happens with sorrow. Suddenly he felt a pang of hunger. Night was coming, and he needed some lodging. He dared not try the other inns.

He noticed he was passing the prison. An iron chain hung from the door and was attached to a bell. He rang.

The grating opened.

"Jailer," he said, respectfully removing his cap, "would you open up and let me spend the night?"

A voice answered, "A prison is not a tavern. Get yourself arrested and we'll gladly take you in."

The grating closed.

He wandered into a small street where there were many gardens, some of them enclosed only by low shrubs which brightened up the street. Night was falling, and the cold Alpine winds were blowing. By the dying light, the stranger saw, in one of the gardens facing the street, a kind of shed that seemed to be covered with earth. He boldly scaled a fence and found himself in the garden. He neared the shed. It had a low, narrow entrance, like the ones that road workers put up for temporary shelter. These huts are usually not occupied at night. He crawled in. It was warm and had a good bed of straw. He rested for a moment, motionless from fatigue. Then, thinking his knapsack would make a fine pillow, he began to unbuckle the straps. Just then, he heard a ferocious growl. Looking up, he saw the head of an enormous bulldog at the opening of the hut.

It was a kennel!

Fortunately he was agile in spite of the fatigue. He seized his stick, made a shield of his knapsack, and got out of the hut as best he could. Even so, he did not escape over the fence without enlarging the rips in his already tattered clothes.

It was about eight o'clock in the evening. He again wandered, not knowing the streets.

Soon he came to the cathedral square. He shook his fist at the church. But, exhausted, he lay down on one of the stone benches.

Just then an old woman came out of the church. She saw him and asked, "What are you doing there, friend?"

He replied harshly and angrily, "As you can see, my good woman, I'm trying to sleep."

"On the bench?" she asked.

"For nineteen years I've had a wooden mattress," said the man. "Tonight I have a stone one."

"You were a soldier?"

"Yes, my good woman, I was a soldier."

"Why don't you go to the inn?"

"Because I have no money."

"You must be very cold and hungry. They should give you food and lodging out of charity."

"Well, I have knocked on every door. And everyone has driven me away."

"You have knocked on every door?" the woman asked.

"Yes."

"Have you knocked on that one over there?" the woman asked, pointing to a little house beside the bishop's palace.

"No."

"Knock there."

Cautionary Advice to the Wise

Mademoiselle Baptistine often told what happened at the bishop's house that night. Many still recall the tiniest details of the story.

At eight o'clock the bishop was still at work. He was writing on small slips of paper, holding a large book open on his knees, when Madame Magloire came in to get the silver from the cupboard near the bishop's bed. A moment later the bishop closed his book and went into the dining room. He knew that the table would be laid for supper and that his sister was probably waiting.

As the bishop entered the room, Madame Magloire was speaking vivaciously. She was talking to Mademoiselle about a familiar subject. The bishop was used to the topic. It concerned a way to lock the front door.

It seems that while Madame was shopping for supper she had heard news of an evil-looking runaway in the town. There was a suspicious tramp who had arrived and was lurking somewhere. Unpleasant adventures might happen to someone coming home late at night. It was up to the intelligent people to protect themselves. Everybody should be careful to shut up, bolt, and bar their doors properly.

The bishop, having come into the warm room, sat down in front of the fire and thought of other things. He made an absentminded query to Madame's comments.

"Monseigneur, it's true. Something will happen tonight in this town. I say this house is not safe. We must have bolts, if only for tonight. Nothing is worse than a door that can be opened by any visitor. And the Monseigneur has the habit of saying, 'Come in!' even at midnight. My heavens! There's no need even to ask permission . . . ."

At that precise moment, there was a violent knock on the door.

"Come in!" called the bishop.

The Heroism of Passive Obedience
The door opened. It opened quickly, quite wide, as if

pushed boldly and energetically.

A man entered. It was the traveler we saw wandering in search of food and shelter.

He came in, took a step, and paused. Knapsack on his back and stick in hand, he had a rough, hard, tired, and fierce look in his eyes. By the firelight, he looked hideous and sinister.

Madame Magloire did not have enough strength to scream. She stood trembling, her mouth open.

Mademoiselle Baptistine started up half alarmed. Then she slowly turned back toward the fire, looked at her brother, and resumed her usual serene posture.

The bishop gazed calmly at the man.

He was opening his mouth to speak when the man said loudly, "Look here! My name is Jean Valjean. I was a convict. I have spent nineteen years in prison. Four days ago I was freed and started out for Pontarlier. For four days I have been walking from Toulon. Today I walked thirty-five miles. When I reached this place tonight I went to an inn. They sent me away because of the yellow passport which I had shown at the mayor's office, as the law requires. They said, 'Get out!' Nobody would have me. I went to the prison, and the jailer wouldn't let me in. I crept into a kennel, and the dog bit me and chased me away. I sought shelter in doorways. In the square I was resting on a stone bench when a good woman pointed out your house and said, 'Knock there.' I have money. I'll pay. I'm so tired . . . and so hungry. Will you let me stay?"

"Madame Magloire," said the bishop, "another place at the table, please."

"Everybody else has thrown me out. Will you take me in? Is this an inn? Can you give me something to eat? A place to sleep? Do you have a stable?"

"Madame Magloire," said the bishop, "put some

sheets on the bed in the alcove."

"It's nineteen years since I've slept in a bed. You're really going to let me stay? You're good people! Besides, I have money. I'll pay well—whatever you say. What's your name? You're an innkeeper, aren't you?"

"I am the priest who lives here," said the bishop.

Madame Magloire brought the silver and set it on the table.

"Madame," said the bishop, "set the places as near the fire as you can." Then facing his guest, he added, "The night wind is raw in the Alps.[1] You must be cold, monsieur."

To be called *monsieur* in this gentle and hospitable voice, was to a convict like water to a man dying of thirst at sea.

"Monsieur Curé," said the man, "you are truly good. You take me into your house, even after I tell you how miserable I am."

The bishop touched the man's hand lightly and said, "You didn't have to tell me who you are. And this is not my house; it is Christ's. It does not ask any guest his name, only whether he is suffering. You are hungry and tired, and you are welcome. You, a traveler, are more at home here than I. Whatever is here is yours. And I knew your name before you told it. Your name is my brother."

Madame Magloire served up supper. It consisted of soup made from water, oil, bread and salt; a little pork; a scrap of mutton; a few figs; a green cheese; and a large loaf of rye bread. On her own she added a bottle of fine old wine.

---

1. **Alps** the major mountain range in Europe, separating France from Italy

"Do be seated!" the bishop said eagerly. As he did whenever he had a guest, the bishop seated the traveler on his right. Mademoiselle Baptistine, as accommodating as usual, sat on his left.

Tranquility

After supper, the bishop said goodnight to his sister and took one of the silver candlesticks from the table. He handed the other one to his guest and said, "Monsieur, let me show you to your room."

The man followed him. They made their way through the bishop's bedroom to the alcove in the oratory.[2] Madame Magloire was putting away the silver in the cupboard at the head of the bishop's bed, as she did every night before going to sleep.

The bishop left his guest in the alcove, in front of a clean white bed. "So now!" said the man. "You let me stay in your house, so near to you! How do you know I am not a murderer?"

The bishop replied, "God will take care of that."

A moment later he was walking in the garden contemplating the great and mysterious works that God shows at night to eyes that are open.

As for the man, he did not even use the clean white sheets. He collapsed onto the bed, fully dressed, and fell into a sound sleep.

Jean Valjean

Jean Valjean was born into a poor peasant family in the Brie[3] region. He lost his parents when he was very young. His mother died of a milk fever; his

---

2. **oratory** small room, or chapel, for praying
3. **Brie** district of northeastern France famous for cheese of the same name

father, a pruner, was killed when he fell from a tree he was working on. An older sister, with seven children of her own, brought up Jean. When she was widowed with her youngest one year old, only Jean—at twenty-five—took on the responsibility of the family. He was never known to have a sweetheart; he did not have time to be in love.

He did whatever work he could find to do. His sister worked, too, but with seven children they were a sad group. One bad winter, Jean had no work, and the family had no bread. Literally no bread, and seven children.

Maubert Isabeau, the baker on the Place de l'Église, was just going to bed when he heard a crash against the barred window of his shop. He arrived downstairs just in time to see an arm thrust through the opening made by the blow of a fist against the glass. The arm grabbed one loaf of bread and took it. Isabeau rushed out. The thief was running away at top speed. Isabeau pursued and caught him. The thief had thrown away the bread, but his arm was still bleeding.

This happened in 1795. Jean Valjean was charged with "burglary at night, in an inhabited house." He also had a gun, which made things worse.

He was found guilty. The penal code was explicit. He was sentenced to five years in prison, and he was shackled at the end of a chain. Probably, to a poor and ignorant man, the penalty seemed excessive. As they riveted the bolt of his iron collar behind his head, he wept. Sobbing, he raised his hand and lowered it seven times, as if touching seven heads of different heights. From this gesture one could guess that what he had done had been done to feed seven little children.

He was taken to Toulon, a journey of twenty-seven days, on a cart, with the chain still around his neck. At Toulon, he was dressed in the red prison uniform. He was no longer Jean Valjean; he became Number 24,601. While at Toulon, he heard once about his sister. I think it was at the end of his fourth year of prison. The news reached him somehow that she was in Paris, living on a poor street. Only the youngest child was with her. Where the other six were, no one knew. Perhaps even she did not know.

Nothing more ever reached him.

Near the end of his fourth year, Jean Valjean had a chance for freedom. He escaped, and for two days he wandered through the fields, nervous and without sleeping or eating for thirty-six hours. The evening of the second day he was captured. They extended his sentence three years for the escape, making his sentence eight years. In the sixth year he tried again to escape but failed. This was punishable by an additional five years. Thirteen years. The tenth year he made another escape attempt without success. Three more years. Sixteen. Finally, I think it was in his thirteenth year, he made yet another escape and was recaptured after only four hours. Three years for those four hours. Nineteen years. In October 1815, he was freed. He had entered prison in 1796 for breaking a pane of glass and taking a loaf of bread.

Profoundest Despair

Jean Valjean entered prison sobbing and trembling; he left hardened. He entered in despair; he left sullen.

What happened to him in prison?

Jean Valjean thought about his crime. He admitted he had done wrong. Then he asked himself if he was the only one to have done wrong in his case. In the first place, was it not a serious thing that he, a work-man, was not able to find work and that he, an indus-trious man, was without bread? Moreover, since he had confessed, was the punishment not excessive? Was this not a crime of society upon the individual? An outrage of stronger people upon weaker ones? Was it not outrageous that society should be so intolerant of those who were poorest and therefore most deserv-ing of tolerance?

With these questions asked and answered, he con-demned society. And he sentenced it with his hatred.

Anger may be foolish and absurd, and one may be wrongly angered. But a person does not feel outraged unless, in some way, he is fundamentally right. Jean Valjean felt outraged.

Society had done nothing to Jean Valjean except injury. No other human had ever touched him except to bruise him. Never, since infancy, since his mother and his sister, had he been greeted with a friendly look. He gradually concluded that life was a war and that he was the defeated. He had no weapon except hatred. He resolved to sharpen the weapon and take it with him when he left prison.

At Toulon, there was a school for the prisoners. Some rather ignorant friars taught the essentials to the poor men who wanted to learn. At forty, he went to school and learned to read, write, and do arithmetic. To increase his knowledge was to increase his hatred.

Sadly, after having tried and convicted society, he tried Providence, which had created society. He con-demned it as well.

Jean Valjean was not, as we have seen, born evil. He was still good when he arrived in prison. But, over the course of nineteen years, he had learned to hate human laws. That hatred had turned into a hatred of society, then of the human race. Finally it became a hatred of creation—revealing itself as a desire to injure some living being, no matter who.

The passport was correct in describing Jean Valjean as "a very dangerous man."

His soul had died. A dead soul is usually accompanied by a dry eye. When he left prison, he had not shed a tear for nineteen years.

There was one more important fact. In physical strength Jean Valjean far surpassed all other inmates of the prison. At hard work, he was equal to four men. He could hold enormous weights on his back. His agility was even greater than his strength. To scale a wall, finding footholds where you could hardly see a projection, was a game for Jean Valjean. Sometimes he would climb to the attic of the prison this way.

The Man Wakes Up

As the cathedral clock struck two, Jean Valjean awoke.

Strangely, what awakened him was too much comfort. The sensation of sleeping in a bed was too new not to disturb his sleep. He had slept for four hours. His fatigue was gone. He was not used to many hours of sleep.

He could not sleep again, so he began to think. Many thoughts came to him, but one kept appearing. The thought was this. He had noticed the silver place settings and the large spoon that Madame Magloire had put on the table. Those six silver sets obsessed him. There they were, just a few steps away.

The clock struck three. He sat up hurriedly in the bed and swung his feet to the floor. He stayed in that position while the clock struck each quarter hour. "Come on!" it seemed to be saying.

He stood up, hesitated, and listened. The house was still. He moved quietly toward the door to the next room which was the bishop's, as we know. When he reached the door, he found it ajar. The bishop had not closed it.

Jean Valjean listened. Not a sound.

He pushed open the door lightly with the tip of his fingers. The hinge made a creak in the darkness.

He stood still, not daring to stir. Nothing moved. Nobody had awakened.

With one step, he was inside the room. He advanced, carefully avoiding the furniture. At the far end of the room he could hear the quiet, even breathing of the sleeping bishop.

Suddenly he stopped. He was near the bed, sooner than he thought.

A ray of moonlight lit up the bishop's face. He slept peacefully. There was something divine in this man, something unconsciously noble.

He did not take his eyes off the old man. It was as if he were hesitating between two realms: the doomed and the saved. He seemed ready either to crack this skull or to kiss this hand.

Suddenly Jean Valjean moved quickly past the bed to the cupboard. He took the basket of silverware, crossed the room hurriedly, reached the door, and entered the oratory. He took his stick, stepped outside, put the silver in his knapsack, threw away the basket. He ran across the garden, leaped the wall like a tiger, and fled.

The Bishop at Work

"Monseigneur, the man is gone! The silver is stolen!" Madame Magloire's cry interrupted the bishop's walk in the garden.

The bishop was silent for a moment; then he said calmly to the woman, "Now first, did this silver belong to us?"

Madame Magloire was speechless. After a moment, the bishop continued, "For a long time I have wrongfully kept the silver. It belonged to the poor. And who was this man? A poor man, obviously."

Just then there was a knock on the door.

"Come in!" called the bishop.

The door opened for a strange and fierce group. Three men were holding a fourth by the collar. The three men were gendarmes;[4] the fourth, Jean Valjean.

"Monseigneur," said the man who seemed to head the group.

At this, Jean Valjean raised his head with a startled look. "Monseigneur!" he murmered.

"Silence!" said a gendarme. "It is his lordship, the bishop."

In the meantime, Monseigneur Bienvenu had approached. "Ah, there you are!" he said, looking at Jean Valjean. "I'm glad to see you. But I gave you the candlesticks, too. They are silver like the rest, and they would fetch two hundred francs. Why didn't you take them with your cutlery?"

Jean Valjean looked at the bishop with an indescribable expression.

The bishop went to the mantelpiece and took the two candlesticks down. He handed them to Jean Valjean. The two women observed without a word, gesture, or look.

Jean Valjean took the two silver pieces with trembling hands and a bewildered expression.

---

4. **gendarmes** policemen

"Now," said the bishop, "go in peace. And do not forget, ever, that you have promised me to use this silver to become an honest man."

Jean Valjean stood dumfounded as the bishop whispered in his ear, "My brother, you no longer belong to evil, but to good. It is your soul I am buying for you. And I give it to God!"

Mysterious Murmurs

When Jean Valjean left the bishop's house he was overwhelmed. His thoughts were unlike any he had ever known before. He understood nothing of what was going on inside him.

One thing was certain, although he did not know it. He was not the same person; everything had changed in him. It was not possible to prevent the bishop from having talked to him and touched him.

His conscience considered in turn these two men before it: the bishop and Jean Valjean. Only the first could have succeeded in softening the second. The bishop grew larger and larger. Jean Valjean shrank and faded away. Finally he disappeared. The bishop alone remained. He filled the whole soul of the miserable man with a magnificent radiance.

Jean Valjean wept for a long time.

While he wept, the light grew brighter and brighter. All of his wrongdoings appeared to him clearly, but in a light he had never seen before. He could see his life, and it seemed horrible. However, there was a gentler light shining on that life and soul.

How long did he weep? Where did he go? What did he do? Nobody ever knew. But that night the stage driver who arrived at Digne about three in the morning saw a man kneeling in prayer on the pavement before the door of Monseigneur Bienvenu.

3 The Year 1817

Double Quartet

In the year 1817 four young Parisians had a good laugh on four others.

The first four of these Parisians were students. To say students is to say Parisian. To study in Paris is to be born there. The four young men were insignificant—neither good nor bad.

The second four were girls. Fantine was the only one of the four girls who had been touched by one alone.

She was one of those beings who come from the heart of people, so to speak. She had never known her parents. She was born when the Revolutionary Directory[1] was still in power. She had no family name because she had no family. She had no baptismal name because there was no church at the time. She was named Fantine by someone who found her as an infant wandering barefoot in the streets. At fifteen Fantine came to Paris to "seek her fortune." She was beautiful, and she remained pure as long as possible. She was a pretty blonde with fine teeth. For a dowry she had gold and pearls. The gold was on her head and the pearls in her mouth.

Fantine loved Tholomyès.

---

1. **Directory** a group that ruled France after the Revolution, from 1795 until 1799

Tholomyès was an older student of the old style. He was rich and he lived high. He was thirty years old and in poor shape.

The four young men made a plan one day to take their girlfriends on a picnic in the country. And they promised the girls a surprise.

Bombarda's

The day of the picnic was sunshine from start to finish. Nature seemed to be on vacation. The flowers and lawns of Saint-Cloud were balmy and perfumed. The breeze from the Seine[2] stirred the leaves, and butterflies settled on the clover and wild oats.

The happy eight glowed in the sunshine, flowers, fields, and trees. Then they thought of dinner and, a little weary, ended up at Bombarda's, on the Champs-Elysées.[3] After dinner the girls inquired about the surprise.

"Precisely. The moment has come," replied Tholomyès. "Ladies, wait for us for a moment."

Each of the men placed a kiss on the forehead of his girlfriend. Then they went to the door, each one laying a finger on his lips.

"Don't be too long," murmured Fantine. "We're waiting for you."

"I wonder what they will bring us," Zéphine said.

"Let's hope it is something pretty," Dahlia said.

"Me, I hope it will be gold," Favourite replied.

Some time passed. Suddenly Favourite started.

"Well!" she said. "And the surprise?"

"Yes," returned Dahlia, "the famous surprise."

"They are taking a long time!" Fantine sighed.

---

2. **Seine** major river in France which flows through Paris
3. **Champs-Elysées** grand boulevard in Paris

The boy who had waited on them at dinner entered. He carried something that looked like a letter.

"The gentlemen left this for the ladies," he said. Favourite snatched the paper from his hands.

"There's no address, but look what is written"

"THIS IS THE SURPRISE."

She unsealed the letter, opened it, and read:

Dear Girls:

We have parents. As you read this, we will be on our way back to our papas and mamas. We are going; we are gone. We are returning to society, to duty and honor. Adieu.

For nearly two years you have made us happy.

Do not think badly of us for it.

Blacheville
Fameuil
Listolier
Tholomyès

P. S. Dinner is paid for.

The girls burst out laughing. Fantine laughed with the others, but an hour later, back in her room, she wept. Tholomyès had been her first love, and she was going to have his child.

4 *To Trust Is Sometimes to Surrender*

One Mother Meets Another

In 1818, at Montfermeil, near Paris, there was a cheap tavern which is no longer there. Above the door, nailed flat against the wall, was a board. At the base of it was this name: THE SERGEANT OF WATERLOO.

There was a fragment of a vehicle blocking the street in front of the Sergeant of Waterloo. Its bulk attracted the attention of passersby. It was the front part of one of those trolleys for carrying heavy articles, the kind used in wooded regions for carrying tree trunks. It consisted of a massive axletree[1] with two enormous wheels. Under the axletree hung a length of huge chain fit for a Goliath. The middle of the chain was hanging close to the ground, and upon it sat two little girls. The little one, eighteen months old, sat in the lap of the larger, who was two and a half years old.

The mother was sitting on the steps of the inn, swinging the two children by a long rope. At each swing, the links gave out a noise like an angry cry. The girls were in ecstasy. The mother sang a popular tune. Singing and watching the two children, she did not see anyone approach.

Suddenly a voice near her ear said, "You have two lovely children, madame."

---

1. **axeltree** bar with bearings on the end on which the wheels turn

The mother sang on but turned her head.

A woman was standing in front of her a few steps away. She also had a child, in her arms. The child was the loveliest creature imaginable, a little girl of two or three. She was asleep, comfortably.

As for the mother, she seemed poor and sad. She looked like a working woman ready to return to peasant life. She was young—and pretty? She was pale, and she looked very tired and somewhat sick. Her figure was covered by a large blue kerchief folded across her bosom. She was Fantine.

Ten months had slipped by since the "good joke." During those months, Fantine had sold all she had to pay her debts. One fine spring morning, at twenty-two years of age, she left Paris carrying her child on her back. She had nothing in the world except this child, and the child had nothing in the world but the woman.

And Félix Tholomyès? We will say only that twenty years later he was a fat provincial attorney, rich and powerful. But he was still, as always, a man of pleasure.

As Fantine passed by the inn, the two girls perched on the monstrous swing had a dazzling effect on her, and she stopped, as we have just read.

"My name is Thénardier," the woman said. "We run this inn."

The two women chatted, and Cosette awakened. Soon the three girls were grouped in an attitude of bliss. They watched a worm that had come out of the ground. Their foreheads touched.

"Children!" exclaimed Madame Thénardier. "How quickly they get to know one another. One would swear they were sisters!"

These words were the spark that the other mother was probably awaiting. She seized the hand of

Madame Thénardier and said, "Will you keep my baby for me?"

Madame Thénardier made a gesture of surprise, neither consenting nor refusing.

Cosette's mother continued. "You see, I can't take her into the country. The work doesn't allow it. With a child I couldn't find a job there. It is the good Lord that led me to your inn. The sight of your little ones, so pretty and clean and happy, overwhelmed me right away. I said to myself, 'There's a good mother. They'll be like three sisters. Then it won't be so long until I come back.' Will you keep my child for me?"

"I must think it over," said Madame Thénardier.

"I will pay six francs a month," said Fantine.

At this point, a man's voice was heard from within. "Not less that seven francs, and six months in advance."

The bargain was concluded. The mother spent the night at the inn, gave over her money, and left her child. She set off the next morning, expecting to return soon.

When she had left, the man said to his wife, "That's enough for my debt which falls due tomorrow. I was fifty francs short. Do you realize the sheriff would have come and they'd have brought charges against me? You've a good mousetrap with your little ones."

"Without even knowing it," the woman replied.

The Lark

Thanks to Fantine's money, Thénardier had been able to avoid a lawsuit. The next month when they were still in need of money, the woman took Cosette's clothes to Paris and pawned them.

There are some people who cannot love on one side without hating on the other. Madame Thénardier was such a person. She loved her own daughters so much that she detested the young stranger. She was unkind to her. So were Eponine and Azelma. The children were simply smaller copies of the mother.

From year to year the child grew, and her misery as well. She was the scapegoat of the other two. When she began to grow a little—that is to say, before she was five years old—she became the servant of the house. Cosette ran the errands, swept the rooms and yard, washed the dishes, and carried heavy loads. The Thénardiers felt doubly justified in treating Cosette this way when Fantine began to miss her monthly payments.

It was terrible to see the small child sweeping the street before daylight, in tattered clothes. In the neighborhood she was called the Lark. She was no larger than a bird, trembling and frightened, and the first to wake every morning before dawn.

Except that the Lark never sang.

5 The Descent

An Improvement in Making Jet Beads

After leaving her little Cosette with the Thénardiers, Fantine had gone on to Montreuil-sur-Mer.

For many years the occupation of the inhabitants of Montreuil-sur-Mer had been imitating English jet[1] beads and German black glass trinkets. The industry had been slow because of the high price of the raw material. At the time of Fantine's arrival in the city, a transformation had taken place. Toward the end of 1815, a stranger to the city had developed several processes for manufacturing better jewelry with cheaper raw materials.

These minor changes caused a revolution. The price of raw material was enormously reduced. This made it possible to raise the wages of the workers—a benefit to the district. It also improved the quality of the goods—a benefit to the consumer. Finally, it was possible to sell the beads at a lower price and three times the profit—a gain for the manufacturer.

In three years the inventor of this idea had become rich. And he made all those around him rich, which was better. He was a stranger. Nothing was known about where he came from or who he was. A man of about fifty, he always seemed preoccupied. That was all that could be said about him.

---

1. **jet** dense black coal that is polished and used as jewelry

In the five years since his arrival, the man—who had come to be called Father[2] Madeleine—had done such service for the region that the king appointed him mayor of the city. He refused, but the people begged him to accept. The insistence was so strong he finally yielded. Father Madeleine had become Monsieur Madeleine, and Monsieur Madeleine now became Monsieur the Mayor.

He remained a simple man. He led a solitary life. He loved books. Books are cold but sure friends. He read to cultivate his mind. It was noted that from year to year, his language became more polished and gentler.

He did a multitude of good deeds without attracting attention. He was good-natured and sad. People would say, "There's a rich man who does not show pride."

In early 1821, the newspapers announced the death of the Bishop of Digne, known as Monseigneur Bienvenu, at the age of eighty-two.

The announcement was carried in the local paper. M. Madeleine appeared next morning dressed in black, with a black band on his hat. One of the women in town ventured to ask him, "The mayor is a relative of the late Bishop of Digne?"

He replied, "No, Madame."

"But," the woman insisted, "you wear mourning clothes."

"In my youth," he answered, "I was a servant in his family."

Flashes on the Horizon

There came a time in 1821 when the words "Monsieur the Mayor" were said in Montreuil-sur-Mer in almost

---

2. **Father**   affectionate title of respect given for age or good acts

the same way as "Monsieur the Bishop" in Digne in 1815. People came from miles around to consult Father Madeleine. He settled differences, he prevented lawsuits, he reconciled enemies.

One man alone kept himself free from this contagious admiration for Monsieur Madeleine. Whatever Father Madeleine did, this man remained indifferent. It was as if an unchangeable instinct kept him awake and on the watch.

Often, when Monsieur Madeleine passed along the street, a tall man wearing a flat hat and an iron-gray coat and carrying a stout cane, would turn around behind him. He would follow him with his eyes until he disappeared.

This individual was Javert, and he was a policeman.

The peasants of the Asturias[3] believe that in every litter of wolves there is one pup that is killed by the mother for fear that it will kill the other ones as it grows up. Put a human face on this wolf's son, and you have Javert.

Javert was born in prison. His mother was a fortune teller. He grew up thinking he was outside of society, and he hated the gypsy race to which he belonged. He entered the police and succeeded. At forty years old he was an inspector.

Javert's face consisted of a snub nose with two deep nostrils, bordered by large bushy sideburns. When Javert laughed, which was rarely, thin lips parted, showing his teeth and gums. When serious, Javert was a bulldog. When he laughed, he was a tiger. His stare was cold and piercing. His whole life consisted of

---

3. **Asturias** region of northwestern Spain

watching and waiting. Woe to anyone who fell into his hands. He would have arrested his own father if he had escaped from prison. He would have turned in his mother for breaking parole. His life included no amusements. It was only duty.

Javert had a suspicious eye always fixed on M. Madeleine. Monsieur Madeleine finally noticed this, but he did not question Javert. He treated Javert as he did everyone, with ease and kindness.

One day, however, his strange behavior appeared to make an impression on M. Madeleine. The occasion was as follows:

One morning M. Madeleine was walking along an alley in Montreuil-sur-Mer. He heard a shout and, seeing a crowd gathered, he went over.   An old man named Father Fauchelevant had fallen under his cart, and his horse was lying on the ground. It had broken two thighs and could not get up. The old man was caught between the wheels. The cart was heavily loaded, and the whole weight rested on the man's chest.   They tried to pull him out but in vain. Any inexpert help, a false push, might have crushed him. It was impossible to get him out without raising up the cart from underneath. Javert, who had arrived at the moment of the accident, had sent for a jack.

"It's crushing me!" cried the old man.

Madeleine met the eagle eye of Javert watching him, and he smiled sadly. Then, without a word, he fell to his knees and went under the cart.

The bystanders held their breath. The wheels were still sinking, and it looked impossible for Madeleine to get out.

All at once the whole mass shook, the cart rose slowly, and the wheels came half way out of the ruts. Everybody rushed to help. The devotion of one man had given strength and courage to all. The cart was now lifted by twenty arms. Old Fauchelevant was saved.

Madeleine arose. He was very pale and dripping with sweat. His clothes were torn and covered with mud. The crowd was weeping. The old man kissed his knees. Madeleine himself had an expression of indescribable joy, and he looked calmly at Javert, who was still watching him.

Fauchelevent Becomes a Gardener and Fantine Becomes the Object of Maliciousness

Fauchelevent had broken his kneecap in the accident. More seriously, his cart was ruined and his horse was dead. Father Madeleine carried him to the infirmary he had set up for the workers of his factory. This infirmary was managed by two sisters of charity. The next morning the old man found a thousand-franc note by his bed and a note from Monsieur Madeleine. Through the help of the sisters, Father Madeleine had got the old man a job as gardener at a convent in the Saint Antoine Quarter in Paris.

There were many stories such as this one that referred to the benevolence of Monsieur the Mayor. In addition, thanks to his business sense, work was abundant and the countryside was rich and happy.

Such was the situation of the region when Fantine arrived. The door of M. Madeleine's factory was like the face of a friend. She went there and was admitted into the workshop for women. The business was new to Fantine, and she did not receive much pay right away. But the problem was solved; she was earning her living.

Fantine was filled with joy. She bought a mirror and was pleased with her lovely blond hair and her fine teeth. She was almost happy, except that she thought constantly of her daughter. She rented a small room and furnished it on credit.

Because she was not married, Fantine never spoke of Cosette, but she was sometimes observed weeping quietly at her work. She wrote often, and that was noticed. The other women began to whisper that she was odd, and that she "put on airs."

There are those people who take time and trouble, just for the pleasure of it, to satisfy their own curiosities. They will follow this person or that, ask questions of carriage drivers, or bribe porters. For what? For nothing. Just to see, to know, to find out. And then they tell the secrets, publish the mysteries, to make lives miserable and ruin families. And this to their great joy, with no other motive than pure instinct. A sad thing.

So Fantine was watched. And more than one woman was envious of her fine hair and teeth. It all took time.

Fantine had been at the factory over a year when one morning the overseer handed her, on behalf of the mayor, fifty francs, telling her to leave the city.

This was at the same time the Thénardiers demanded more money. Fantine was devastated. She could not leave the city. She was in debt for her furniture and room.

Fantine sold first her long hair to pay her creditors, and then two of her beautiful front teeth to send money for clothes for Cosette. Still she needed more money. Thénardier wrote to say that unless he had one hundred francs immediately Cosette, who was just recovering from a sickness, would be turned out to fend for herself. How to earn a hundred francs?

She spent whole days weeping and thinking. There

was a constant pain in her shoulder and she coughed a great deal. She hated Father Madeleine profoundly, and she never complained. She sewed for a contractor seventeen hours a day, but she could not earn enough to keep up with the demands of the furniture creditor and the Thénardiers.

What to do? Cosette knew only one way. The unfortunate creature became a woman of the street.

And the busybody, seeing Fantine walking bent over and sickly, commented, "I knew that woman would come to a bad end!"

The Idleness of M. Bamatabois

There is in all small towns a set of young men who would be clowns and think themselves gentlemen. They whistle at actresses in the theater to prove they have good taste. They quarrel with the local army officers to show they are gallant. They hunt, smoke, stare, drink, play billiards, live at the cafes, and generally do no good but also not much harm.

Félix Tholomyès, if he had never seen Paris, would have been such a man.

In early January 1823, one snowy evening, one of these "dandies" was amusing himself by tormenting a poor creature who walked back and forth before the windows of the officers' cafe.

Each time the woman walked past him, he threw out some remark that he thought was witty and pleasant, such as "Why don't you try hiding your face?" or "Where are your front teeth?" The dandy's name was M. Bamatabois. The woman did not answer but continued pacing in silence. This lack of attention irked the dandy, and he came up behind her with a handful of snow from the sidewalk and stealthily threw it down her back. The girl roared with anger and rushed the man. She buried her nails into his face, and she threw shocking insults at him. It was Fantine.

At the noise, the officers came out of the cafe, and a crowd gathered. They watched the tornado composed of two beings. A man defending himself, his hat knocked off. A woman kicking and thumping, her head bare and her face gray with some terrible anger.

Suddenly a tall man advanced, seized the woman by the shoulders, and said, "Follow me!"

The woman's eyes were glassy, and she shuddered with terror. She recognized Javert.

The dandy took advantage of the moment to run away.

Some Questions from the Municipal Police

Javert brushed aside the bystanders, broke up the circle, and walked rapidly toward the police station, dragging the poor woman with him. Neither spoke a word.

Javert sat down, drew from his pocket a sheet of stamped paper, and began to write. At this moment he felt filled with justice. He conducted a trial, trying and condemning. He examined the conduct of the young woman. It revolted him. Clearly he had seen a crime committed. He wrote in silence. When he finished, he signed his name, folded the paper, and handed it to the sergeant of the guards. "Choose three men and take this girl to jail," he said. Turning to Fantine, he said, "You are in for six months."

"But Monsieur Javert, good Monsieur Inspector!" Fantine cried. "Others saw it. Perhaps I was wrong to get mad. Have pity on me, Monsieur Javert!"

Javert turned his back.

A man had entered the office unnoticed. He had closed the door and stood with his back to it. Just as the soldiers put their hands on the girl, he stepped forward. "One moment, if you please!"

Javert looked and recognized M. Madeleine. "Monsieur Mayor," he said.

At this, Fantine broke loose from the soldiers and walked straight to M. Madeleine. She spat directly in his face.

M. Madeleine wiped his face and said, "Inspector Javert, set this woman free."

Javert felt as if he were losing his mind. He was stupefied. Thought and speech alike failed him.

Fantine was no less astonished.

Finally, Inspector Javert tried again. "But, M. Mayor, permit me—"

"Not another word."

"However,—"

"You may go," said Monsieur Madeleine.

Javert received the blow. He bowed deeply before the mayor and went out.

Fantine stood by the door and looked at him as he went past her.

When Javert was gone, M. Madeleine turned to Fantine and said slowly and with difficulty, "I have seen you over the past months. Why did you not come to me when you had difficulty? Now, I will pay your debts. I will have your child come to you, or you go to her. You shall live here, or in Paris, or wherever you wish. I take charge of your child and you. You will not have to work again, if you don't want to. I will give you what you need. You will become honest again. Poor woman!"

This was more than Fantine could bear. She looked with astonishment at the man speaking to her. She began to weep quietly. Her limbs gave way and she fell to her knees in front of M. Madeleine. Then she fainted.

6 Javert

Now, Rest

Monsieur Madeleine had Fantine taken to the infirmary, which was in his house. She spent part of the night with a violent fever. Finally she fell asleep.

Just before noon the next day, Fantine woke up. M. Madeleine had spent the night and morning learning about Fantine. He knew everything about her life now, including all the details.

That same night, Javert wrote a letter. In the morning he carried it to the post office. It was directed to Paris and bore this address: "To Monsieur Chabouillet, Secretary to Monsieur the Prefect of Police." The postmistress and some others saw the envelope before it was sent. Since they had heard about the events of the night before, they thought Javert was sending in his resignation.

Monsieur Madeleine wrote a letter also. Fantine owed the Thénardiers one hundred twenty francs. He sent them three hundred and asked them to bring the child at once to Montreuil-sur-Mer, where her mother—who was sick—wanted her.

Monsieur Madeleine came to see Fantine twice a day. At each visit she asked him, "Will I see Cosette soon?"

He answered, "Perhaps tomorrow. I expect her any moment."

And Fantine's pale face would brighten. "Ah," she would say, "how happy I will be!"

But Cosette did not arrive. The Thénardiers asked for more money and invented a hundred reasons for not sending Cosette.

"I will send somebody for Cosette," said M. Madeleine. "If necessary, I will go myself." And he wrote this letter, which Fantine signed.

> Monsieur Thénardier:
> You will deliver Cosette to the bearer.
> He will settle all small debts.
> I have the honor of greeting you with kind regards,
>
> Fantine

How Jean Can Become Champmathieu

One morning M. Madeleine was in his office when he was informed that Javert, the police inspector, wished to speak with him. On hearing the name, M. Madeleine felt some displeasure. Since the business at the police station, Javert had avoided him.

"Have him come in," he said.

Javert entered.

Monsieur Madeleine remained seated near the fire, pen in hand, looking over some papers. He did not interrupt his work for Javert. He could not help thinking of poor Fantine, and it seemed right to greet him coldly.

Javert respectfully greeted the mayor, whose back was to him. The mayor did not look up.

Javert advanced a few steps and paused without breaking the silence. He waited in real humility until it pleased Monsieur the Mayor to turn toward him. He stood, calm, hat in hand, and eyes cast down. Nothing was on his face except a gloomy sadness. He looked courageously dejected.

Finally, the mayor put down his pen and turned part way around.

"Well, what is it, Javert?"

Javert stood silent a moment; then he raised his voice solemnly: "A criminal act has been committed, Monsieur Mayor. I have come to ask you to be kind enough to make charges against me and ask for my dismissal."

Amazed, M. Madeleine opened his mouth. Javert interrupted. "You will say that I might hand in my resignation, but that is not enough. To resign is honorable; I have done wrong, and I ought to be punished. I must be dismissed."

He continued, "Monsieur Mayor, you were severe with me the other day unjustly. Today, you should be justly so. Dismiss me."

"That's very odd. I don't understand."

"You will, Monsieur Mayor," sighed Javert. "Six weeks ago, after the scene about the girl, I was furious and I denounced you to the Prefecture[1] of Police in Paris."

"As a mayor who interfered with the police?" asked M. Madeleine, laughing.

"As a former convict."

The mayor's face turned ashen.

Javert did not raise his eyes, but he continued. "I suspected it for a long time. Your skill as a marksman, your leg that drags a little, your immense strength. At last I recognized you as a man named Jean Valjean."

"Named what? What is that name?"

"Jean Valjean. A convict I saw twenty years ago, when I was a guard of a chain gang at Toulon. For

---

1. **Prefecture** main office

eight years his whereabouts have been unknown. I imagined—in other words,—I did this thing. I denounced you to the prefect."

In a tone of perfect indifference, M. Madeleine said, "And what answer did you get?"

"That I was crazy."

"Well!"

"Well, they were right. I must be, for the real Jean Valjean has been found."

M. Madeleine dropped the paper he was holding, but his tone did not change when he asked Javert to continue.

Javert did. "Apparently, in the countryside there was a simple sort of man called Father Champmathieu. He was very poor. Nobody paid any attention to him.   Finally, last fall, Father Champmathieu was arrested for stealing apples. There was a theft, a wall scaled, branches of the trees broken. When arrested, he had the branch of an apple tree in his hand. He was taken to Arras prison, where there is a former convict named Brevert who is turnkey.[2] No sooner was Champmathieu brought in than Brevert cried, 'Ha, ha! I know that man. Look at me! You're Jean Valjean! You were in a work gang in Toulon twenty years ago! We were there together.'

"Champmathieu denied it all. You understand. They investigated it in depth. There is nobody now at Faverolles who knew Jean Valjean. But a search was made at Toulon. Besides Brevet, there are only two convicts who have seen Jean Valjean. They are Cochepaille and Chenildieu, both serving life sentences. Those men were brought in to confront the

---

2. turnkey official who locks and unlocks prison cells

alleged Champmathieu. Without hesitation they said the man was Jean Valjean. Same age (fifty-four), same height, same appearance. Same man. It was at this time that I sent my letter to the Prefecture in Paris. They replied that I was out of my mind—that Jean Valjean was at that moment in the hands of justice. You can imagine how astonished I was. The justice sent for me and brought in Champmathieu."

"Well?" interrupted the mayor.

"Monsieur Mayor, the truth is the truth. That man *is* Jean Valjean. I recognized him, too."

"Are you sure?" asked Monsieur Madeleine in a very low voice.

Javert laughed. "Oh, yes! Positive!"

"That will do, Javert. Actually, the details interest me very little. We are wasting time, and we have urgent business." And he dismissed Javert with a wave of his hand.

Javert did not go. "Your pardon, monsieur," he said.

"What more is there?" asked M. Madeleine.

"Monsieur Mayor, there is one more thing. I ought to be dismissed."

Monsieur Madeleine rose.

"Javert, you are a man of honor. You exaggerate your fault. Besides, this offense concerns only me. You deserve a promotion, not dismissal. I want you to keep your job."

Javert looked at Monsieur Madeleine with his calm eyes. He said in a still voice, "I cannot agree to that. But I will continue in the service until I am replaced."

He went out. Monsieur Madeleine sat thinking, listening to the sound of Javert's firm step as it died away along the corridor.

7   *The Champmathieu Affair*

A Tempest Within a Brain

The reader has undoubtedly guessed that Monsieur Madeleine is none other than Jean Valjean.

We have already looked into the depths of that conscience; the time has come to look there again. There is nothing more terrifying than this kind of study. There is one spectacle greater than the sea; that is the sky. There is one spectacle greater than the sky; that is the interior of the soul.

We have little to add to what the reader already knows about what happened to Jean Valjean. What the bishop had wished for him, he had carried out. It was more than an improvement—it was a complete change.

He succeeded in disappearing from sight. He sold the bishop's silver, keeping only the candlesticks as souvenirs. He quietly slipped from city to city across France, came to Montreuil-sur-Mer, thought of the invention we have described, and accomplished what we have related. When Javert pronounced the name he had so deeply buried, he was dazed. He felt clouds of thunder and lightning gathering above his head. Even while he listened to Javert, his first thought was to go, to run, to give himself up, to drag this Champmathieu out of prison and go back in his place.

He felt that it would perhaps be necessary to go to Arras. He said to himself that, since he was entirely free of suspicion, there would be no danger in going to see what might occur there. He hired a carriage to be prepared for any emergency. He ate dinner with a reasonable appetite. Then he returned to his room to collect his thoughts.

Everything he had done up to now was merely a hole he was digging, in which to bury his name. What he dreaded, in the sleepless nights, was the thought of ever hearing that name pronounced. He felt that it would be the end of everything for him; his new life would vanish from around him. He shuddered at the thought.

All he had to do was leave things alone.

His place in prison was empty; it was always waiting for him. It would await him until he returned there. It was his inevitable fate. And then he said to himself: at this very moment he had a substitute there—a man named Champmathieu had that bad luck. He had nothing to fear; he was safe in society under the name of M. Madeleine.

"Well, then!" he said, "what am I afraid of? Why am I pondering these things? Now I'm safe. This Javert who has troubled me for so long, that fearful instinct which guessed the truth, that followed me everywhere, that terrible bloodhound always trailing me—he is thrown off the track, busy elsewhere. He is satisfied; he will leave me in peace; he has caught his Jean Valjean! Leave the matter alone."

He questioned his decision. Everything he had been thinking was monstrous, simply horrible. To let this mistake of fate and man happen, not to prevent it, was ultimately to do everything! It was hypocritical and wrong! He was robbing another man of his existence, his life!

On the other hand, to give himself up, to reassume his name, becoming again the convict Jean Valjean—

that was really his salvation. He must do it! All he had done was useless if he did not do that. His whole life was useless. So he had to go to Arras, save the false Jean Valjean, and turn in the real one. He had to do it! Painful fate!

"Well," he said, "Let's take the course—do our duty! Let's save the man!"

He said these words without knowing he was speaking aloud.

And all of a sudden he thought of Fantine. "But wait!" he said. "What about that poor woman!"

Here was a new crisis.

"And that child I wanted to bring here, whom I promised to the mother! Don't I owe something to this woman, too? If I should disappear, what would happen to her?"

What should he do, great God! What should he do?

He felt in his pocket, drew out his purse, and took from it a little key. He put this key into a lock whose hole was scarcely visible. It was lost in the dark shading of figures on the wallpaper. A secret door opened. There was nothing in it except a few things: a yellow smock, an old pair of trousers, an old knapsack, and a large stick iron-tipped at each end. Anyone who had seen Jean Valjean when he passed through Digne in October 1815 would easily have recognized the remains of his miserable outfit.

He had kept them, as he had kept the silver candlesticks, to remind him of what he had been. He took it all—rags, stick, knapsack—and threw it into the fire. He put the candlesticks on the mantel. Then he took up a slow monotonous pacing.

The clock struck three. For five hours he had been pacing that way, without interruption. He dropped into his chair. He fell asleep and dreamed.

He woke up freezing. A cold wind had swung open the window sashes. The fire had gone out. From his window he could look down onto the street. A harsh rattling noise from the ground made him look down. He saw below him two red stars. "Of course," he thought, "there are none in the sky. Now they're on earth."

The confusion, however, faded away. A second noise awakened him completely. He looked and realized the two stars were the lamps of a carriage. It took some moments before he remembered he had hired it for the possible trip to Arras.

"Tell the driver I'm coming down," he called to the concierge who tapped at his door.

Fantine's Courage Put to the Test

While M. Madeleine set out on what would turn out to be a very long trip to Arras, Fantine was doing poorly.

She had spent a very bad night. Terrible cough, high fever, nightmares. In the morning when the doctor came, she was delirious. He was alarmed and asked to be informed as soon as M. Madeleine arrived.

All morning she was in low spirits. Her eyes were sunken and staring. Whenever she was asked how she felt, she would reply, "Well, thank you, but I would like to see Monsieur Madeleine."

At noon the doctor came again, left some prescriptions, and inquired about the mayor. M. Madeleine almost always visited Fantine at three o'clock. Since promptness is kindness, he had always been prompt in his daily visits.

At about half past two, Fantine grew restless. In the space of twenty minutes, she asked more then ten times, "Sister, what time is it?"

The clock struck three. At the third stroke, Fantine

rose up in bed. Ordinarily she could hardly turn over. She joined her two shrunken yellow hands in a sort of clasp. Then Fantine looked toward the door.

Nobody came in. The door did not open.

She sat that way for fifteen minutes, eyes fixed on the door and as if holding her breath. When the clock struck the quarter hour, Fantine fell back on her pillow.

Hours passed, but no one came. Every time the clock struck, Fantine sat up and looked toward the door, then she fell back.

Then the sister heard her speak: "Since I am going away tomorrow, he is wrong not to come today!"

No one understood M. Madeleine's absence. The sister sent someone to the mayor's quarters to ask if he had returned. The servant explained that the mayor had gone away in the morning and that he might not be expected that night. One of the sisters explained to Fantine.

Fantine sprang up and sat on her feet. Her eyes sparkled. A marvelous joy spread over her face.

"Gone away!" she exclaimed. "He has gone for Cosette! I know it. I'm so happy! God is kind, and Monsieur Madeleine is good. Just think! He has gone to Montfermeil to get my little Cosette."

Anyone who had seen Fantine some minutes before would not have believed this. She had been weak and delirious. Now she was all rosy, talking in a lively voice, her whole face a smile.

Between seven and eight o'clock, the doctor returned. Hearing no sound, he thought she was asleep. He went close and drew open the curtains. By the glow of the nightlight, he saw Fantine's huge eyes gazing at him.

"Monsieur, you will let her lie by my side in a little

bed, won't you?" she asked.

The doctor thought she was feverish. She added, "Look, there is just enough room. Then, you see, in the morning I can say good morning to the poor kitten. At night, when I'm awake, I can hear her sleeping."

"Give me your hand," said the doctor.

"Of course," she laughed. "It's true you don't know that I'm cured. Cosette is coming tomorrow."

The doctor was surprised. Her paleness was gone and her pulse was stronger. A new life seemed to be reviving the poor exhausted being. He recommended quiet, more medicine, and a soothing potion. On leaving the infirmary, he told the sister, "She is better. If the mayor does come back with the child, who knows? We've seen diseases instantly cured by great joy. I know very well this is an organic disease, and far advanced. But let us see, it is all a mystery. Perhaps we will save her!"

The Traveler Arrives

It was nearly eight in the evening when the carriage bearing M. Madeleine arrived in Arras. Fearing he might have missed the trial, he immediately asked a citizen directions to the courthouse.

The citizen said to him, "If Monsieur wants to see a trial, he is rather late. Usually the sessions end at six o'clock."

However, when they arrived at the great square, the citizen pointed to four long lighted windows. "Just look, monsieur, you're still in time. The lights are still burning. The case must have dragged on. The door-keeper is up there, from the main stairway."

He followed the citizen's directions and soon found himself in front of a double-paneled door, now closed. A bailiff stood near the door, which opened into the courtroom.

"Monsieur," he asked. "Will the door be opened again soon?"

"It will not be. The session has just resumed, but the door will not be opened. The hall is full."

"What! There are no more seats?"

"Not a one. No one can enter."

He opened his coat, took out his billfold, found a pencil and a piece of paper, and wrote this line: "Monsieur Madeleine, Mayor of Montreuil-sur-Mer." He passed the paper to the bailiff and said with authority, "Hand this to Monsieur the Judge."

The officer took the paper, glanced at it, and obeyed.

Admission by Privilege

Without being aware of it, the mayor of Montreuil-sur-Mer had become quite a celebrity. Besides the considerable service he rendered by reviving the jet-bead industry, every one of the hundred forty-one communities in the district was indebted to him for some favor or another. The name of Monsieur Madeleine was spoken only with the greatest respect.

Like everyone else, the judge who was presiding at the trial was familiar with this honored name. When the officer handed him the paper on which the line was written, adding, "This gentleman wishes to witness the trial," the judge hastily replied. "Let him enter."

In a few minutes the mayor found himself alone in a small room. The words of the bailiff who had just left rang in his ears: "Monsieur, you are now in the counsel chamber. Just turn the brass knob of that door and you will be in the courtroom, just behind the judge's bench."

The officer had left him alone. He was in the place
where the judges deliberate and decide. He looked at
the walls; then he looked at himself. He was astonished that it could be this chamber and that this could
be he. His expression, at first calm, now fell. His
eyes, fixed on the brass knob, became wild and filled
with dismay. Drops of sweat started above the hair-
line and rolled down his temples.

Who says I have to? He quickly turned, saw the
door by which he had entered, went to it, opened it,
and went out. He was no longer in the little room.
He took a deep breath and listened. Not a sound
behind him; not a sound in front of him. He ran as if
he were pursued. When he had rounded several turns
of the passage, he listened again. There was still the
same silence. He was out of breath; he tottered; he
leaned against the stone of the wall. It was cold; the
sweat was icy on his forehead.

A quarter of an hour passed. Finally, he bowed his
head, sighed, let his arms droop, and retraced his
steps. He walked as though he had been caught in
flight and brought back.

He entered the counsel chamber again. The first
thing he saw was the brass handle. His eyes did not
leave it. Slowly he stepped near to the door. He seized
the knob convulsively; the door opened.

He was in the courtroom.

A Place for Convictions

Nobody in the crowd paid any attention to him. All
eyes were converged on a single point, a wooden bench
against a little door, to the left of the judge. On this
bench sat a man between two gendarmes.

This was the man.

He did not look for him; he saw him. His eyes went

toward him naturally, as if they had known in advance where he was.

He thought he was seeing himself, older undoubtedly. Not exactly the same in features, but alike in attitude and appearance—just as he had been on the day he entered Digne all those years before.

He said to himself with a shudder, "Great God! Will I return to that?"

The man seemed at least sixty years old. There was something crude, dull-witted, and terrified in his appearance.

As he opened the door, people stood to make room for him. The judge greeted him with a bow. The prosecuting attorney recognized him and bowed also. He scarcely noticed them. He looked around as if hallucinating.

There was a chair behind him; he sank into it, terrified of being seen. Now his face was hidden by a pile of folders on the judge's desk. He could see without being seen. He regained some sense of reality. Little by little he regained enough composure to be able to listen.

Monsieur Bamatabois was one of the jurors.

He looked for Javert but could not see him. The witnesses were hidden by the clerk's table, and the room was dimly lit.

As he entered, the defense was finishing his plea. Everyone's attention was fully engaged. The trial had been in progress for three hours. Four witnesses had positively and without hesitation identified Champmathieu as Jean Valjean. The man had persisted in denying everything—both the theft and the fact that he had been a convict. He probably expected to escape punishment by admitting nothing. It was a mistake, but his intellect should be taken into consideration. The man was clearly dull-witted.

The prosecutor began his attack on the accused, who listened open-mouthed. His expression was one of astonishment mingled with admiration. He seemed surprised that a man could speak so well. From time to time, at the most forceful parts of the prosecutor's arguments, he slowly turned his head from right to left, then left to right.

The time came to close the case. The judge ordered the accused to rise, and he asked the usual question, "Have you anything to add in your defense?"

The man stood and twirled a hideous cap in his hands. He seemed not to hear.

The judge repeated the question.

This time the man heard and appeared to understand. He started like someone awaking from sleep and began to speak. It was like an explosion. Words escaped his lips—senseless, hasty, helter-skelter. He spoke words in a loud, rapid, harsh voice. He made no sense. Once, he stopped to nod to someone in the crowd. When the flow of words stopped, the spectators burst out laughing. He looked at them and, seeing them laughing and not knowing why, he began to laugh himself.

The judge, a kind man, raised his voice. He questioned the witnesses again. They repeated their identification of the man. Each of the assertions, obviously sincere and in good faith, raised a murmur from the audience. The prisoner himself listened with that astonished expression. The gendarmes at his side heard him mutter between his teeth "Good!" then "O, well! So much for him!" and lastly "Splendid!"

The judge addressed him, "Prisoner, you have heard. What do you have to say?"

He replied, "I say—splendid!"

A buzz ran through the crowd. It was obvious that the man was lost.

"Bailiffs," said the judge, "enforce order. I am about to sum up the case."

At that moment, there was a movement near the judge. A voice was heard to cry out, "Brevet, Chenildieu, Cochepaille, look this way!"

So terrible was the voice that all who heard it felt their blood run cold. All eyes turned to the point from which it came. A man, who had been sitting among the privileged spectators behind the judge, had risen and was standing in the center of the room. The judge, the prosecuting attorney, Monsieur Bamatabois, and twenty other persons recognized him and cried out simultaneously, "Monsieur Madeleine!"

Champmathieu More and More Astonished

It was indeed he. He had his hat in his hand; his overcoat was carefully buttoned. He was very pale and he trembled slightly. His hair, already gray when he came to Arras, was now perfectly white. It had turned white during the hour he had been there.

Turning toward the jurors and court, M. Madeleine said in a mild voice, "Gentlemen of the jury, release the accused. Your honor, order my arrest. He is not the man you seek. I am. I am Jean Valjean."

Not a breath stirred. The room was touched with the sort of awe that takes place when something enormous has taken place.

The judge's face reflected sympathy and sadness. He exchanged glances and then a few whispers with the prosecuting attorney. Then he turned to the crowd and asked, "Is there a physician in the room?"

The prosecuting attorney added, "Gentlemen of the jury, you all know—at least by reputation—the honorable Monsieur Madeleine, Mayor of Montreuil-sur-Mer. If there is a doctor in the audience, we join the judge in asking him to kindly help Monsieur Madeleine to his residence."

M. Madeleine did not let the prosecutor continue. These are the words he spoke, just as they were written down immediately after the trial. And they still ring in the ears of those who heard them nearly forty years ago.

"I thank you, Monsieur Prosecuting Attorney, but I am not mad. You'll see. You were on the point of committing a grave error. Release that man. I am carrying out a duty; I am the unfortunate convict. I am the only one who can see this clearly, and I am telling you the truth. What I am doing at this moment, God on high is witnessing, and that is enough. You can take me, since here I am. Yet I have done my best. I have hidden under another name; I have become rich; I became a mayor. I wanted to live among honest people. It seems this cannot be. Make of this what you will. Before prison I was a poor peasant, unintelligent, a sort of idiot. Prison changed me. I was stupid; I became wicked. Later I was saved by indulgence and kindness. Take me. Good God! The prosecuting attorney shakes his head. He thinks I have gone mad. How I wish Javert were here. He would recognize me!"

He turned to the three convicts. "Brevet, do you remember those checkered knit suspenders you had in prison? Chenildieu, you nicknamed yourself to repudiate God! Your entire left shoulder has been deeply burned from trying to erase the letters T.F.P. Cochepaille, on your left arm you have a date marked in blue letters with burned powder. March 1, 1815.

"So you see," he said, "I am Jean Valjean."

The fact was beyond dispute. The arrival of this man had been enough to clear up the case. Without need for any further explanation, the whole crowd understood the simple story of a man giving himself up so that another man would not be condemned in his place.

"I will not disturb the proceedings further," continued Jean Valjean. "I am leaving since you are not arresting me. I have many things to do. Monsieur Prosecuting Attorney knows who I am, and he knows where I am going. He will have me arrested when he chooses. Monsieur," he said as he walked toward the door, "I am at your disposal."

He went out, and the door closed as it had opened.

Less than an hour later, the jury dismissed all charges against Champmathieu, who went on his way thinking all men mad and understanding nothing of the whole event.

8 Counterstroke

The Mirror in Which M. Madeleine Looks at His Hair

Fantine spent a night that was feverish but filled with happy visions. At daybreak, when Fantine fell asleep, Sister Simplice went to the infirmary laboratory to arrange her medicines. Suddenly she turned and let out a cry. M. Madeleine was standing in front of her.

"How is the poor woman?" he asked in a low voice.

"Better just now. But we have been very worried."

She explained Fantine's sudden improvement when she believed that the mayor had gone to get her child. She did not question him, but she could see that all had not gone well wherever he had been. As daylight streamed into the room, the sister looked up.

"O, God, monsieur," she exclaimed. "What has happened to you? Your hair is completely white!"

"White?" he asked.

The sister rummaged and found a little mirror in a case of instruments. M. Madeleine looked at his hair and said again, "White!"

He asked, "Can I see her? It will take two or three days, at least, to bring back her child. But I cannot wait; I may not have much time."

Fantine was sleeping calmly despite the labored breathing. M. Madeleine stood still for some time near the bed, just as he had done two months ago when she first came to the shelter. They were in the same attitude: she sleeping, he praying. Only now her hair had become gray and his was white.

She opened her eyes, saw him, and calmly said with a smile, "Cosette?"

Fantine Happy

"Where is Cosette?" Fantine continued. "Why didn't you put her on my bed so I might see her the moment I woke up?"

Fortunately the doctor had arrived. He came to the aid of M. Madeleine.

"Soon," the doctor said, "not right now. You still have some fever. First we must cure you."

Although showing restraint, she asked M. Madeleine a hundred questions about the trip, about Cosette, about the treatment her daughter had received from the Thénardiers.

He took her hand. "Cosette is beautiful," he said. "You will see her soon, but right now you're talking too much, which makes you cough."

In fact, coughing fits did interrupt Fantine at almost every word. But suddenly Fantine stopped talking, and M. Madeleine raised his eyes. Fantine looked terrible.

She did not speak; she did not breathe. She half raised herself on the bed. Her face, radiant a moment before, had turned deathly pale. Her eyes, wide with terror, seemed fastened on something at the other end of the room. She touched his arm with one hand and, with the other, gestured for him to look behind him.

He turned and saw Javert.

Javert Satisfied

This is what had happened.

After the revelations of M. Madeleine—the real Jean Valjean—the case against Champmathieu was dismissed. But the prosecuting attorney required a

Jean Valjean in custody. Having lost one, he wanted the other. The order of arrest was granted, and it was sent by courier, at top speed, to Police Inspector Javert.

Javert was just waking up when the courier arrived. He went immediately to the infirmary. On reaching Fantine's room, he turned the knob gently and entered.

As Fantine's glance met that of Javert, Javert—without moving or approaching—became terrible. It was the face of the devil who has just regained his victim.

Javert's satisfaction radiated from his commanding attitude. Triumph spread across his narrow forehead.

Although hideous in his gratitude, Javert was not base. Without suspecting it, Javert—in his terrible happiness—was pitiful. He was an ignorant man in triumph. Nothing is more terrible than such a face.

Authority Gains Its Power

Fantine had not seen Javert since the day the mayor had saved her from him. Her sick brain could only grasp that he had come for her. She hid her face with both hands and shrieked in anguish, "Monsieur Madeleine, save me!"

Jean Valjean—from here on we will call him only by that name—stood up. He said to Fantine in his gentlest and calmest tone of voice, "Don't be afraid. He hasn't come for you."

Then he turned to Javert and said, "I know what you want."

Javert answered only, "Hurry up."

"Monsieur," Jean Valjean said, "I would like a word with you in private."

"Aloud, speak out loud," said Javert. "People speak

out loud to me."

Jean Valjean went on, "It is a request I have to make of you. Give me three days! Three days to go for the child of this woman. I'll pay whatever it takes. You may accompany me if you like."

"Are you laughing at me?" cried Javert. "I didn't think you were that stupid! You're asking me for three days to get away, and you tell me you're going for this girl's child! Ha, ha, that's a good joke!"

Fantine shuddered.

"My child!" she exclaimed. "Going for my child? Then she is not here! Where is Cosette? Monsieur Madeleine, Monsieur Mayor!"

Javert stamped his foot. He stared at Fantine and added, grabbing Jean Valjean's tie and collar, "I tell you there's no Monsieur Madeleine, no Monsieur the Mayor. There's only a thief, a convict named Valjean! And I've got him!"

Fantine sat upright. She looked at Jean Valjean, then at Javert. She opened her mouth as if to speak. A guttural sound emerged; then she clamped her teeth shut. She spread her fingers and groped like someone drowning, then suddenly fell back against the pillow.

Her head struck the head of the bed and fell forward onto her chest. Her mouth gaped open; her eyes were open and glazed.

She was dead.

In a corner of the room there was an old iron bedstead with a loose head bar. Jean Valjean went to the bed and pulled out the loose bar—easy for a man as strong as he was—and held it in his clenched fist.

He walked slowly to Fantine's bed and said to Javert in a voice that could scarcely be heard, "I advise you not to disturb me now."

It is certain that Javert shuddered.

Jean Valjean bent down to Fantine and spoke to her in a whisper. What he said to her was heard by no one on earth. Sister Simplice, the only witness to what happened, said that as Jean Valjean whispered in Fantine's ear, she clearly saw a smile spread across those pale lips and eyes.

Jean Valjean took Fantine's head in his hands and arranged it on the pillow as a mother would do. He fastened the string of her nightgown and tucked her hair under her cap. This done, he closed her eyes.

Then he rose and, turning to Javert, said, "Now I am at your disposal."

A Fitting Grave

Javert put Jean Valjean in the city prison.

Monsieur Madeleine's arrest caused a sensation, an extraordinary commotion, at Montreuil-sur-Mer. Only three or four persons in the city remained faithful to his memory. One among those was the old concierge who had been his servant.

On the evening of that same day, the old woman was sitting alone, no one in the house except the two nuns, Sister Perpétue and Sister Simplice, who were beside Fantine's body.

About the time M. Madeleine had usually come home, the concierge rose without thinking and gathered the key to his room as well as the candle he used to light the way to his room. She hung the key on its usual nail, then sat down.

More than two hours passed before she realized what she had done and exclaimed about it.

Just then, the window near her chair opened, and a hand reached in and took the key and the candle.

The concierge was dumbfounded, a stifled cry in her throat. She knew the hand, the arm.

It was M. Madeleine.

"My God! Monsieur Mayor!" she finally exclaimed, "I thought you were —- "

"In prison," he completed her thought. "I was. I broke a window bar, I jumped from the top of the roof, and here I am. I am going to my room. Go for Sister Simplice."

He went up, drew the shutters, and sat down at his table. He took a paper and began to write.

Two gentle taps were heard, and Sister Simplice entered. Jean Valjean had written a few lines, which he handed to the nun, explaining that they were instructions about the dispersal of his monies.

He had scarcely done that when they heard a loud noise on the staircase. The clump of climbing feet was followed by the concierge's voice claiming loudly, "I swear that nobody has come in here all day or evening."

They recognized Javert's voice answering, "But there is a light in the room."

Jean Valjean quickly placed himself in the corner behind the door.

Sister Simplice fell on her knees near the table.

The door opened. Javert entered.

The sister did not look up. She was praying.

Javert saw the sister and stopped, embarrassed. His first impulse was to leave the room. His second was to remain and ask at least one question.

This was the Sister Simplice who had never lied in her life.

"Sister, are you alone in this room?" asked Javert.

"Yes," replied the sister.

"Excuse me if I persist, Sister, but we are searching for a person—Jean Valjean—you have not seen him?"

"No," answered the sister.

Two lies in succession, one upon the other, without hesitation, as if she were used to it.

Javert withdrew, bowing. "Your pardon!" he said reverently.

An hour later a man walked rapidly through the fog near the trees, leaving Montreuil-sur-Mer in the direction of Paris. The man was Jean Valjean.

A final word about Fantine.

Fantine was buried in the common grave of the cemetery, which belongs to everybody and to nobody. God knows these places where the poor are lost. Fortunately He knows where to find the soul.

Cosette

1 The Ship Orion

Number 24601 Becomes Number 9430

Jean Valjean had been recaptured.

Pardon us for passing over the painful details. We shall merely reproduce an item that was published in the newspaper, a few months after the events at Montreuil-sur-Mer.

The article is from the *Drapeau Blanc,* dated July 25, 1823.

> A district in the Pas-de-Calais has just been the scene of an unlikely occurrence. A newcomer to the region, known as Monsieur Madeleine, had within a few years, thanks to certain new processes, restored the manufacturing of jet and black glassware—formerly a local industry. He had made his own fortune by it, and that of the entire district. In acknowledgement of his services he had been appointed mayor. The police have discovered that Monsieur Madeleine is none other than an escaped convict, condemned in 1796 for robbery, one Jean Valjean. This Jean Valjean has been sent back to prison. It appears that before his arrest he was able to withdraw from

Lafitte's a sum amounting to more than half a million, which incidentally he had quite legitimately earned from his business. Since his return to the prison at Toulon, it has been impossible to discover where Jean Valjean concealed the money.

Jean Valjean's new prison number was 9430.

Before going on, we will relate a remarkable incident that took place around the same time at Montfermeil.

An old road worker named Boulatruelle was known to have a "fancy" for the woods. He was distrusted by the people of the neighborhood; he was too quick to doff his hat to everybody, and he always trembled and smiled at the gendarmes. He had nothing in his favor.

One morning about daybreak, as he was going to work, Boulatruelle was surprised to see a pickax and spade concealed under a bush in the woods. That same evening he saw, without being seen himself as he was concealed behind a large tree, a person who did not come from that region but whom Boulatruelle knew well. It was "an old comrade from prison," as someone translated his story, who turned off the main road toward the thickest part of the woods. The stranger carried a square package, like a large box or small trunk. Boulatruelle was so surprised it took several minutes before it occurred to him to follow. He was too late. The stranger was already in the dense woods, and night had fallen. Boulatruelle made up his mind to watch at the edge of the woods. Two or three hours later he saw the man come out of the woods, this time carrying not the little trunk but a pickaxe and spade. From this he concluded that the man had dug a hole with the pickaxe, buried the chest, and covered the hole with the spade. Now, Boulatruelle reasoned that, as the chest was too small to contain a corpse, it must contain money. He proceeded to explore, delve into, and comb through the whole forest. He had dug in every spot where the earth seemed to have been freshly disturbed. But all in vain. He turned up nothing.

Nobody in Montfermeil thought anything more about Boulatruelle's story, except for a few gossips who said, "I'm sure the road worker didn't make all that fuss for nothing. The Devil must have been there."

The Shackle Must Have Undergone Some Preparation to Be Broken with One Hammer Blow

Toward the end of October in that same year, 1823, the inhabitants of Toulon saw, returning to port for some damage repair, the ship Orion.

The presence of a warship in port has something about it that attracts and occupies a crowd. It is because it is imposing, and the crowd likes imposing things. Every day, from dusk to dawn, the wharfs and piers of Toulon harbor were crowded with a throng whose occupation consisted of gazing at the Orion.

It was moored near the arsenal. The hull had not been damaged on the starboard[1] side, but some planks had been removed here and there to allow air into the framework.

One morning, the throng witnessed an accident.

The crew was busy furling[2] sail. The seaman whose duty was to take in the starboard head of the mainsail lost his balance. He was seen tottering; the dense throng on the arsenal[3] wharf cried out. The man

---

1. **starboard** right side of a boat
2. **furling** folding
3. **arsenal** place where weapons or ammunition is stored

tipped over head first and he spun across the yard,[4] his arms outstretched toward the deep. As he went by, he grabbed the foot rope with one hand and then the other. He hung suspended there. The sea lay far below him, and the poor man dangled back and forth like a stone in a sling.

Anyone going to his aid took a terrible risk. None of the crew dared try. In the meantime the poor man was tiring. The agony showed in his face. His arms strained in horrible contortions. Every attempt to pull himself up only increased the swing of the rope. He did not cry out, saving his strength. The throng awaited the moment when he would let go of the line and fall like ripe fruit.

Suddenly a man was seen clambering up the rigging with the agility of a wildcat. He was dressed in red—a convict; he wore a green cap—a convict for life. As he reached the top, a gust of wind blew off his cap, revealing entirely white hair. He was not a young man.

It had happened that one of the convicts had run up to the officer of the watch and, amidst all the panic and confusion, asked permission to save the seaman's life at risk of his own. At a nod from the officer he broke the chain riveted to the iron ring at his ankle with one hammer blow. He then grabbed the rope and began the climb. At the time nobody noticed the ease with which the chain was broken. It was only later that anyone remembered.

In a twinkling he was up. He paused a few seconds. Finally he lifted his eyes to heaven and took a step forward. He ran along the yard. On reaching its

---

4. yard cylinder, perpendicular to the mast, on which the sail is fastened

tip, he fastened one end of the rope he had with him and let the other fall. He let himself down the rope hand over hand. Now, terrifyingly, instead of one man, two were now dangling at that dizzying height.

Ten thousand eyes were fixed on the pair. Not a cry, not a word was uttered. Nobody dared breathe.

The convict managed to make his way down to the seaman. It was just in time. The man, exhausted and despairing, would have fallen into the deep. The convict firmly tied him to the rope to which he clung with one hand. He moved back up the yardarm,[5] hauling the sailor after him. He supported him there to recover his strength; then he lifted the seaman in his arms and carried him across the yard to the crosstrees. From there he took him to the roundtop, where he left him in the hands of his mates.

Then the throng applauded. Seasoned prison guards wept; women hugged each other. On all sides, voices exclaimed, "The man must be pardoned!"

The man, however, had began his descent immediately. He slid down the rigging and started to run along a lower yard. Every eye followed him. Suddenly terror gripped the crowd. Whether from dizziness or exhaustion, the man hesitated and staggered. The crowd shouted as he fell into the sea.

The fall was dangerous. There was a frigate close by the Orion. It was feared he would go down under one vessel or the other. Four men sprang immediately into a small boat. The people cheered them on, but with apprehension. The man had not appeared at the surface. He had disappeared without even a ripple. They sounded and dredged the place. All in vain. The search continued until nightfall, but the body was not found.

---

5. yardarm either end of the yard

The next morning the *Toulon Journal* published the following item.

November 17, 1823. Yesterday a convict at work aboard the Orion, after rescuing a sailor, fell into the sea and drowned. His body was not recovered. It is presumed he was caught under the piling at the pier head of the arsenal. The man was registered under the number 9430, and his name was Jean Valjean.

2 Fulfillment of the Promise

The Water Question

Montfermeil was a peaceful and charming village. Its inhabitants enjoyed an easygoing life, but water was scarce because of the height of the plateau on which the town was situated. They had to go a considerable distance for it, to a little spring on the side of a hill.

The man who made the water supply his business worked only up to seven o'clock in summer and five in the winter. Those who arrived later had to haul in their own water or wait until the next day.

This was the terror of little Cosette. Remember that Cosette was useful to the Thénardiers in two ways: they got money from the mother and work from the child. When Fantine ceased to pay, the Thénardiers kept Cosette. She became their servant. She ran upstairs and downstairs. She washed, brushed, scrubbed, swept, slaved away breathless. She lifted heavy things and, puny as she was, did the hardest work. The Thénardiers were ferocious and spiteful. The tavern was like a web in which Cosette had been caught. It was something like a fly serving spiders.

It was also Cosette who ran for water when it was needed. The child was terrified by the idea of going to the spring at night.

Horses Must Have Water

Four new guests had arrived at the Thénardier tavern.

Cosette was sad. At eight years old she had alre. suffered so much that she brooded like an old woman. Today she had a bruised eyelid from a blow of Mme. Thénardier's fist, which made the family say from time to time, "How ugly she is with her black eye!"

Cosette was thinking that it was dark outside. The bowls and pitchers in the rooms of the last travelers had needed filling, so there was no more water in the cistern.[1] She counted the minutes as they rolled by and eagerly wished for morning to arrive.

All at once one of the travelers came in and said with a harsh voice, "You haven't watered my horse!"

Cosette came out from under the table.

"Oh, yes, monsieur, your horse did drink. He drank a whole bucketful, and I carried it to him and I talked to him."

It was not true. Cosette lied.

"Here is a girl as big as my fist who can tell a lie as big as a house," exclaimed the man. "I tell you he has had no water! He has a way I know quite well when he has had no water! Just give my horse his water and shut up!"

Cosette went back under the table.

"What's become of that wretched girl?" cried Mme. Thénardier, looking around. "Are you going?" she shouted. Cosette came out from where she had hidden.

"Little Miss No-Name, go get some water for the horse."

"But, madam," said Cosette faintly, "there isn't any more water."

"Then go fetch some!"

Cosette hung her head and went to get the empty bucket from the chimney corner. It was larger than

---

1. cistern tank for catching and storing rainwater

she was. She remained motionless in front of the open door. It was as if she was waiting for someone to come to her aid.

"Get out!" cried Mme. Thénardier.

Cosette went out. The door closed.

A Doll Enters the Scene

Since it was Christmas, a row of booths stretched along the street from the church to the Thénardier tavern. The last one, set up right opposite the tavern door, was a toy shop. It glittered with trinkets, glass beads, and wonderful things made of tin. In the first row in front, the merchant had placed—on a bed of white cloth—a huge doll nearly two feet tall. It wore a dress of pink crepe, with gold garlands on its head, real hair, and enamel eyes. All day this marvel had been on display, but there was no mother rich or generous enough to give it to her child. Eponine and Azelma spent hours staring at it. Cosette herself had furtively dared to look at it.

Now, as Cosette left the house, bucket in hand and gloomy as she was, she could not help raising her eyes toward the magnificent doll—"the lady," as she called it. She had never seen the doll up close before.

The whole booth seemed a palace to her. This doll was not a doll; it was a vision. It was joy, splendor, riches, happiness. She gazed at the beautiful pink dress, the beautiful smooth hair, and she thought, "How happy that doll must be!" The longer she looked, the more she was dazzled. She thought she was seeing Paradise.

In this adoration, she forgot everything—even the errand on which she had been sent. Suddenly, Mme. Thénardier's loud voice brought her back to reality: "What's this, you halfwit? Haven't you gone yet? Just you wait; I'm coming after you! You little monster!"

Cosette fled with her bucket, running as fast as she could.

The Little Girl All Alone

The Thénardier tavern was in the part of Montfermeil near the church, so Cosette had to go to the spring in the woods in Chelles to draw water.

She did not look again at the booths. As long as she was near the church, the lighted booths showed the way, but soon the last gleam from the last stall disappeared. The poor girl found herself in darkness. She went on, only she rattled the handle of the bucket as much as she could. The noise kept her company.

The farther she went, the denser the dark became. There was nobody on the streets. She was terrified. She began to run. She ran out of the village, into the woods, seeing nothing and hearing nothing. She stopped running only when she ran out of breath; and even then she kept going, desperate.

It was only several minutes' walk from the edge of the woods to the spring. Cosette knew the path from traveling it several times a day, so she did not lose her way. Instinct guided her. But she turned her eyes neither left nor right, for fear of seeing things in the trees and bushes. This is the way she reached the spring.

Cosette did not take time to rest. It was very dark, but she felt with her left hand for a young oak that bent across the pool and served as a support for her. She found a branch, hung on, leaned down, and plunged the bucket into the water. For a moment her strength was tripled. She drew out the bucket nearly full and set it on the grass. This done, she felt all her strength used up. She was anxious to start back, but the effort of lifting the bucket had been so great it was impossible to take a step. She had to sit down. She dropped to the grass and stayed crouching there.

Darkness is dizzying. We need light; whenever we plunge into the opposite of day we feel our hearts chilled. When the eye sees darkness, the mind sees trouble. In an eclipse, at night, in sooty darkness, even the strongest heart feels anxiety. Nobody walks alone at night in the forest without trembling. There are fierce shapes on the horizon. You are afraid and are tempted to look behind you. The socket of night, the profiles that fade away as you approach, angry clumps, the immensity of silence, the possible unknown things, swaying mysterious branches, frightful torsos of the trees, long wisps of shivering grass— you are defenseless against it all. There is no bravery that does not shudder. This darkness is inexpressibly sinister for a child.

By some sort of instinct that she did not understand, Cosette began to count aloud: one, two, three, four, up to ten. When she finished she began again. This restored some sort of reality to things around her. Her hands, wet from drawing the water, felt cold. She stood up. She grasped the handle of the bucket with both hands. She could hardly lift it.

She went a dozen steps this way, but the bucket was full and heavy. She had to rest it on the ground. She caught her breath an instant, then walked on, this time a little longer. But she had to stop again. After resting, she started on. She walked bending forward, head down, like an old woman. The iron handle was numbing and freezing her little hands. Every time she stopped, the cold water sloshed against her bare knees. She could not make much progress like this, and she was moving very slowly. As hard as she tried to walk farther between stops, she realized that it would take her more than one hour to get to

Montfermeil and that Mme. Thénardier would beat her. She gathered all her strength, took up the handle, and began to walk on courageously. But the poor thing could not help crying out, "Oh my God! Oh God!"

At that moment, she felt the weight of the bucket was gone. A hand, which looked enormous to her, had taken the handle and was carrying it easily. She looked up. A large dark form, straight and tall, was walking beside her in the darkness. A man, whom she had not heard, had come up behind her. Without saying a word, this man had taken the handle of the bucket she was carrying.

There are instincts that operate in all crises of life. Cosette was not afraid.

Which May Prove the Intelligence of Boulatruelle

Earlier that same day, Christmas Day in 1823, a man dressed in an old yellow coat hired a seat in a carriage bound for Lagny.

About six o'clock in the evening, when the driver stopped to rest his horses in Chelles, the man got off. A moment later he disappeared and, when the coach started off again for Lagny, it did not overtake the man on the main street.

The driver turned to the other passengers. "There," he said, "is a man who is not from these parts, because I don't know him. He looks like he hasn't a cent to his name, but he doesn't care about money. He pays to Lagny but goes only to Chelles. It's night, all the houses are shut, he doesn't go to the tavern, and we don't see him on the road. He must have sunk into the ground!"

The man had, in fact, hurried along the dark main street, turned left before reaching the church, and gone along the road to Montfermeil as though he knew the area.

He rapidly followed the road. At an intersection he heard footsteps approaching and concealed himself in a ditch until the people had gone well past. The precaution was probably not necessary since, as we have said, it was a dark December night.

At this point in the road, the hill begins to rise. The man did not return to the road; he turned to the right across the fields, and he reached the woods with fast strides. When he got there, he slowed his pace and began to examine the trees carefully, as if he were seeking and following a mysterious route known only to him. He finally reached a clearing with a heap of large whitish stones. The man went toward the stones and examined them as though in review. There was a large ash tree covered with warts a few steps away from the stones. The man touched the ash and then looked opposite it to a chestnut tree that had a wound staunched with a tacked-on square of zinc. The man rose on tiptoe and touched the square. Then he stamped on the ground between this tree and the stones, like someone who wanted to be sure the earth had not been freshly dug.

This was the man who had fallen in step with Cosette. He had seen the little shadow struggling along with a sob, setting her burden down, then taking it up again. He had approached her and seen that it was a small child carrying an enormous bucket of water. He had gone to her and silently taken the handle from her hands.

Cosette with the Unknown Man in the Dark

As we have said, Cosette was not afraid. She let go of the bucket. The man walked along with her.

"It certainly is very heavy," he said to himself. Then he added, "Little girl, how old are you?"

"Eight, monsieur."

"Are you going far?"

"At least fifteen minutes from here."

For a moment the man did not speak; then he asked abruptly, "Don't you have a mother?"

"I don't know," said the child. Before the man could say a word, she added, "I don't think I do. Everyone else does. But I don't think I have one."

And after a pause, she added, "I don't think I ever had one."

The man stopped, put the bucket on the ground, bent down, and put his hands on the child's shoulders. He tried to see her face in the darkness.

"What is your name?" he asked.

"Cosette."

It was as though an electric shock ran through the man. He looked at her again and then, letting go of her shoulders, took up the bucket and walked on.

A moment later, he asked, "Little one, where do you live?"

"At Montfermeil, if you know where that is."

Another pause; then he began again. "Who sent you out into the woods for water at this time of night?"

"Madame Thénardier."

The man continued in a voice that sounded casual though it trembled strangely: "What does she do, this Madame Thénardier?"

"She is my mistress," said the child. "She runs the tavern."

"The tavern," said the man. "Well, I'm going there to stay tonight. Show me the way."

They reached the village. Cosette guided the stranger through the streets. As they drew close to the tavern, Cosette shyly touched the man's arm.

"Monsieur? We are close to the house. Will you let

me take the bucket now?"

"Why?"

"Because if Madame sees that someone carried it for me, she will beat me."

The man gave her the bucket. A moment later they were at the tavern door. Cosette knocked.

Entertaining a Poor Man Who May Be Rich

"Madame," said Cosette, trembling as Mme. Thénardier opened the door, "there is a gentleman who has come for lodging."

"Is it you, monsieur?" she asked with an amiable sneer.

"Yes, madame," answered the man, touching his hat.

Rich travelers are not so polite. That gesture and the sight of the stranger's clothes and baggage made the amiable sneer disappear. "Come in, fellow," she added with a surly look.

The "fellow" entered and, after leaving his walking stick and bundle on a bench, sat down at a table on which Cosette had placed a bottle of wine and a glass.

Cosette took her usual place under the kitchen table and began to knit.

The man hardly touched the wine he had poured. He watched the child with a strange intensity.

Everything about this child—her walk, her attitude, the sound of her voice, the pauses between one word and another, her look, her silences, her slightest gesture—portrayed a single idea: fear.

Fear was spread all over her; she was covered with it. Fear squeezed her elbows against her sides, drew her heels up under her skirt, made her shrink into the least possible space, prevented her from breathing more than was absolutely necessary, and had become her bodily habit. In the depths of her eyes, there was an expression of astonishment mingled with terror.

This fear was so strong that, on coming into the house wet as she was, Cosette had not dared dry herself by the fire but had gone silently to her knitting work.

Now the door opened, and Eponine and Azelma entered. They were two really pretty girls, very charming. Both were so lively, neat, plump, fresh, and healthy that it was a pleasure to look at them. They shed light around them. Besides, in the tavern they were royalty. In all they did, there was authority.

When they entered, Mme. Thénardier said to them in a scolding tone full of adoration, "Ah, there you are, you two!" Then taking them on her knee one after the other, she smoothed their hair and retied their bows, then let them go with a gentle shake.

They went and sat by the fire. They had a doll that they turned back and forth on their knees amidst playful babbling. From time to time, Cosette raised her eyes from her knitting and watched them sadly as they played.

Eponine and Azelma did not notice Cosette. To them she was like the dog.

The Thénardier sisters' doll was very faded, old, and broken, but it seemed wonderful to Cosette, who had never in her life had a doll—a real doll, as children understand.

"Madame," said the stranger, "why don't you let her play?"

She replied sharply, "She has to work, since she eats. I don't feed her to have her do nothing."

"What is she knitting?" asked the stranger in his gentle voice which contrasted sharply with his beggar's clothes and worker's shoulders.

"Stockings. Stockings for my girls, who have none worth speaking of and would soon have to go barefoot," Mme. Thénardier condescended to answer.

The man looked at Cosette's poor red, bare feet and went on, "How long will it take her to finish that pair of stockings?"

"It will take her at least three or four good days, the lazy thing."

"And how much would this pair cost, when it is finished?"

Mme. Thénardier glared at him scornfully. "At least thirty sous."

"Would you take five francs for them?" asked the man.

Monsieur Thénardier now thought it was time for him to speak.

"Yes, monsieur, if that's your wish, you can have that pair of stockings for five francs. We can't refuse travelers, but you'll have to pay for them now."

"I'll buy that pair of stockings," answered the man, "and," he added, taking a five-franc piece out of his pocket and laying it on the table, "I'll pay for them."

Then he turned to Cosette.

"Now your work belongs to me. Play, my child."

Thénardier returned to his drink. His wife whispered in his ear, "Who can that yellow-coated man be?"

"I have seen," answered Thénardier in an authoritative tone, "millionaires with coats like that."

Cosette had stopped knitting, but she had not moved from her spot. She always stirred as little as possible. From a little box behind her she had taken out a few old rags and a little lead sword.

As birds make nests out of everything, children do the same with dolls. While Eponine and Azelma were dressing up the tavern cat, Cosette dressed up her sword. That done, she cradled it on her arm and was singing it softly to sleep.

Suddenly Cosette stopped. She had just turned and seen the Thénardiers' doll, which they had dropped to play with the cat. It was on the floor a few steps from the kitchen table.

She let go of the sword, which only half satisfied her, and looked around the room. Everyone was occupied; no one was looking at her. She didn't have a minute to lose. She crept out from under the table on her hands and knees, darted to the doll, and grabbed it. An instant later, she was back in her spot, sitting still, but turned so as to cast a shadow on the doll she held in her arms. The joy of playing with a doll was so rare for her that she seemed for once like a happy child.

Nobody had seen her except the traveler, who was slowly eating his supper.

The joy lasted for nearly fifteen minutes.

Suddenly the two girls stopped, amazed. Cosette had dared to pick up their doll.

Eponine got up, went to her mother, and tugged at her skirt.

"Leave me alone," said the mother. "What do you want?"

"Mother," said the child, "look at that!"

And she pointed to Cosette.

Madame Thénardier's face took on an expression of terrible fury. Cosette had stepped over all barriers. She had laid her hands on the doll of the "young ladies."

"Cosette!" she cried with a voice harsh with indignation.

Cosette took the doll and placed it gently on the floor. Then, without moving her eyes, she clasped her hands, and—frightful to say about a child of that age—she wrung them. None of the other experiences of her day had been able to draw any show of emotion from her—neither the trip through the woods nor the weight of the water bucket nor the sight of the whip nor even the cruel words she heard from her mistress. But now she burst into tears. She sobbed.

The traveler rose to his feet.

"What is the matter?" he asked Mme. Thénardier.

"Don't you see? That beggar has dared to touch the children's doll!"

The man walked straight to the street door and went out.

As soon as he left, the woman took advantage of his absence to give a sharp kick under the table to Cosette, who shrieked in response.

The door opened again, and the man reappeared, holding the fabulous doll we have mentioned, which all the children in town had admired since morning. He stood before Cosette and said, "Here you are, this is for you."

Cosette raised her eyes. She looked at the man; she looked at the doll; then she backed up under the table in the far corner of the room. She was no longer crying, but she looked as if she no longer dared to breathe.

Madame Thénardier began to question herself again: "What could this man be? A pauper? A millionaire?"

Her husband approached and whispered in her ear. "That thing cost at least thirty francs. No mistake about it. Get down on your knees to the man."

"Well, Cosette," said Mme. Thénardier in a voice entirely composed of sour honey, "aren't you going to take your dolly? Monsieur's giving you a doll. Take it. It's yours."

Cosette was looking at the doll with a sort of terror. Her face was still flooded with tears, but her eyes began to fill with the strange glow of joy. It seemed to her that if she touched the doll, thunder would erupt from it.

The attraction overcame her. She finally approached and shyly murmured, "Can I, madame?" "Good lord," said the woman, "it's yours. Monsieur is giving it to you."

"Is it true, monsieur? Is the lady for me?"

The stranger's eyes seemed to be brimming with tears. He seemed to be at the stage of emotion in which one does not speak for fear of weeping. He nodded to Cosette and put the hand of "the lady" in her little hand.

Cosette hastily removed her hand as if burned. Then, all at once she turned and seized the doll eagerly.

"I'll call her Catherine," she said.

It was a strange moment when soiled rags pressed against the ribbons and fresh pink crepe of the doll.

Thénardier Maneuvering

On the following morning, at least two hours before daybreak, Thénardier was at a table in the barroom making out a bill for the traveler in the yellow coat.

After a quarter hour and some erasures, Thénardier produced his masterpiece:

Bill of Monsieur in No. 1	
Supper	3 frs.
Room	10 frs.
Candle	5 frs.
Fire	4 frs.
Service	1 frs.
Total	23 frs.

"Monsieur Thénardier, you're right; he certainly owes it," murmured the woman, thinking of the doll given to Cosette in the presence of her daughters. "It's right, but it's too much. He won't pay it."

"Certainly he'll pay!" Thénardier said with his cold laugh.

What was said with that authority must be. The woman did not insist. The husband began to pace back and forth. A moment later he added, "I owe at least fifteen hundred francs."

"Ah ha!" replied the woman. "Remember I'm kicking Cosette out of the house today! The monster! It tears my guts to see her with that doll! I won't keep her in the house another day!"

Thénardier lit his pipe and answered only, "You present the bill to the man."

Then he left.

He was scarcely out of the room when the traveler entered.

"Up so soon?" said the woman. "Is monsieur going to leave us already?"

He answered, "Yes, madame, I am going away."

The woman handed him the bill, which he unfolded and looked at, but his thoughts were elsewhere.

"Madame," he asked, "do you do a good business here?"

"So-so, monsieur," said the woman, surprised not to get an explosion at the bill. She continued in a tragic way, "Oh, monsieur, the times are hard. This is a very little place, and we have so many expenses! Why, that little girl eats us out of house and home."

"Ah," said the man, "suppose you were relieved of her?"

"Who? Cosette?"

"Yes."

The woman's face lit up with a hideous expression.

"Ah, monsieur! My good monsieur! Take her, keep

her, take her away, carry her off, and be blessed by
the holy Virgin and all the saints in heaven!"

"Agreed."

"Really? You will take her?"

"I will."

"Immediately?"

"Immediately. Call the child."

"Cosette!" shouted the woman.

"In the meantime," continued the man, "I will pay
my bill. How much is it?"

He glanced at the bill and made a gesture of surprise. "Twenty-three francs?" he inquired.

The woman had had time to prepare for the shock.
"Yes, of course, monsieur! Twenty-three francs."

The stranger placed five five-franc pieces on the
table. "Go for the little girl," he said.

At that moment Thénardier moved to the middle of
the room and said, "As for the girl, I must talk with
monsieur about that. Leave us alone, please, my
dear."

Thénardier continued, "It's strange how we become
attached! What is all this silver? Take back your
money. I adore that child. And you want to take her
from us? I cannot consent to it. I would miss her. I
have had her since she was very small. It's true she
costs us money; it's true she has her faults. It's true
we're not rich; it's true I paid four hundred francs once
when she was sick. But we must do something for
God. She has neither a father nor a mother. I raised
her. In fact, I'm fond of this child. You understand, we
all have affections. I'm a simple sort, myself; I don't
think; I love this little girl. My wife is hotheaded, but
she loves her, too. You see, she's like our own child. I
feel the need of chatter around the house."

The stranger was staring at him all the time. He

continued: "Pardon me, monsieur, but I cannot give up the child just like that to a stranger. I mean you look like a very fine man. But I have to know for sure. I would want to know where she is going. I would not want to lose sight of her. I would want to know whom she is with, so I could come and see her once in a while. Well, some things just aren't possible. I don't even know your name. If you should take her away I must see a proper slip of paper, a passport or something."

The stranger, without lifting his eyes, answered severely and firmly.

"Monsieur Thénardier, people do not take a passport to travel fifteen miles from Paris. If I take Cosette, I take her. That is the end of it. You will not know my name, you will not know my address, you will not know where she is going. My intention is that she will never see you again in her life. Do you agree to that? Yes or no?"

Thénardier was a man who made up his mind at a glance. He decided that this was the moment to advance straight ahead and quickly. He abruptly showed his hand.

"Monsieur," he said, "I must have fifteen hundred francs."

The stranger took an old black pocketbook from his side pocket, opened it, and removed three banknotes, which he placed on the table. He then put his large thumb down on the bills and said to the tavern keeper, "Bring Cosette."

At her husband's command, the woman went to look for Cosette. She did not give her the usual slap or even call her names.

"Cosette," she said, almost gently, "come quickly."

An instant later, Cosette entered the room.

The stranger took a bundle he had brought and untied it. The bundle contained a little wool dress, an apron, a coarse cotton undergarment, a petticoat, a scarf, wool stockings, and shoes—a complete outfit for a girl of seven. It was all black.

"My dear," said the man, "take these things and dress yourself quickly."

The day was breaking when the people of Montfermeil who were beginning to open their doors saw going by on the road to Paris a poorly dressed man leading a little girl in mourning carrying a large pink doll. They were going toward Livry. It was the stranger and Cosette.

Number 9430 Comes Up Again

When Jean Valjean fell into the sea, or rather threw himself in, he was free from his irons. He swam underwater to a ship at anchor, where a boat was fastened.

He found a way to hide in the boat until evening. At night he again took to the water, and he reached shore a short way from Cap Brun.

There, as he did not lack for money, he bought clothes. Then Jean Valjean followed an obscure and wandering path. He found shelter in a dozen or more hamlets, until he finally reached Paris. We have just seen him at Montfermeil.

His first concern, on reaching Paris, had been to buy mourning clothes for a small girl and to find lodging. This done, he went to Montfermeil.

On the very day that Jean Valjean had rescued Cosette, he was back in Paris. He entered the city at night with the child. There he took a carriage as far as the Observatory, where he and the child got out. He paid the driver, he took Cosette by the hand, and both of them walked in the dark night toward the

Boulevard de l'Hopital.

The day had been strange and filled with emotion for Cosette. They had eaten bread and cheese behind hedges; they had changed carriages and traveled short distances on foot. She did not complain, although she was tired. Jean Valjean knew that from the way she pulled more heavily on his hand while they walked. He picked her up in his arms. Cosette, without letting go of Catherine, laid her head on Jean Valjean's shoulder and went to sleep.

3 *The Old Gorbeau House*

Forty years ago, anyone who ventured into the part of the city where Jean Valjean walked would have reached certain places where Paris seemed to disappear. It was not the country, for there were houses and streets. It was not a city, because the streets had ruts like the highways and grass grew along the borders. It was not a village, for the houses were too large. What was it then? It was a boulevard of a great city that was wilder at night than a forest and gloomier by day than a graveyard.

It was the old quarter of the Horse Market.

There, near a manufacturing building and behind some garden walls, could be seen an old ruined dwelling that at first sight seemed small as a cottage yet was in reality as huge as a cathedral. Nearly the whole house was hidden. Only the door and one window could be seen. The old house had only one story.

The door was merely a collection of worm-eaten boards tacked together with crosspieces that looked like firewood clumsily split. It opened directly onto a steep staircase with high steps that seemed to rise like a ladder and disappear into the shadow between two walls.

The staircase led to a very spacious interior, which looked like a barn converted into a house. This structure had a long hall on which there opened, on either side, apartments of different sizes resembling booths rather than rooms. These rooms looked out onto the

shapeless grounds of the neighborhood. It was altogether dark and dull and dreary.

The letter carrier called the house No. 50-52, but it was known in the neighborhood as the Gorbeau House.

A Nest for Owl and Wren

Jean Valjean stopped in front of this Gorbeau tenement.[1] He had chosen this lonely place to make his nest.

He fumbled in his coat and took out a sort of night key, opened the door, entered, carefully closed the door again, and climbed the staircase, still carrying Cosette.

At the top he drew from his pocket another key, with which he opened another door. The room he entered and closed immediately again was a kind of attic, rather roomy, furnished only with a mattress on the floor, a table, and a few chairs. A stove containing a fire, the coals of which were still visible, stood in one corner. At the further end there was a little room containing a cot bed. On this Jean Valjean laid the child without waking her.

The little girl had fallen asleep without knowing with whom she was, and she continued to sleep without knowing where she was.

Jean Valjean bent down and kissed the child's hand. Nine months before, he had kissed the hand of the mother, who had also just fallen asleep.

He knelt by the bedside of Cosette.

Two Misfortunes Equal One Happiness

Dawn found Jean Valjean still near Cosette's bed. He waited there motionless, to see her wake up.

---

1. **tenement** a low-rent apartment building or rooming house

Something new was entering his soul.

Jean Valjean had never loved anything. For twenty-five years he had been alone in the world. He had never been a father, lover, husband, or friend. At the galleys, he was cross, sullen, ignorant, and stubborn.

When he saw Cosette, when he had taken her away, he felt his heart move. All that he had of feeling and affection extended toward Cosette. He would approach the bed where she slept and would stand there delighted. He did not comprehend the feelings of the first love he had known in all his fifty-five years.

Poor old heart, so young!

This was the second white vision he had had. The bishop had caused the dawn of virtue in him; Cosette evoked the dawn of love.

On her part, Cosette, too, underwent a change. She could not recollect her own mother. Like all children, she had tried to love, but she had not been able to succeed. Everything had repelled her—the Thénardiers, their children, other children. She had loved the dog, but it died, and after that no person or thing had anything to do with her. At the age of eight, her heart was cold. It was not her fault; she did not lack the ability, only the opportunity. So, from the first day, she began to love this kind new friend. He no longer impressed her as old and poor. In her eyes, Jean Valjean was handsome, just as the garret room was pretty.

Jean Valjean had chosen a hiding place well. He was there in a state of security that seemed complete. The room with the side chamber he occupied was the one whose window looked out onto the street. The window being the only one in the house, there were no neighbors' prying eyes. And although the upper floor of the house had several rooms and lofts, except for an old woman, all the rest was uninhabited. It was

this old woman who collected the re
room as we have described it, and ki
the stove the evening of their arrival.

Jean Valjean had begun to teach
To do this and to watch her playing w
his life. And then, he would talk to
mother and teach her to pray.

She called him "Father" and knew him by no other
name.

The Beggar and the Five-Franc Piece

There was, in the neighborhood, a beggar who sat
crouching over the edge of a condemned public well.
Jean Valjean often gave alms; in fact he never passed
without giving the man a few pennies. Sometimes he
spoke to him. Those who were envious of the poor
creature said he was in the pay of the police.

One evening, as Jean Valjean was passing that way
alone, he noticed the beggar sitting in his usual place.
The man, as usual, seemed to be praying and was bent
over. Jean Valjean went up to him and put a piece of
money in his hand as usual. The beggar suddenly
looked up and gazed intently at Jean Valjean; then he
quickly dropped his head. The movement was like a
flash. Jean Valjean shuddered; it seemed to him he
had seen not the calm face of the old man but a terrible and well-known face. He experienced the sensation of someone finding himself face-to-face with a
tiger. He was horror stricken, not daring to breathe or
to speak. Some instinct prevented Jean Valjean from
speaking. The beggar had the same rags, the same
general appearance as every other day. "Pshaw!" said
Jean Valjean to himself. "I am dreaming! It cannot
be!" But he went home, anxious and ill at ease.

He scarcely dared to admit, even to himself, that

.ce he thought he had seen was that of Javert.

.'he next day, at dusk, he went out again. The beggar was at his place. "Good day! Good day!" said Jean Valjean with a strong voice as he gave the man the usual alms. The beggar raised his head and answered in a whining voice, "Thanks, kind sir, thanks!" It was only the old beggar.

Some days later, near eight o'clock in the evening, he was giving Cosette her spelling lesson, which the child was repeating in a loud voice. Suddenly he heard the door of the building open and close again. That seemed odd. He made a sign for Cosette to be quiet. He heard someone coming up the stairs. The footstep was heavy; it sounded like a man's; but the old woman next door wore heavy shoes. However, Jean Valjean blew out his candle.

He sent Cosette to bed, telling her to lie down very quietly. The footsteps stopped. Jean Valjean remained silent and motionless, his back to the door, still seated on his chair, and holding his breath in the darkness. After a time, not hearing anything, he turned around without making any noise. As he raised his eyes toward the door, he saw a ray of light through the keyhole. There was, evidently, someone outside with a candle and who was listening.

A few minutes later the light disappeared. There was no sound of footsteps, which seemed to mean the person had removed his shoes.

Jean Valjean threw himself on the bed without undressing. But he did not shut his eyes that night.

At dawn, as he was falling asleep, he was awakened again by the creaking of the door of a room at the end of the hall. Then he heard the same footsteps that had climbed the stairs the previous night. The steps approached. He placed his eye against the keyhole, hoping to get a glimpse of the person. It was a man, indeed, who passed by the door, this time without stopping. When the man reached the stairs, a ray of light made his figure stand out in profile. The man was tall, wore a long frock coat, and carried a stick under his arm. It was unmistakably the figure of Javert.

The man had entered by means of a key. Who had given him the key? And what did this mean?

At seven o'clock, he made a roll of a hundred francs he had in a drawer and put it in his pocket. A five-franc piece escaped his grasp and rolled away jingling across the floor.

At dusk, he went to the street door and looked up and down. No one was to be seen. The street seemed utterly deserted. It's true that there might have been someone hidden behind a tree.

He went upstairs again.

"Come," he said to Cosette.

He took her hand and they went out.

4 A Dark Chase Needs a Silent Hound

Zigzags

Jean Valjean immediately left the main street and began to thread his way through the streets, making as many turns as possible, returning sometimes on his own tracks to be sure he was not being followed.

The moon was full. Jean Valjean was not sorry for that. He could glide along the house walls on the dark side of the street and observe the light side. He felt sure that no one was behind him.

At eleven o'clock he crossed the street in front of the Police Commissary. The instinct we have spoken about made him turn his head. At that moment he saw clearly three men following him quite near. They passed under the lamp on the dark side of the street. One of the men entered the passage leading to the commissioner's house. The one in the lead seemed very suspicious.

"Come, child!" he said to Cosette, and he hurried out of the street. He made a circle around to the square nearby.

The square was well lighted. Jean Valjean concealed himself in a doorway, thinking that if the men were still following him he could get a good view of them when they crossed the lighted area.

No more than three minutes passed when the men appeared. There were now four of them; all were tall, dressed in long brown coats, with round hats, and with large clubs in their hands. They stopped in the center

of the square to converse. They appeared to be undecided. The man who seemed to be the leader turned
and pointed in the direction in which Jean Valjean
was. One of the others seemed stubbornly to insist on
the opposite direction. The instant the leader turned,
the moon shone fully on his face. Jean Valjean recognized Inspector Javert.

Happily, the men were uncertain. Jean Valjean
took advantage of their hesitation to gain time. He
picked up Cosette in his arms and left the doorway at
a fast pace. He hurried until he reached the quay. It
was deserted. The streets were deserted. Nobody was
behind him. He took a breath. He had arrived at the
Austerlitz Bridge.

A large cart was passing the river and going toward
the right bank at the same time as he was. This could
be useful. He could go the whole length of the bridge
in the shadow of the cart.

From his vantage point, he could see the whole
length of the bridge. At that moment, four shadows
entered the bridge. It was the four men.

Jean Valjean felt a shudder. One hope was left him.
By plunging into the little street before him, if he
could reach the woods, the marshes, the fields, the
open ground, he could escape. He entered it.

Three hundred paces on, the street forked. Jean
Valjean had to choose a direction. Which? Without
hesitation, he took the right. The left, he knew, led to
the more inhabited section of the city. The right
branch headed to the country.

He turned from time to time and looked back. The
first few times he saw nothing, and he continued reassured. Suddenly on turning again he thought he saw,
from where he had just passed, far in the darkness,
something which stirred.

He came to a wall. Here again he must decide; should he take the right or left?

He looked to the right. The end of this blind alley was plain to see—a great white wall.

He looked to the left. That alley was open and, about two hundred paces on, ran into a street. That way was safety.

The instant Jean Valjean decided to turn to the left, to try to reach the street, he saw—at the corner of the alley and the street where he wanted to go—a black motionless statue. It was a man who had just been posted there and who was waiting for him, guarding the passage.

Jean Valjean was startled. There was no doubt. He was being watched. What should he do?

There was no time to turn back. What he had seen moving behind him was undoubtedly Javert and his squad of men. To turn back was to fall into their hands. To advance was to fall into the hands of this man. Jean Valjean felt as if he were caught by a chain that was slowly winding up. He looked up into the sky in despair.

Groping to Escape

At that moment a muffled, regular sound could be heard in the distance. Seven or eight soldiers, formed in a platoon, had turned into the street. Jean Valjean saw the gleam of their bayonets. They were coming towards him. At their head, he could make out the tall form of Javert, advancing slowly and with precaution.

There was only one thing possible. Jean Valjean measured with his eye the wall, above which he saw a lime tree. It was about eighteen feet high, and it was topped by a flat stone without any projections.

The difficulty was Cosette. She did not know how

to scale a wall. To abandon her was unthinkable; to carry her was impossible. He needed all his strength to accomplish the climb. The least burden would make him lose his center of gravity. He needed a cord. He had none. Where could he find some cord at midnight? At that instant, Jean Valjean would have given anything for a rope.

His despairing eye encountered the lamp-post in the little alley.

Now, at this time in Paris, there were no gaslights. At nightfall, the street lamps were lowered for lighting by means of a rope running the length of the street, running though grooves in the posts.

Jean Valjean, with the energy of a final effort, crossed the street with the point of his knife ready. An instant later, he was back at Cosette's side. He had a rope.

Meanwhile the place, the late hour, the darkness, Jean Valjean's actions—all this began to disturb Cosette. Any other child would have let out loud cries before now. She just pulled on the skirt of Jean Valjean's coat. The sound of the patrol was coming closer.

"Father," she whispered, "I am afraid. Who is that coming?"

"It is Mme. Thénardier," answered the man.

Cosette shuddered. He added: "Don't make a sound. I'll take care of her. If you cry, she will hear you. She is coming to catch you."

Then, without any haste or any hesitation, he removed his cravat[1] and wrapped it around Cosette's body under the arms, attached it to the end of the rope, took the other end of the rope in his teeth,

---

1. **cravat** scarf worn around the neck

removed his shoes and stockings and threw them over the wall. He began to pull himself up with as much steadiness and sureness as if he had a ladder. Only half a minute had passed before he was on his knees on the wall.

Cosette was astonished. All at once she heard Jean Valjean's voice calling her in a low whisper: "Put your back against the wall."

She obeyed.

"Don't speak, and don't be afraid," added Jean Valjean.

She felt herself lifted from the ground. Before she had time to think, she was on top of the wall. Jean Valjean grabbed her and put her on his back, lay down flat, and crawled along the top of the wall. As he thought, there was a building there, the roof sloping very gently, almost to the ground.

Just as Jean Valjean reached the roof of the building, a violent uproar signaled the arrival of the patrol. He heard Javert's thundering voice.

"Search the alley! The street's guarded!"

Jean Valjean slid down the roof, keeping hold of Cosette. He reached the lime tree and jumped to the ground. Whether from terror or from courage, Cosette had not made a sound. Her hands were a little scraped.

An Enigma

Jean Valjean found himself in a very large garden, one of those gloomy gardens that seemed made to be seen at night or in winter. He saw a row of large poplar trees, some very tall forest trees in the corners, a clear space in the center where stood a single very large tree, then a few fruit trees, some vegetable beds, a melon patch, and an old well. Here and there were stone benches. The garden walks were bordered with perfectly straight little shrubs. The grass covered some of them, and green moss covered the rest.

Jean Valjean's first business was to find his shoes and put them on. Then he headed for the shed with Cosette, who trembled and pressed close to his side. They heard the racket of the patrol, the calls from Javert to the watchmen he had stationed.

After some time, the rumbling began to recede. Still Jean Valjean did not breathe. He had placed his hand over Cosette's mouth.

The solitude about them was strangely calm. Suddenly, in the midst of the calm, a new sound arose. It was a hymn which came from the darkness, a mingling mixture of prayer and song in the silence of the night—voices of women. The song came from the gloomy building which overlooked the garden. At the moment when the sounds of the demons receded, the song was like a choir of angels approaching in the darkness.

Cosette and Jean Valjean fell on their knees.

The voices had a strange effect. They did not prevent the building from appearing deserted. It was like a supernatural song in an uninhabited dwelling.

The chant stopped. Everything lapsed again into silence. There was nothing more in the street, nothing more in the garden.

Cosette laid her head on a stone and went to sleep.

Jean Valjean sat near her and looked at her. He plainly saw the truth, the basis for his life henceforth. So long as he should have her with him, he would need for nothing else and he would fear nothing except on her account.

During this wandering of his thoughts, Jean Valjean had for some time heard a strange noise in the garden. It sounded like a little bell which someone was shaking.

The noise made Jean Valjean turn. He looked and saw that there was someone in the garden.

Something which resembled a man was walking among the glass domes in the melon patch. He watched the strange motions of the man. The sound of the bell followed every movement of the man. It seemed evident the bell was attached to the man. What could that mean?

While he asked himself these questions, he touched Cosette's hands. They were icy.

"Oh, God!" he said.

He called to her in a soft voice: "Cosette!"

She did not open her eyes.

He shook her firmly.

She did not awaken.

"Could she be dead?" said he, jumping up.

He listened for her breathing. She breathed but with breaths that seemed feeble and about to stop.

The Bell-Ringer

Jean Valjean walked directly to the man he saw in the garden. He had taken out the roll of money from his vest pocket.

The man had his head down. He did not see anyone approaching. With a few strides, Jean Valjean was at the man's side.

"A hundred francs!"

The man jumped and raised his eyes.

"A hundred francs for you," continued Jean Valjean, "if you will give me refuge tonight."

The moon shone fully in his face.

"Why, it is you, Father Madeleine!" said the man.

The name, said that way, in this unknown place,

by this unknown man, made Jean Valjean step back.

"Who are you?   And what is this house?" asked Jean Valjean.

"Indeed! I am the one you got the job for here, and this house is the one you got me a job in. What? You don't remember me?"

"No. How do you know me?" asked Jean Valjean.

"You saved my life," said the man. And as he turned a ray of light lit up the side of his face. Jean Valjean recognized old Fauchelevent.

"I remember you," added Jean Valjean. "What are you doing here?"

"Oh! I am covering my melons. There is going to be a frost."

"And what is that bell you have on your knee?"

"That!" answered Fauchelevent, "is to warn the women of where I am, so they keep away."

"Keep away from you? What is this house?"

"Why, you should know that very well. You got me the job here as gardener. It is the Convent of the Petit Picpus."

Jean Valjean remembered. He said aloud, "Well, I must stay here."

"Oh! My God!" exclaimed Fauchelevent.

Jean Valjean approached the old man and said in a grave voice:

"Father Fauchelevent, I saved your life."

"I was the first to remember that," answered the old man.

"Well, you can do for me now what I once did for you."

"Oh! That would be a blessing if I could do something for you in return for that! I can save your life? Monsieur the Mayor, this old man is at your disposal. What do you want me to do?"

"I will explain. You have a room?"

"I have a small shanty over there, in the corner that nobody ever sees. There are three rooms."

The shanty was so well hidden behind the ruins of the old convent that no one could see it. In fact, Jean Valjean had not seen it.

"Good," he said; "I ask two things."

"What are they, Monsieur Madeleine?"

"First that you not tell anyone what you know about me. Second that you will not attempt to learn more."

"As you please. I know you would not do anything dishonorable and that you are a man of God. Besides, you put me here. It is your place. I am yours."

"Very well. Then come with me. We will go for the child."

"Ah!" exclaimed Fauchelevent. "There is a child." He said not another word but followed Jean Valjean like a dog follows his master.

In half an hour Cosette was warm before a good fire and asleep in the gardener's bed.

The two men warmed themselves, with their elbows on a table, on which Fauchelevent had set a piece of cheese, brown bread, a bottle of wine, and two glasses.

"Ah, Father Madeleine! You didn't know me at first? You save people's lives and then forget them? That's bad; they remember you. You are ungrateful!"

5   *Cemeteries Take What Is Given Them*

The Way to Enter a Convent

Before going to sleep, Jean Valjean had said: "From here on, I must remain here." Those words chased one another around Fauchelevent's brain all night.

To tell the truth, neither man slept.

Jean Valjean felt that he was discovered and that Javert was on his trail. He knew that he and Cosette were lost if they ever returned to the city. The convent was both the safest and the most dangerous place to be. It was the most dangerous because, if he was discovered, it was a serious crime. It was the safest, for who would come to look for him there? To live in an impossible place—that is safety.

For his part, Fauchelevent was racking his brain. How did Monsieur Madeleine get there, with such walls? The walls of a convent are not so easily crossed. How did he happen to be with a child? A man does not scale a steep wall with a child in his arms! Who is the child? Where did they both come from? Fauchelevent saw nothing clearly except this: Monsieur Madeleine had saved his life. That single certainty was enough, and it determined him. He said to himself: "It's my turn now." And he added in his conscience: "Monsieur Madeleine did not deliberate so long when the question was to squeeze himself under a wagon to draw me out." He decided that he would save Monsieur Madeleine.

But to have him remain in the convent? That was a

problem. But he did not shrink from it. The man—
who had for a ladder only his devotion, his good will,
and a little country know-how—was committed to his
good intention.

He formed his resolution then: to devote himself to
Monsieur Madeleine.

Fauchelevent Confronts the Difficulty

Father Fauchelevent rapped softly at a door, and a
soft voice answered, "Come in."

The door was that of the sitting room that was set
aside for use in communicating with the gardener. It
was near the back of the convent. The prioress was
seated in the only chair, waiting for Fauchelevent.

The gardener made a timid bow. The prioress, who
was saying her rosary, raised her eyes and said: "Ah!
It is you, Father Fauvent."

This abbreviation of the man's name had been
adopted in the convent.

"Father Fauvent, I have called you."

"I am here, reverend mother."

"I wish to speak to you."

"And I, for my part," said Fauchelevent with a boldness that surprised even him, "I have something to
say to the most reverend mother."

The prioress looked at him. "You have a communication to make to me?"

"A petition!"

"What is it?"

Fauchelevent, with the confidence of someone who
knows he is appreciated, began to talk. He spoke at
length of his age, of his infirmities, of the weight of
years on him, of the growing demands of his work, of
the size of the garden, of the nights to be spent like
last night, for example, when he had to put awnings

over the melons. He finally ended with this: that he had a brother (The prioress jumped); that the brother was not young (The prioress was reassured); that if it was desired, this brother could come and live with him and help him; that he was an excellent gardener; and that the brother had a little girl that he would bring with him. The girl would be reared under God in the house, and she—who knows—might one day become a nun.

When he finished, the prioress said: "Can you between now and nighttime procure a strong iron bar?"

"For what work?"

"To be used as a lever."

"Yes, reverend mother," answered Fauchelevent.

The prioress, without another word, got up and went into the next room, where the vocal mothers were probably assembled. Fauchelevent waited alone.

Mother Innocent

About fifteen minutes passed. The prioress returned and took her seat.

We shall report, as well as possible, the dialogue that followed.

"Father Fauvent?"

"Reverend mother?"

"You are familiar with the chapel?"

"Yes, reverend mother."

"A stone there is to be raised."

"Heavy?"

"The slab of pavement at the side of the altar, covering the vault."

"That is a piece of work where it would be well to have two men."

"The stone is arranged to turn on a pivot."

"Very well, reverend mother. I will open the vault."

"And the four mother choristers will help you."

"And when the vault is opened?"

"It must be shut again."

"Is that all?"

"No."

"Give me your orders, most reverend mother."

"Something must be let down."

There was silence. The prioress, after hesitating, spoke:

"Father Fauvent, you know that a mother died this morning."

"No, reverend mother."

"Father Fauvent, we must do what the dead want done. To be buried in the vault under the altar of the chapel, not to go into the ground, is the last wish of Mother Crucifixion."

"But it is forbidden. If it should come to be known?"

"We have confidence in you."

"I shall obey."

"It is well."

"Reverend mother, I need a lever at least six feet long."

"Where will you get it?"

"Where there are gratings, there are always iron bars. I have my pile of old iron at the back of the garden."

"Father Fauvent, be at the high altar with the iron bar at eleven o'clock. It must all be finished within forty-five minutes."

"I will do everything to prove my commitment to the community. Reverend mother, is that all?"

"No."

"What more is there, then?"

"There is still the empty coffin. What will be done

with the empty coffin?"

"It will be put in the ground."

"Empty?"

"Reverend mother, I will put some earth into it. That will have the effect of a body."

"So you will prepare the coffin?"

"I will attend to that."

The prioress's face, until then dark and worried, became serene again. She dismissed Fauchelevent, who moved toward the door. As he was going out, the prioress gently raised her voice:

"Father Fauvent, I am pleased with you. Tomorrow, after the burial, bring your brother to me. And tell him to bring his daughter."

Cosette Learns to Laugh

Jean Valjean was regularly installed. He had his leather kneecap and bell. From then on he had his commission. His name was Ultimus Fauchelevent.

The prioress immediately took Cosette into her friendship and gave her a place in the school as a charity pupil.

A very pleasant life began for Jean Valjean. He worked in the garden every day, and he was very useful there. He had formerly been a pruner and now found it quite comfortable to be a gardener. He knew all kinds of tips and secrets of field work. Nearly all the orchard trees were wild stock; he grafted them and made them bear fruit.

Cosette was allowed to come each day to spend an hour with him. She adored him. At the appointed hour she would hurry to the little building. When she entered the place, she filled it with pleasure. Jean Valjean basked in her presence and felt his own happiness increase because of the happiness he gave to

Cosette. The delight we inspire in others returns to us stronger than ever. At the recreation hours, Jean Valjean watched her playing from a distance, and he could tell her laugh from that of the others.

For now Cosette laughed. Her face had changed. Its gloomy look had disappeared. Laughter is sunshine; it chases winter from the human face.

When the recreation time was over and Cosette went in, Jean Valjean watched the windows of her schoolroom. At night he would rise from his bed to look at the windows of the room in which she slept.

God has his own ways. The convent, like Cosette, served to complete in Jean Valjean the work of the bishop.

Everything around him—this quiet garden, these flowers, these children shouting with joy, these meek and simple women, this silent convent—gradually entered into all his being. Little by little, his soul subsided into silence, peace, simplicity, and joy. He reflected on the two houses of God that had come into his life at critical times. Had it not been for the first, he would have fallen back into crime. Had it not been for the second, he would have fallen into punishment.

His heart melted with gratitude, and he loved more and more.

Several years passed this way. Cosette was growing up.

Marius

1 *Little Gavroche*

Whose Family Lives at No. 50-52

The events we are about to relate occurred about eight or nine years after Jean Valjean and Cosette arrived at the convent.

There was a little boy of eleven or twelve years of age, with the laughter of youth on his lips but a heart that was absolutely dark and empty. This child was muffled up in a pair of man's trousers, not from his father, and a woman's shirt, not inherited from his mother. Strangers had clothed him in these rags out of charity. Still, he had a father and a mother. But his father never thought of him, and his mother did not love him. He was one of those children who are so deserving of pity because they have father and mother yet are orphans.

This little boy never felt so happy as when he was in the street. The pavement was not as hard to him as the heart of his mother.

His parents had thrown him out into life with a kick.

He laughed when people called him an errand boy, and he got angry when they called him a ragamuffin. He had no shelter, no food, no fire, no love. But he was lighthearted because he was free.

It happened sometimes, every two or three months,

that he would say to himself, "Come, I'll go and see my mother!" Then he would go down along the quays, cross the bridges, reach the suburbs, walk and arrive—where? Precisely at that double number 50-52, which is known to the reader as the Gorbeau House.

The tenement 50-52, usually empty and permanently decorated with the sign Rooms to Let was, wonder of wonders, inhabited by several persons who, in all other respects, had no relation to or connection with each other. All of them belonged to the population of scavenger and ragpicker.

The landlady from the time of Jean Valjean was dead and had been replaced by another exactly like her. I do not remember which philosopher it was who said: "There is never any shortage of old women."

The new old woman was called Madame Burgon, and her life had been remarkable for nothing except a series of three parakeets which had held her affections.

Among those who lived in the building, the most miserable was a family of four persons—father, mother, and two daughters nearly grown. All four lodged in the same garret room, one of those cells we have already described.

This family of four at first sight presented nothing peculiar except its extreme poverty. The father, in renting the room, had given his name as Jondrette.

Now this was the family of this happy little barefooted urchin. When he came in, they would ask: "Where have you come from?" He would answer: "From the street." When he was going away, they would ask him: "Where are you going to?" He would answer: "Into the street." His mother would ask him: "What have you come here for?"

The child felt no suffering from this method of existence, and he bore no ill will to anybody. He did not know how a father and mother ought to be.

But yet his mother loved his sisters.

We had forgotten to say that on the Boulevard this boy went by the name of Little Gavroche. Why Gavroche? Probably because his father's name was Jondrette.

The room occupied by the Jondrettes in the Gorbeau tenement was the last one at the end of the hall. The adjoining cell was inhabited by a very poor young man who was called Monsieur Marius.

Let us see who and what Monsieur Marius was.

2 *The Grand Bourgeois*

Over Ninety Years Old

Monsieur Gillenormand was as much alive as any man can be, in 1831. He was one of those men who have become curious simply because they have lived a long time. They are strange because formerly they were like everybody else and now they are no longer like anybody else.

He had spent his ninetieth year, walked erect, spoke in a loud voice, saw clearly, drank hard, ate, slept, and snored. He had all of his thirty-two teeth. He wore glasses only when reading. For ten years past he had given up women. He was no longer pleasing, he said. He did not add that he was too old, only that he was too poor. If anyone contradicted him, he raised his cane. He beat his servants. He had an unmarried daughter over fifty years old to whom he was nasty when he was angry.

He lived in the Marais,[1] rue des Filles du Calvaire, No. 6.

The house was his own. He occupied an ancient and large apartment on the first floor, between the street and the gardens. It was covered to the ceiling with fine Gobelin and Beauvais tapestry showing pastoral scenes. The subjects of the ceiling and the panels were repeated in miniature on the armchairs. Long, full

---

1. **Marais** section of Paris where royalty and wealthy people lived

curtains hung at the windows and made great, magnificent folds. The garden, which was immediately below his windows, was connected with the angle between them by means of a staircase of twelve to fifteen steps, which the old man went up and down easily.

He had kept up with the fashions. His coat was of light cloth, with wide lapels, a long tail, and large steel buttons. Add to this knee-length breeches and shoe buckles. He always carried his hands in his pockets. He said authoritatively: "The French Revolution is a mess of scamps."

Always Gillenormand worshipped the Bourbons[2] and held 1789[3] in horror. He was constantly telling how he saved himself during the Reign of Terror[4] and how—if he had not had some humor and wit—his head would have been cut off. If any young man went so far as to praise the Republic[5] in his presence, he turned black in the face and was angry enough to faint.

He had two servants, "a male and a female." He always gave the men the name of the province where they had lived. As for the females, they were always called Nicolette.

He had had two wives. By the first he had one daughter, who had never married. By the second he had another daughter, who died when about thirty years old. She had married, for love, a soldier of fortune who had served under Napoleon. The old man

---

2. **Bourbons** royal family that ruled in France from 1589 until 1793 and again from 1814 to 1830
3. **1789** date of the French Revolution
4. **Reign of Terror** period (1793-1794) during the French Revolution when thousands of people were executed and anyone could be arrested
5. **Republic** period in France between 1792 and 1804

called the son-in-law "the disgrace of my family." He had very little belief in God.

He was a perfect man of the eighteenth century, frivolous and great.

Two Do Not Make a Pair

As for the two daughters of Monsieur Gillenormand, they were born ten years apart. The younger had married the man of her dreams, but she was dead. The elder, unmarried and now fifty, lived with her father. Outside of the immediate family nobody had ever known her first name. She was called Mademoiselle Gillenormand the elder.

She was sad, with a sadness even she did not understand. There was in her entire being the stupor of a life that had ended but had never begun. She took care of her father's house.

Besides this old woman and the old man, there was a child—a little boy, always trembling and quiet before Monsieur Gillenormand. The old man always spoke to the child in a stern voice and sometimes with a raised cane: "Here! You rascal! Come here! Answer me! Let me see you," etc. etc. He idolized the boy.

It was his grandson. We shall see this child again.

3

The Grandfather and the Grandson

The First Baron Pontmercy

Anyone who passed through the little city of Vernon would have noticed a man of about fifty with a leather casque[1] on his head, dressed in pantaloons and waistcoat of coarse gray cloth, to which something yellow was stitched which had a red ribbon. He was shod in wooden shoes, his face was browned by the sun, his hair was almost white, and he had a large scar running from his forehead down his cheek. He walked bent over, older than his years, with a pruning knife in his hand.

The man thus dressed lived, in 1817, in a small, humble house. He lived there alone, in silence and poverty, with a woman who was neither young nor old, neither pretty nor ugly, neither a peasant nor a bourgeois, who took care of him. The square of earth which he called his garden was famous in the town for the beauty of the flowers he grew in it. Flowers were his occupation.

Anyone, at the same time, who had read the military memoirs or biographies or newspapers or bulletins of the Grand Army[2] would have often seen the name George Pontmercy. When young, this George Pontmercy was a soldier at Waterloo.[3] It was

---

1. **casque** kind of hat like a helmet
2. **Grand Army** the army of Napoleon
3. **Waterloo** place in Belgium where Napoleon was finally defeated on June 18, 1815

he who carried the flag to the emperor's feet. He was covered with blood, having received a saber stroke across the face as he seized the colors. The emperor, pleased, cried: "You are now a Colonel, you are a Baron, you are an Officer of the Legion of Honor!"[4] Pontmercy answered: "Sire, thank you for my widow." An hour later he was struck down.

The government put him on half pay and then sent him to a residence at Vernon. King Louis XVIII refused to recognize his position as officer of the Legion of Honor, as well as his rank of colonel and his title of baron. On his part, he never passed up an opportunity to write Colonel Baron Pontmercy. He had only one old blue coat, and he never went out without putting on the badge of an officer of the Legion of Honor.

He took the smallest house he could find in Vernon and lived there alone, as we have seen. Between the two wars, he had found time to marry Mademoiselle Gillenormand. The old bourgeois was outraged but consented. In 1815, Madame Pontmercy, a noble woman in every respect, died, leaving a child. The child would have been the colonel's joy, but the grandfather demanded his grandson, declaring that—unless he were given up to him—he would disinherit him. The father gave in for the sake of the little boy and, not being able to care for his child, he set about loving flowers.

Monsieur Gillenormand had no communication with his son-in-law. To him, the colonel was "a bandit," and he made fun of "his barony." It was clearly understood that Pontmercy should never try to see his

---

4. **Legion of Honor** award given for distinguished service to the country

son or speak to him. The Gillenormands intended to bring up the child to their liking. Perhaps the colonel did wrong to accept these conditions, but he submitted thinking he was doing the right thing for the child.

The child, whose name was Marius, knew that he had a father, but nothing more. Nobody spoke a word about him. Little by little, the boy came to think of his father only with shame and with a closed heart.

While he was growing up, every two or three months the colonel would go to the church Saint Sulpice, at the hour when Aunt Gillenormand took Marius to mass. There, concealed behind a pillar and motionless, he watched his child. This battle-scarred veteran was afraid of the woman.

Twice a year, Marius wrote letters to his father, which his aunt dictated. That was all that Monsieur Gillenormand allowed, and the father replied with very tender letters that only found their way into the grandfather's pocket, unread.

The Bandit's End

Like all children, Marius Pontmercy went through various studies. After Aunt Gillenormand's tutoring, he was passed on to a professor of the classics. He then had his years at college and entered law school. He was a royalist,[5] fanatical in his ideas, and unsociable. He had little love for his grandfather, and the place of his father was a dark void.

In 1827, Marius was eighteen years old. On coming in one evening, he saw his grandfather with an envelope in his hand.

"Marius," said Monsieur Gillenormand, "you will leave tomorrow for Vernon to see your father."

---

5. royalist one who favors royal government

Marius shuddered. He was convinced that his father, "the saberer" as his grandfather called him in his kinder moments, did not love him. That was clear since he had abandoned him and left him to others. Feeling unloved, he felt no love back. Nothing more natural, he said to himself.

He was so astounded he did not ask any questions. The grandfather continued:

"It appears that he is sick. He is asking for you."

The next day at dusk, Marius arrived at Vernon. Candles were just being lighted. He asked the way to "the house of Monsieur Pontmercy," for he also did not recognize his father as baron or colonel.

He rang the bell of the house that had been pointed out to him. A woman opened the door with a small lamp in her hand.

"Monsieur Pontmercy—is he here?" asked Marius. The woman remained motionless for a moment and then gave an affirmative nod of the head.

"Can I speak with him?"

The woman gave a negative sign.

"But I am his son!" continued Marius. "He expects me."

Then he noticed that she was in tears.

She pointed to the door of a low room.

In this room there were three men: one of them standing, one on his knees, and one stripped to his shirt and lying at full length upon the floor. The one on the floor was the colonel. The two others were a physician and a priest praying.

The colonel had been attacked with a brain fever three days earlier. He had just died. The doctor and priest had been called. The doctor had arrived too late; the priest had come too late. The son had come too late, too.

Marius looked at the man whom he was seeing for the first time and the last. He thought that this man was his father and that this man was dead, and he was unmoved. The sorrow he experienced was the sorrow he would have felt for any other man whom he might have seen stretched out in death.

Marius felt ashamed that he was too little moved by his father's death. At the same time he felt something like remorse. Was it his fault? He did not love his father!

The colonel left nothing. The sale of his furniture hardly paid for his burial. The woman found a scrap of paper, which she handed to Marius. It was in the handwriting of the colonel:

> *For my son.* The emperor made me a baron on the battlefield of Waterloo. Since the government contests this title which I bought with my blood, my son will take it and bear it. I need not say that he will be worthy of it.

On the back was added:

> At the battle of Waterloo, a sergeant saved my life. The man's name is Thénardier. Not long ago, he owned a tavern in a suburb of Paris, at Chelles or Montfermeil. If my son meets him, he will do anything he can for Thénardier.

Marius remained in Vernon only forty-eight hours. After the burial, he returned to Paris and back to studying law. He thought no more about his father. In two days the colonel had been buried; in three days forgotten.

Marius wore black crepe on his hat, as a sign of mourning. That was all.

The Advantage of Going to Mass

One Sunday Marius went to hear mass at Saint Sulpice, the same chapel to which his aunt took him when he was a boy. He took a place behind a pillar and knelt down without noticing that on the back of the velvet chair was inscribed: Monsieur Mabeuf, Churchwarden. The service had hardly begun when an old man approached and said to Marius:

"Monsieur, this is my place."

Marius moved away readily, and the old man sat down on his chair.

After the mass, the old man approached and said, "I beg your pardon for having disturbed you. You must have thought me rude, and I must explain."

"Monsieur," said Marius, "it is not necessary."

"Yes!" said the old man. "I do not want you to have a bad opinion of me. I think a great deal of this place. I have seen for ten years, regularly, every two or three months, a poor brave father come here to this place to see his son. He had no other opportunity or means of seeing his child, being prevented from doing so because of some family arrangements. The little one never suspected that his father was here. The father, for his part, stayed behind the pillar so no one would see him. He looked at his child and wept. The poor man worshipped this little boy. I saw that. I was even acquainted slightly with the unfortunate gentleman. He had a father-in-law, a rich aunt, or some relative— I do not remember exactly—who threatened to disinherit the child if the father should see him. They were of different political opinions, but bless me! Because a man was at the battle of Waterloo, he is not a monster.

A father is not separated from his child for that. He was one of Bonaparte's colonels. He is dead, I believe. His name was Pontmercy, I think. He had a handsome saber cut."

Marius turned pale. "Monsieur," he said, "he was my father."

"Ah! You are the child! Yes, you would be a man now. Well! You can say that you had a father who loved you well."

The next day Marius said to his grandfather, "We have arranged a hunting party with a few friends. Will you permit me to be absent for three days?"

"Go and amuse yourself," answered the old man with a wink, thinking Marius's absence was due to a girl.

To Meet a Churchwarden

Marius went to Vernon and spent several hours at his father's grave. Then he returned to Paris and went straight to the library of the law school and asked for the records of the French Army.

There he read everything he could find about the activities of the Grand Army and found his father's name. He visited the generals under whom George Pontmercy had served. The churchwarden, Mabeuf, gave him an account of his father's life at Vernon— his flowers and his solitude. Marius came to understand the lion-lamb who was his father. He was on the way to adoration for him.

At the same time, an extraordinary change took place in his ideas.

First was bewilderment. The Republic and the Empire had been, till then, monstrous words. Little by little, as he read and learned, the confusion passed away. He saw in the Revolution the grand figure of the people, and out of the Empire the grand figure of France. He declared to himself that all that had been good.

At the same time he became more serious, surer of his beliefs and his thought. It was like an interior growth. He felt a sort of natural expansion, which these two new things—his father and his country— brought to him. As he read the bulletins of the Grand Army, his father's name appeared regularly, and the emperor's name was everywhere. He felt as if a tide was rising within him. It seemed at moments that his father passed like a breath and whispered to him. He was transported, trembling, breathless. Suddenly he arose, stretched his arms out of the window, and cried, *"Vive l'empereur!"*[6]

From that moment it was all over. To Marius the emperor had become the incarnation of France. Napolean became to him the people-man, as Jesus is the God-man.

All these revolutions were accomplished in Marius without a suspicion of it from his family. He had cast off his old royalist skin. When he became fully a revolutionary, thoroughly democratic and almost a republican, he went to an engraver and ordered a hundred cards bearing the name Baron Marius Pontmercy.

By a natural consequence, as he drew nearer to his father's memory and all the things he fought for, he drew further away from his grandfather. He reached almost an aversion for his grandfather, although nothing of this showed. Only he became more and more cold, and he was scarcely ever in the house.

On one of his journeys, Marius went to Montfermeil and sought the innkeeper Thénardier. Thénardier had failed, the inn was closed, and nobody knew what had

---

6. Vive l'empereur long live the emperor

become of him. When this visit lasted four days, the grandfather decided Marius was going astray.

They thought they noticed something he wore under his shirt, hung from his neck by a black ribbon.

Marble Against Granite

One morning Marius returned from Vernon very tired and felt the need to make up for his lack of sleep with an hour in the swimming pool. He took time only to take off his traveling coat and the black ribbon he wore around his neck. Then he went away to the bath.

Monsieur Gillenormand, hoping to see Marius, went to his room. A moment later, he entered the parlor where Mademoiselle Gillenormand was seated.

"We are about to solve the mystery of Marius's absences. We shall even perhaps have the portrait of the girl!"

In fact the black box fastened to the ribbon did look much like a medallion. It opened by pressing a spring. Inside was only a folded piece of paper.

Thinking it a love letter, the aunt and grandfather opened it eagerly, to find it read thus:

> *For my son.* The emperor made me a baron upon the battlefield of Waterloo. Since the government contests this title which I bought with my blood, my son will take it and bear it. I need not say that he will be worthy of it.

The feelings of the father and daughter cannot be described. They felt chilled as by the breath of a death's head. They did not say a word. The aunt examined the paper, turned it on all sides, and put it back in the box.

At that moment, a little oblong package wrapped in blue paper fell from a pocket of the coat. Mademoiselle Gillenormand picked it up and unfolded the blue paper. It was Marius's hundred cards: Baron Marius Pontmercy.

An hour passed before Marius appeared. Before he entered the room, he saw his grandfather holding one of his cards. As he entered he heard the crushing, superior tone of voice:

"Stop! Stop! You are a baron now. I present you my compliments. What does this mean?"

"It means that I am my father's son. My father was a humble and heroic man who served the republic and France gloriously and who died forgotten and abandoned. He had but one fault; he loved two ingrates, his country and me."

At the word republic, Monsieur Gillenormand could bear no more. He sprang to his feet, his face purple and glowing.

"Marius!" he exclaimed. "I don't know who your father was! I don't want to know. They were all beggars, assassins, redcaps,[7] and thieves! Do you hear, Marius? You are as much a baron as my slipper! They were all bandits who served B-u-o-naparte![8] All traitors who betrayed their legitimate king. That is all I know. If your father is among them, I don't know him."

Marius shuddered. He did not know what to do; his head burned. His father had been trodden underfoot and stamped on in his presence, and by his grandfather. How should he avenge the one without outraging the other? It was impossible for him to

---

7. **redcaps** name for revolutionaries, who wore red caps
8. **Bonaparte** Napoleon's family name

insult his grandfather, and it was equally impossible for him not to avenge his father. He raised his eyes, looked straight at his grandfather, and cried in a thundering voice: "Down with the Bourbons and the great hog Louis XVIII."

Louis XVIII had been dead for years, but it did not matter to him.

The old man, scarlet as he was, became whiter than his hair. Then he walked twice, slowly and in silence, from the fireplace to the window, and back again, crossing the whole length of the room. The second time, he bent toward his daughter and said to her with a smile that was almost calm:

"A baron like monsieur and a bourgeois like me cannot remain under the same roof. He straightened up, pointed toward Marius, and cried to him:

"Be off!"

Marius left the house. He went away without saying where he was going and without knowing where he was going. He had thirty francs, his watch, and a few clothes in a carpetbag. He hired a carriage by the hour, jumped in and drove away.

What was Marius to do?

4 The Friends of the A B C

A Group That Almost Became Famous

At this period, something of a revolutionary thrill was vaguely felt. People were transformed almost without suspecting it, by the very movement of the time. Royalists became liberals; liberals became democrats.

Some groups were very serious. They understood principle; they attached themselves to right. They longed for absolute. There was in Paris, among other groups of this kind, the Society of the Friends of the A B C.[1]

Who were the Friends of the A B C? In appearance, their aim was the education of children; in reality, their goal was to elevate mankind. They called themselves the Friends of the A B C. The abaissés were the people. The group wished to raise them up.

The Friends of the A B C were not numerous; it was a secret society. They met in Paris in two places: near the Halles[2] in a wineshop called Corinthe, and in the back room of a little coffeeshop on the Place Saint Michel, called Le Cafe Musain. The first of these two places was near the workingmen, the second near the students.

The room at the back of the cafe was connected by quite a long passageway and had two windows and an

---

1. **ABC** pronounced AH-BAY-SAY sounding in French like the word *abaissé,* meaning "brought down"
2. **the Halles** at the time, a large open-air market place

exit by a private stairway. Here the students smoked, drank, played, and laughed. They talked very loudly about everything and in whispers about something else. On the wall was an old map of France as it existed under the republic.

Most of the Friends of the A B C were students, with a few workingmen. The principals were Enjolas, Combeferre, Jean Prouvaire, Feuilly, Courfeyrac, Bahorel, Lesgle (or Laigle), Joly, and Grantaire. These young men made up a sort of family among themselves, because of their friendship. All except Laigle were from the South of France.

Enjolas named first, was an only son and was rich. He was a charming young man who was capable of being terrible. He was as beautiful as an angel. He represented the logic of the revolution.

Combeferre represented its philosophy. Between the logic of the revolution and its philosophy, there is a difference. Logic could conclude with war while its philosophy could only end in peace. In all of Combeferre's views, there was something attainable and practicable.

Jean Prouvaire was a little more subdued than Combeferre. Prouvaire was addicted to love. He cultivated flowers, played the flute, wrote verses, loved people, mourned over women, wept over childhood. All day long he pondered social questions. Like Enjolas, he was rich and an only son. He spoke gently, bent his head, cast down his eyes, smiled with embarrassment, dressed badly, had an awkward air, blushed at nothing, and was very timid yet brave.

Feuilly was a fanmaker, an orphan, who had only one thought: to deliver the world. He had still another desire: to instruct himself. He had taught himself to read and write. All that he knew, he learned alone. Feuilly had a generous heart, and he had a huge embrace.

Enjolas was the chief, Combeferre the guide, Courfeyrac was the center. The others gave more light; he gave more heat. The truth is, he had all the qualities of a center, rounded and radiant.

Bahorel was a creature of good humor and bad company. He was brave, bold, a spendthrift, talkative almost to eloquence, and bold almost to offensiveness. He was always ready to break up something to see the effect of it. He served as a liaison between the Friends of the A B C and other groups which were undefined now but which would take shape later.

In this group of young heads there was one bald member: Lesgle or Laigle (de Meaux). For the sake of brevity, his comrades called him Bossuet. He was a cheery fellow who was unlucky. He succeeded at nothing, and he laughed at everything.

Joly was a young hypochondriac. What he had learned in medicine had prepared him to be a patient rather than a physician. At twenty-three, he spent his time looking at his tongue in a mirror. Nevertheless, he was the happiest of all. He was an eccentric and an agreeable person.

All these young men, as different as they were, had the same religion: Progress.

All were legitimate sons of the revolution. They secretly sketched out their ideas.

Among these passionate hearts and undoubting minds, there was one skeptic: Grantaire. All of the words—rights of the people, rights of man, French Revolution, republic, democracy, civilization, religion, progress—were, to Grantaire, nearly meaningless. He smiled at them. He lived in irony. Still he had a fanaticism. The fanaticism was not an idea, nor an art, nor a science. It was a man: Enjolas. Grantaire admired, loved, and worshipped Enjolas.

Funeral Oration

On a certain afternoon, Laigle de Meaux was leaning lazily against the doorway of the Cafe Musain. He was looking at the square, Place Saint Michel. His eyes were wandering when he noticed a two-wheeled vehicle turning into the square, moving slowly as if undecided. What did this carriage want? There was inside, besides the driver, a young man; and before the young man there was a large carpetbag. Written in big letters upon a card sewed to the bag: Marius Pontmercy.

This name changed Laigle's attitude. He straightened up and addressed the young man in the carriage:

"Monsieur Marius Pontmercy? I was looking for you."

"How is that?" inquired Marius, raising his eyes. "I don't know you."

"You were not at school yesterday."

"You are a student?" inquired Marius.

"Yes, monsieur, like you. The day before yesterday I happened to go to school. You know, sometimes one has such notions. The professor was about to call the roll. You know that if you miss the third call they erase your name."

Marius had begun to listen. Laigle continued:

"It was Blondeau who was calling the roll. You know he delights in smelling out the absent. The roll went on well; no names to erase; the universe was present. Suddenly, Blondeau calls: 'Marius Pontmercy'; nobody answers. Blondeau, full of hope, repeats the call louder: 'Marius Pontmercy?' He seizes his pen. Monsieur, I said to myself rapidly: 'Here is a brave fellow who is going to be erased. Attention. Let us save him. Death to Blondeau!' At that moment Blondeau dipped his pen into the ink, cast his eyes over the room, and repeated for the third time: 'Marius Pontmercy!' I answered for you: 'Present!' In that way you were not erased."

"Monsieur—!" said Marius.

"And I was," added Laigle de Meaux.

"I don't understand you," said Marius.

Laigle resumed:

"The professor was looking at me with a certain fixedness. Suddenly he leaps to the letter L. L is my letter. He calls 'Laigle'; I answer 'Present!' Blondeau smiles like a tiger and says: 'If you are Pontmercy, you are not Laigle.' So saying he erases me."

"Monsieur, I am sorry—"

Laigle burst out laughing. "And I am in rapture. I was on the brink of becoming a lawyer. This saves me. I intend to pay you a solemn visit of thanks. Where do you live?"

"In this carriage," said Marius.

Just then Courfeyrac came out of the cafe.

Marius smiled sadly.

"I have been paying this rent for two hours, and I hope to get out of it. But it is the usual story; I do not know where to go."

"Monsieur," said Courfeyrac, "come home with me."

And that evening Marius was installed in a room at the Hotel de la Porte Saint Jacques, side by side with Courfeyrac.

Marius Amazed

In a few days, Marius was the friend of Courfeyrac. In Courfeyrac's presence, Marius breathed freely, a new thing for him. Courfeyrac asked no questions. It didn't occur to him.

Courfeyrac introduced Marius to the Cafe Musain. He whispered in Marius's ear with a smile, "This is your admission into the revolution." And he presented him to the other Friends of the A B C, saying in an undertone, "A pupil."

Marius was bewildered by this flock of young men. All these different progressives attacked him at once. He heard talk of philosophy, of literature, of art, of history, of religion. On abandoning his grandfather's opinions for his father's, he had thought he was settled. He now suspected, with anxiety, that he was not. Even the angle under which he saw things was beginning to change.

There were no "sacred" topics. Marius heard a similar language about every subject.

None of the young men uttered the word "emperor." Jean Prouvaire alone sometimes said "Napolean"; all the rest said "Bonaparte." Enjolas pronounced Buonaparte. Marius became confused and astonished.

The Cafe Musain

Of the conversations among these young men which Marius heard, and in which he sometimes took part, one shocked him severely. It was held in the back room of the Cafe Musain. Nearly all the Friends of the A B C were together that evening. The large lamp was ceremoniously lighted. They talked of one thing and another, without passion and with noise. A stern thought suddenly crossed the tumult of speech in which Grantaire, Bahorel, Prouvaire, Bossuet, Combeferre, and Courfeyrac were confusedly fencing. In the midst of the uproar, Bossuet suddenly ended some comment to Combeferre with this date:

"The 18th of June, 1815: Waterloo."

"Pardieu!"[3] exclaimed Courfeyrac, "that number 18 is strange and striking to me."

Enjolas, until now quiet, broke the silence and addressed Courfeyrac.

"You mean the crime by the atonement."

The word, "crime," exceeded Marius's endurance. He turned toward Enjolas, and his voice rang:

"I am a newcomer among you, but I confess that you astound me. Where are we? Who are we? Who are you? I thought you were young men. Where is your enthusiasm then? And what do you do with it? Whom do you admire, if you do not admire the emperor? And what more must you have? If you do not like that great man, what great men would you have? Be just, my friends! To be the grand nation and to bring forth the grand army, to send your legions flying over the whole earth as a mountain sends its eagles upon all sides, to vanquish, to rule, to thunderstrike, to be in Europe a kind of golden people through much glory, to sound through history a trumpet call, to conquer the world twice—this is sublime, and what more can be grand?"

"To be free," said Combeferre.

Marius bowed his head. When he raised his eyes, Combeferre was no longer there. Suddenly they heard somebody singing as he went downstairs. It was Combeferre, and he was singing:

> If Caesar had given me
>   glory and war
> and if I needed to abandon
>   my mother's love,

---

3. **Pardieu!** By God!

I would say to Caesar,
Take back your scepter and your carriage,
I prefer my mother, oh me!
I love my mother more.

Marius repeated mechanically, "my mother—."

At that moment, he felt Enjolas's hand on his shoulder. "Citizen," said Enjolas, "my mother is the republic."

Marius left the cafe in a gloomy state. He had just found a faith; could he reject it so soon? He feared, after having taken so many steps which had brought him closer to his father, now to take any steps which would separate them. He was on good terms neither with his grandfather nor with his friends. He felt isolated. He did not go to the cafe again.

Meanwhile the Aunt Gillenormand had discovered where Marius was. One morning he found a letter from her and some money in a sealed box. He sent the money back with a respectful letter telling her he had the means to live and that he would henceforth provide for all his own necessities. At the time he had three francs in his pocket.

Marius left the hotel, unwilling to take on any more debt.

5 The Excellence of Misfortune

Marius Indignant

Life became harsh for Marius. He chewed the cud of bitterness. A horrible thing, which included days without bread, nights without sleep, evenings without a candle, a hearth without a fire, weeks without work, a future without hope, a coat worn out at the elbows, an old hat that makes young girls laugh, the door shut against you at night because you have not paid the rent, the jibes of the neighbors, outrages against your self-respect, disgust, bitterness—Marius learned how one swallows down all those things and how sometimes they are the only things to swallow.

There was a period in Marius's life when he swept his own hall, when be bought a pennyworth of Brie cheese, when he waited for night to make his way to the bakery to buy a loaf of bread. If he went to the meat market to buy a mutton cutlet, he cooked it himself and ate for three days on it. The first day he would eat the meat; the second he ate the fat; and the third day he gnawed the bone. On several occasions Aunt Gillenormand made overtures and sent him the allowance from his grandfather. Marius always sent it back, saying he had no need of anything.

Through all this, Marius was admitted to the bar.[1] He occupied Courfeyrac's room, which was decent and where a certain number of law books, filled in with

---

1. **admitted . . . bar** allowed to practice law

other odd volumes, made up the library required by the rules.

When Marius became a lawyer, he informed his grandfather of it in a letter that was cold but respectful. Monsieur Gillenormand took the letter with trembling hands, read it, and threw it away. He was overheard to say aloud: "If you were not a fool, you would know that a man cannot be a baron and a lawyer at the same time."

Marius Poor

With misery as with everything else, it gradually becomes endurable. It ends by becoming fixed. This is the way Marius's life was arranged. Through hard work, he succeeded in earning about seven hundred francs a year. He had learned German and English, thanks to Courfeyrac, who introduced him to a publisher. There, Marius worked in the literary department in the role of a utility person. He lived on what he earned. He paid his rent for the little room in the Gorbeau house, paid a little to the old woman who swept his room and brought him some bread and eggs in the morning. He ate dinners, bought some clothes and washed them, and had some money left over. He was rich. He occasionally lent ten francs to a friend.

Marius had two suits: one old "for everyday," the other quite new and for special occasions. Both were black. He had three shirts: one he had on, another in the drawer, and the third at the washerwoman's. He bought a new one as each wore out. They were usually ragged, so he buttoned his coat to his chin.

It required years for Marius to achieve this condition. He had never given up, not for a single day. He had undergone everything, except getting into debt. He gave himself this credit: he didn't owe a cent to

anybody. For him, a debt was the beginning of slavery. He felt that a creditor was worse than a master; for a master owns only your body, but a creditor owns your dignity. Rather than borrow, he did not eat. He watched jealously over his pride.

In all his trials, he felt encouraged and sometimes carried along by a force within him. The soul helps the body and at certain moments lifts it up.

Marius a Man

Marius was now twenty years old. It had been three years since he left his grandfather. They remained on the same terms on both sides, without attempting a reconciliation or seeking to meet.

In fact, Marius was mistaken about his grandfather's heart. He imagined that Monsieur Gillenormand had never loved him. Marius was wrong. In reality, Monsieur Gillenormand worshipped Marius. When the young man left, he felt a dark void in his heart. He had ordered everyone not to speak of Marius again, and he regretted that he was so well obeyed. "But I could not do otherwise than to turn him away," said the grandfather. He asked himself if it were to be done again, would he do it? His pride promptly answered "yes," but his old head, which he shook in silence, answered "no." He had his hours of dejection. He missed Marius. He never inquired about him, but he thought of him constantly. He said sometimes: "Oh! If he would come back, what a good box on the ear I would give him."

As for the aunt, she thought too little to love very much. Marius was nothing to her but a sort of dim, dark outline. She busied herself a good deal less about him than with the cat or parakeet which she probably had.

While the old man was regretting, Marius was rejoicing. Misery had been good to him. He had a hundred coarse amusements. And he had two good friends, one young and one old: Courfeyrac and Monsieur Mabeuf. He was inclined toward the old friend. First, he was grateful to him for the revolution through which he had gone. He was also indebted to him for having known and loved his father.

Certainly the old churchwarden had been decisive. However, he had not been anything more than the calm, passive agent of Providence. He had enlightened Marius accidentally and without knowing it.

As for the internal political revolution in Marius, Monsieur Mabeuf was not capable of comprehending it or directing it.

As we shall meet Monsieur Mabeuf hereafter, a few words about that man will be worthwhile.

Monsieur Mabeuf

The day that Monsieur Mabeuf said to Marius, "Certainly, I approve of political opinions," he expressed the real condition of his mind. All political opinions were indifferent to him, and he approved them all without any distinction. Monsieur Mabeuf's political opinion was a passion for plants and a still greater one for books.

He did not understand how men could busy themselves with hating one another about such things as the charter, democracy, the monarchy, the republic, etc., when there were such things as mosses, herbs, and shrubs which they could look at. He had taken great care not to be useless. Having books did not prevent him from reading; being a botanist did not prevent him from being a gardener. He lived alone, with an old governess. He had written and published a book on flowers called *Flora of the Environs of Cauteretz* with color illustrations. It was a highly praised work, and people came two or three times a day to buy plates from it. He detested the sight of guns or swords. In his whole life he had never been near a cannon. He had a brother who was a priest. He had two friends: a bookseller and Marius. His servant, also a variety of innocent, was called Mother Plutarch.

Toward 1830, the whole horizon of Monsieur Mabeuf darkened. His brother the priest died. By a failure of a notary he lost the money that he possessed in his and his brother's name. The revolution in July brought on a crisis in bookselling, and his business stopped abruptly. Weeks went by without a purchaser. Soon Monsieur Mabeuf resigned his position as churchwarden, gave up his church, sold a part of the prints from his books, and moved into a small house on Montparnasse Boulevard. He stayed only three months, however, since the rent was high and the house was near a shooting gallery. He heard pistol shots, which was unbearable for him. Soon he moved to a sort of cottage in the village of Austerlitz.

Only two visitors—his friend the bookseller of Porte Saint Jacques and Marius—were admitted into his cottage.

As all this darkness was gathering around him and all his hopes were going out one after another, Monsieur remained serene, childishly but thoroughly so. His mind habits swung like a pendulum. Once he was wound up by an illusion, he went a long time— even after the illusion had disappeared. A clock does not stop the moment you lose the key.

Poverty the Neighbor of Misery

It was Marius's delight to take long walks. He sometimes spent half the day looking at a vegetable garden. Passersby looked at him with surprise; some thought him suspicious-looking. He was only a poor young man dreaming.

It was on one of these walks that he had discovered the Gorbeau tenement, where he took a room. He was known there only as Monsieur Marius.

Marius's political fevers were over. The revolution of 1830 had satisfied him. Properly speaking, he held opinions no longer; he had sympathies.

Toward the middle of the year 1831, the old woman who waited on Marius told him that his neighbors, the poor Jondrette family, were about to be turned into the streets. Marius spent so much time outdoors he hardly knew that he had neighbors.

"Why are they to be turned out?" Marius asked.

"Because they don't pay their rent. They owe for two terms."

"How much is it?"

"Twenty francs," said the old woman.

Marius had thirty francs at home in a drawer.

"Here," he said to the old woman. "There are twenty-five francs. Pay for these poor people, give them five francs, and do not tell them it is from me."

6 The Conjunction of Two Stars

The Nicknames

Marius was now a good-looking young man. He was of medium height, with thick black hair, a high and intelligent brow, large and passionate nostrils, a frank and calm expression, and something that beamed thoughtfulness and innocence from every feature. His manners were cold and polished, far from free. But since his mouth was pleasant and his teeth the whitest possible, his smile corrected any severity in his looks. At certain times there was a strange contrast between the serious brow and the sensual smile. His eyes were small, but his look was vast.

At the time of his worst poverty, when girls turned to look at him he ran away or hid. He thought they were looking at his old clothes or were laughing at him. The truth is that they looked at him because of his pleasant appearance. There were, however, two women from whom Marius never fled. In fact, Marius would have been surprised if anybody had told him they were women. One was the old woman who looked after his room. The other was a little girl whom he saw very often but never looked at.

For more than a year Marius had noticed, in a secluded walk of the Luxembourg Gardens, a man and a quite young girl, nearly always sitting side by side, on the same bench at the farthest end of the walk. The man might have been sixty years old; he seemed sad and serious. His expression was kind but

it did not invite approach, and he never returned a look. He wore a blue coat and trousers, a broad-brimmed hat that always looked new, a black tie, and a brilliantly white shirt of coarse texture. His hair was perfectly white.

The first time the young girl that accompanied him sat down on the seat they seemed to have adopted, she looked like a girl of about thirteen or fourteen. She was thin almost to the point of being ugly and awkward, yet promising perhaps to have fine eyes. She wore the black dress of a convent schoolgirl. They appeared to be father and daughter.

For two or three days Marius studied the old man who was not yet aged and the little girl who was not yet a woman; then he paid no more attention to them. They did not even seem to see him. They talked with each other peacefully, indifferent to everything else.

Marius had developed a habit of strolling along this walk. He always found them there.

He would usually start on the walk opposite their bench, stroll the whole length of it—walking in front of them—and return to where he had started. He would do this five or six times in his walks, but they never exchanged greetings.

Because of the dress of the girl and the hair of the man, Marius had named them Mademoiselle Lanoire (black) and Monsieur Leblanc (white). He saw them this way nearly every day at the same hour for a year. He found the man very interesting and the girl rather disagreeable.

Sweet Fifteen

The second year, it happened that Marius broke off his habit of going to the Luxembourg Gardens, and there were six months when he did not set foot on the walk. At last he went back one day, on a calm summer morning.

He went straight to "his walk," and as soon as he reached it he saw—still on the same bench—the well-known pair. When he approached, however, he saw that it was the same man, but it seemed no longer the same girl. This was a woman: a noble, beautiful creature. Beautiful chestnut hair shaded with strands of gold, a brow that seemed chiseled marble, cheeks which seemed made of roses, an exquisite mouth from which came a smile like a ray of sunshine, and a voice like music. The nose was not beautiful; it was pretty, neither Italian nor Greek. It was the Parisian nose— that is, something sprightly, fine, irregular, and pure— the despair of painters and the charm of poets.

When Marius passed near her, he could not see her eyes, which were always cast down. He saw only her long chestnut lashes, eloquent of mystery and modesty. But this did not prevent the beautiful girl from smiling as she listened to the white-haired man who was speaking to her.

At first Marius thought it was another daughter of the same man. But when he looked at her carefully, he recognized that she was the same. In six months, the little girl had become a young woman; that was all.

As for the man, he was still the same.

The second time Marius passed by her, the young girl raised her eyes. They were of deep celestial blue. She looked at Marius with indifference, and he continued his walk thinking of something else. He passed by the bench four or five more times without so much as turning his eyes toward her.

On following days he came as usual to the Luxembourg; as usual he found the father and daughter there, but he paid no attention to them. He passed by the bench on which she sat, because that was his habit.

Spring

One day the air was particularly mild. The Luxembourg was flooded with sunshine and shadow, and the sky was as clear as if the angels had washed it in the morning. Marius opened his whole soul to nature, he was thinking of nothing, he passed near their bench, and the young girl raised her eyes. Their glances met.

But what was there now in the glance of the young girl? Marius could not have told. There was nothing, and there was everything. It was a strange flash.

There is a time when every young girl looks thus. Woe to him upon whom she looks!

That night, on returning to his room, Marius cast a look at this clothes and, for the first time, perceived that he had the indecency and stupidity to stroll in the Luxembourg in his "everyday" suit, a hat with its band broken, coarse working boots, black pants shiny at the knees, and a coat threadbare at the elbows.

The next day, at the usual hour, Marius took out his new coat, pants, hat, and boots. He dressed, put on his gloves, and went to the Luxembourg.

On reaching the Gardens, Marius walked around the fountain and looked at the swans. Then he remained a long time studying a statue. Finally he went toward "his walk" slowly and as if with regret. He was unconscious of this and thought he was doing what he did every day.

When he entered the walk, he saw Monsieur Leblanc and the young girl on their seat. He buttoned his coat and smoothed it down to rid it of any wrinkles and marched upon the bench.

As he drew near, his step became slower and slower. At some distance he stopped and turned back. He did not know how it had happened; he did not plan it. It was doubtful the girl could even see him so far off, much less notice his fine appearance. However, he stood up straight so that he might look well, in case anybody who was behind should happen to notice him.

He reached the opposite end of the walk and returned, this time coming a little nearer to the bench. He came to within three trees of it before he felt powerless to go on and hesitated. He thought he had seen the young girl's face bent toward him. He made a great effort, conquered his hesitation, and went on. In a few seconds, he was passing before the seat, straight and tall, blushing to his ears, not daring to look right or left, and with his hand under his coat like a statesman. He heard what might be "her voice." She was talking quietly. She was very pretty. He felt it, although he made no effort to see her.

He passed the bench, went to the end of the walk, which was very near, then turned and passed again before the beautiful girl. This time he was very pale. He walked away from the bench and from the young girl. Although his back was turned, he imagined she was looking at him, and that made him stumble.

He did not try to approach the bench again but stopped midway along the walk and sat down. At the end of fifteen minutes, he rose as if to resume his walk toward the bench. However, he stood motionless. For the first time in fifteen months, he told himself that this gentleman, who sat there every day with his daughter, had surely noticed him.

He remained thus for some minutes with his head

down, tracing designs on the ground with a little stick he had in his hand. Then he turned abruptly away from the seat, away from Monsieur Leblanc and his daughter, and went home.

That day he forgot to go to dinner.

Thunderbolts

A fortnight rolled away. Marius no longer went to the Luxembourg to walk, but to sit down always in the same place and without knowing why. Once there he did not stir. Every morning he put on his new suit.

She was indeed a marvelous beauty. The only criticism which could be made is the contrast between her look, which was sad, and her smile, which was joyous.

On one of the last days of the second week, Marius had been seated in his usual place for two hours without moving. Suddenly he trembled. A great event was commencing at the end of the walk. Monsieur Leblanc and his daughter had left their seat. The daughter had taken the father's arm, and they were slowly coming along the walk where Marius was. Marius closed his book; then he opened it; then he made an attempt to read. He trembled. "Oh, dear!" he thought, "I will not have time to assume a posture." However, the man with the white hair and the young girl were advancing. He was overwhelmed. He heard the sound of their steps approaching. He bowed his head; when he raised it they were quite near him. The young girl passed, and in passing she looked at him. She looked at him steadily, with a sweet and thoughtful look that made Marius tremble from head to foot.

He felt as if his brain were on fire. She had come to him! What happiness! And then, how she had looked at him! She was more beautiful than she had ever seemed before. He felt as if he were swimming in the deep blue sky. At the same time he was horribly upset because he had a little dust on his boots.

He was sure that she had seen his boots in this condition.

He followed her with his eyes until she disappeared; then he began to walk like a madman. It is probable that at times he laughed, alone as he was, and spoke aloud.

Taken Prisoner

A whole month passed this way. Marius went to the Luxembourg every day. Nothing could keep him away. He lived in ecstasy. It is certain that the young girl looked at him.

He grew bolder, and he approached the bench. However, he passed it no longer. He did not want to attract the attention of the father. He stood behind trees and statues, so as to be seen as much as possible by the girl and as little as possible by the man. Sometimes he stood for hours motionless behind some statue. The girl, for her part, turned her charming profile toward him, smiling. While yet talking in the most natural way with the white-haired man, she rested her eye on Marius. Her tongue replied to one man; her eyes to the other.

We must suppose, however, that Monsieur Leblanc noticed some of this, because often when Marius came, he would rise and walk. He had left their usual place and had taken a bench at the other end of the walk as if to see if Marius would follow them. Marius did not understand, and he committed that blunder. The father became less punctual and did not bring his daughter every day. Sometimes he came alone. When he did that, Marius would not stay. Another blunder.

Finally Marius committed a third blunder, a monstrous one. He wanted to know where she lived. He followed them. He followed them every day for a week and stood below their windows until they became dark. Worse, one night, after he had followed them home, he entered the building and boldly questioned the porter about the man who had just come in.

The next day, Monsieur Leblanc and his daughter did not come to the Luxembourg. Marius waited all day, in vain. That night he went to the house where they lived. There was a light in the windows. He walked beneath them until the light went out. He spent a week this way.

On the eighth day there was no light. Marius knocked on the door and said to the porter:

"The gentleman and his daughter?"

"Moved," answered the porter.

Marius tottered and said feebly, "When?"

"Since yesterday."

"And did he leave his new address?"

"No."

7 *Patron-Minette*

The Evil Quartet

From 1830-1835, a quartet of bandits ruled over most of the crime in the lowest levels of Paris society. They were Claquesous, Gueulemer, Babet, and Montparnasse. These four men were not four men; they were a sort of mysterious robber with four heads preying on Paris. They were a monstrous evil which inhabits the depths of the city.

Gueulemer was a Hercules in appearance. He was six feet tall and had a huge chest and a bird's skull. He could have subdued monsters; he found it easier to become one.

The thinness of Babet contrasted with the meatiness of Gueuelemer. Babet was puny and shrewd, transparent but impenetrable. You could see the light through his bones but nothing through his eye.

Claquesous was night. Before showing himself, he would wait until the sky was black. He came out of his hole only then, and he went in again before day. He was a ventriloquist, restless, and terrible. Claquesous being a nickname, it was not certain he had a voice—or even a face. He sank into the ground and came out like an apparition.

Montparnasse was a mournful sight. Less than twenty years old with a pretty face, lips like cherries, charming black hair, he had all the vices and aspired to all crimes. The digestion of what was bad gave him an appetite for what was worse. He was effeminate, graceful, weak, and ferocious.

Anyone who wanted a crime committed went to these four. They were always prepared to put together a plan of action, always in condition to furnish a company appropriate for any plan. They had a company of actors of darkness at their disposition.

The name given to this group of four was the Patron-Minette. In old language, Patron-Minette means "morning." The name probably came from the hour at which their work usually ended—the dawn being the time for phantoms to disappear.

The police knew the quartet well. When the chief judge of the Assizes once visited a criminal in prison to question him about some crime, the man denied it. "Who did do it?" the judge asked. The man made a reply that puzzled the judge but was very clear to the police: "Patron-Minette, perhaps."

8 *The Noxious Poor*

A Rose in Misery

Summer and autumn passed; winter came. Neither Monsieur Leblanc nor the young girl had set foot in the Luxembourg. Marius had but one thought—to see that sweet, adorable face again. He searched everywhere, continually; he found nothing. He fell into a melancholy. It was all over for him. Work disgusted him, walking tired him, solitude wearied him.

He still lived in the Gorbeau tenement. But he paid no attention to anyone there.

At the time only himself and the Jondrettes, whose rent he had once paid, remained.

One day, in the winter, he had gotten up and breakfasted, and was trying to set about his work, when there was a gentle rap at his door. As he owned nothing, he never locked his door. Even when absent, he left his key in the lock.

There was a second rap, very gentle, like the first.

"Come in," Marius said.

The door opened.

"I beg your pardon, Monsieur—"

It was the voice of an old man—hollow, cracked, and rasping.

Marius turned quickly and saw a young girl.

She was quite young, pale and puny, covered in nothing but a chemise and a skirt. A string for a belt and for a headdress, sharp shoulders sticking out from the chemise, dirty shoulder blades, red hands, mouth

159

open and sunken, some teeth gone, eyes bold but dull and drooping.

Marius rose and, staring, asked, "What do you wish, mademoiselle?"

Without waiting for an invitation, the girl entered and answered, "Here is a letter for you, Monsieur Marius."

She really had a letter in her hand, which she presented to Marius. He read:

My amiable neighbor, young man!

I have learned your kindness toward me, that you paid my rent six months ago. I bless you, young man. My eldest daughter will tell you we have been without bread for two days, four persons, and my wife sick. I hope that your generous heart will soften and that the desire might overcome you to lavish upon me some small gift.

I remain —
Jondrette

P.S. My daughter will await your orders, dear Monsieur Marius.

Meanwhile the girl was walking around Marius's room, moving chairs and looking at things on the bureau.

"Ah," said she, "a mirror!"

She went to the table.

"Ah!" she said, "books!"

She resumed, "I can read, I can," and she picked up a book and read fluently. She put down the book and picked up a pen. "And I can write, too! Would you like to see? Here, I am going to write something to show you."

Before Marius could answer, she wrote on a sheet of blank paper from the middle of the table:

"The Cognes are here."[1]

Marius had been feeling through his pockets. After a thorough exploration, he had gotten together five francs and sixteen sous. This was at the time all he had in the world. "That is enough for my dinner today," thought he. "Tomorrow we will see." He took the sixteen sous and gave the five francs to the young girl.

She took the piece eagerly.

"Good," said she, "there is some sunshine!"

She made a low bow to Marius and a familiar wave of the hand; then she went out the door, saying:

"Good morning, monsieur."

Providence

Marius almost reproached himself with the fact that he had been so absorbed in his dreams and passion that he had not until now paid any attention to his neighbors. Paying their rent was a mechanical impulse, but he should have done better. A mere wall separated him from these abandoned beings. Every day, at every moment, he had heard them through the wall, and he did not lend his ear!

While he thus preached to himself Marius looked at the wall which separated him from the Jondrettes. It was as if he could send his pitying glance through that partition. The wall was a thin layer of plaster, held up by laths and joists, through which voices and words could be heard perfectly. Nobody but the dreamer Marius would not have noticed this before. There was no paper hung on the wall, on either the side of the

---

1. **Cognes** French slang for *cops*

Jondrettes or Marius. Almost unconsciously Marius examined this partition. Suddenly he arose. He noticed, toward the top, near the ceiling, a triangular hole where three laths left a space between them. The plaster which should have stopped up this hole was gone. By getting up onto the bureau he could see through that hole into the Jondrettes' room. "Let us see what these people are," thought Marius, "and to what they are reduced."

And he climbed up onto the bureau, put his eye to the crevice, and looked.

The Savage in His Lair

What Marius saw was a hole.

Marius was poor and his room was poorly furnished, but his place was clean. The den into which he looked was abject, filthy, smelly, infectious, gloomy, unclean. All the furniture was two straw chairs, a rickety table, a few old and broken dishes, and two indescribable pallets in the corners. All the light came from a dormer window of four panes, curtained with spider webs. Just enough light came through to make a man's face look like the face of a phantom. The walls were covered with seams and scars like a face disfigured by some horrible sickness.

The room Marius occupied had a broken brick pavement. This one was neither paved nor floored. The dust was encrusted there, among random socks, old shoes, and hideous rags. However the room had a fireplace, so it rented for forty francs a year. In the fireplace there was a little of everything—a frying pan, a kettle, some broken boards, rags hanging on nails, a bird cage, some ashes, and even a little fire. Two embers were smoking sullenly.

By the table, upon which Marius saw a pen, ink,

and paper, was seated a man of about sixty: small, thin, haggard, and with a keen, cruel, and restless air—a hideous harpy. The man had a long, gray beard. He was dressed in a woman's chemise, which showed his saggy chest and his naked arms bristling with gray hairs. Below this chemise were a pair of muddy trousers and boots from which the toes stuck out. He had a pipe in his mouth and was smoking. There was no more bread in the den, but there was tobacco.

A big woman, who might have been forty years old or a hundred, was squatting near the fireplace, upon her bare feet. She was also dressed only in a chemise and a knit skirt patched with pieces of old cloth. A coarse apron covered half the skirt. Although this woman was bent and drawn up into herself, it could be seen that she was very tall. She was a kind of giantess by the side of her husband. She had hideous hair, light red sprinkled with gray, that she pushed back from time to time with her huge hands which had flat nails.

Upon one of the pallets Marius could make out a sort of slender little girl seated, almost naked, with her feet hanging down. She had the appearance of neither listening nor seeing nor living. The younger sister, doubtless, of the one who had come to his room. She appeared to be eleven or twelve years old.

Marius looked for a time into that funereal interior. It was more fearful than the interior of a tomb, for here were felt the movements of a human soul and the palpitation of life.

The man was silent and the woman did not speak; the girl did not seem to breathe.

Then the man muttered, "Rabble! Rabble! All is rabble!"

Strategy and Tactics

Marius, with a heavy heart, was about to get down from the sort of observatory he had arranged when a sound attracted his attention and made him stay in his place.

The door of the room next door opened, and the elder daughter appeared. She came in, pushed the door shut behind her, stopped to catch her breath, then cried with joy and triumph:

"He is coming!"

The father turned his eyes, the woman turned her head, and the younger sister did not move.

"Who?" asked the father.

"The gentleman!"

"There, true he is coming?"

"In a carriage."

"Are you sure then, sure that he is coming? I will bet the old fool—"

Just then a light tap on the door made the man rush forward and open it. He exclaimed with many low bows and smiles of respect:

"Come in, monsieur! Please, come in my noble benefactor, as well as your charming young lady."

A man of mature age and a young girl appeared at the door.

Marius had not left his place. What he felt at that moment escapes human language.

It was she.

It was indeed she. Marius could barely see her through the mist which suddenly spread over his eyes. She had disappeared and was now reappearing in this gloom, this shapeless den, this horror!

Marius shuddered. What! It was she! The beating of his heart disturbed his sight. He felt ready to melt into tears. It seemed to him that he had just lost his soul and that he had just found it again.

She was still the same, a little paler only. She was still accompanied by Monsieur Leblanc.

She stepped into the room and laid a large package on the table.

The elder Jondrette girl had retreated behind the door and was looking at the young girl with an evil eye.

Jondrette Nearly Weeps

Monsieur Leblanc approached the father with his kind and compassionate look and said:

"Monsieur, you will find in this package some new clothes, some stockings, and some new coverlets."

"Our angelic benefactor overwhelms us," said Jondrette, bowing down to the floor. But stooping to his daughter's ear, he whispered:

"You see! What did I tell you? Rags! No money! They are all the same!"

For some time Jondrette had been looking at the man in a strange way. He passed by his wife, who was lying on her bed appearing to be overwhelmed and stupid, and said in a very low tone:

"Notice that man!"

Then turning to Monsieur Leblanc, he continued:

"You see, monsieur! Tomorrow is the fatal day, the last delay my landlord will give me. I must pay him the rent or we shall all be turned outdoors. You see, monsieur, I owe four quarters, a year! Sixty francs!"

Jondrette was lying. Four quarters would have made only forty francs, and he could not have owed for four quarters, since it was not that long since Marius paid for two.

Monsieur Leblanc took five francs from his pocket and threw them on the table. Then he took off a large brown overcoat and put it over the back of the chair.

"I will be here at six o'clock," said he, "and I will bring you the sixty francs."

"My benefactor!" cried Jondrette. And he added in an undertone, "Take a good look at him, wife!"

Just then the overcoat on the chair caught the eye of the elder daughter.

"Monsieur," said she, "you are forgetting your coat."

The man turned and answered with a smile: "I am not forgetting it; I leave it."

"O, my patron," exclaimed Jondrette. "I am melting into tears! Permit me to show you to your carriage."

"If you go out," replied Monsieur Leblanc, "put on the overcoat. It is really very cold."

He put the overcoat on very quickly, and they went out, all three, Jondrette preceding the two strangers.

Marius had seen everything, yet in reality he had seen none of it. His eyes had remained fixed on her entirely, from her first step into the room. When she went out, he had one thought: to follow her, not to let her leave without knowing where she lived, not to lose her again! He leaped down from the bureau and took his hat. He waited a little, then went out. There was nobody in the hall. He ran to the stairs. Nobody there. He hurried down and reached the street in time to see a carriage turning the corner on its way back into the city.

Offers of Service

Marius went back upstairs slowly, entered his room, and pushed the door closed behind him. It did not close. He turned and saw a hand holding it partly open. It was the Jondrette girl.

"Is it you?" Marius said almost harshly. "You again? What do you want of me?"

"Can I serve you in anything? Let me. I do not ask your secrets, yet I may be useful. I can certainly help you, since I help my father. When it is necessary to carry letters, go into houses, inquire from door to door, find out an address, follow somebody, I do it."

An idea came into Marius's mind. He approached the girl.

"Listen," he said to her kindly. "You brought the old gentleman here with his daughter."

"Yes."

"Do you know their address?"

"No."

"Find it for me."

"What will you give me?"

"Anything you wish."

"Anything I wish?"

"Yes."

"You shall have the address."

She looked down and then with a hasty movement closed the door.

Marius was alone. He dropped into a chair, with his head and both elbows on the bed, swallowed up in thoughts which he could not grasp and as if he were in a fit of vertigo.

Suddenly he was awakened from his reverie.

He heard the loud, harsh voice of Jondrette pronounce these words, full of the strangest interest:

"I tell you that I am sure of it and that I recognized him!"

Of whom was Jondrette talking? He had recognized whom? Monsieur Leblanc? Did Jondrette know him? Oh! Heavens!

He sprang up onto the bureau and took up his place near the little opening in the partition.

The Five-Franc Piece

Nothing had changed in the room, except that the wife and daughters had opened the package and put on the woolen stockings and the underclothes. Two new coverlets were thrown over the two beds.

Jondrette had evidently just come in. He had not yet recovered his regular breathing. He was walking up and down with rapid strides. His eyes had an extraordinary look.

The woman, who seemed timid and stricken with stupor before her husband, ventured to say:

"What, really? You are sure?"

"Sure! It was eight years ago! But I recognize him! Ah! I recognize him! I recognized him immediately. What! It did not strike you?"

"No."

"And I told you to pay attention. But it is the same. He is better dressed, that is all! Mysterious old devil, I have you all right!"

He checked himself and said to the two daughters:

"You go out!" and to his wife, he continued: "It is queer that it did not strike your eye."

As the girls were passing out the door, he caught the elder by the arm and said, with a strange tone:

"Be here at five o'clock exactly. Both of you. I shall need you."

Marius increased his attention.

Jondrette began to walk the room, and he took two or three turns in silence. Suddenly he turned toward the woman, folded his arms, and exclaimed:

"And do you want me to tell you one thing? The young lady—"

Marius could not doubt any longer. It was indeed of her that they were talking. He listened intently. His whole life was concentrated in his ears.

But Jondrette bent down and whispered to his wife. Then he straightened up and finished aloud:

"It is she!"

"That girl?" said the wife.

"That girl!" said the husband. "I tell you it is she. You will see."

At that, the woman raised her big red and blond face and looked at the ceiling with a hideous expression. At that moment she appeared to Marius still more terrible than her husband.

"What!" she fumed. "This horrible beautiful young lady who looked at my girls with pity, can she be that beggar? Oh! I would like to stamp her heart out!"

She sprang off the bed, hair flying, nostrils distended and mouth half open, her fists clenched and drawn back. The she fell back upon the bed.

After a few minutes the man approached her and stopped in front of her with folded arms and said:

"And do you want me to tell you one thing?"

"What?" she answered.

"My fortune is made."

The woman stared at him with a look that means: Has this person gone crazy?

He continued:

"Listen carefully. He is caught. It is all right, already done. Everything is arranged. He will come this evening at six o'clock. To bring the sixty francs, the rascal! Our neighbor is gone to dinner then. Mother Burgon is washing dishes in the city. There is nobody in the house. The girls will stand watch. You shall help us. He will be his own executor."

And he burst into a laugh. It was the first time Marius had heard him laugh. It was cold and feeble, and it made him shudder.

Just then the clock struck one.

Does Honesty Fear Authority?

On reaching No. 14, Marius went upstairs and asked for the commissioner of police.

"The commissioner is not in," said one of the office boys, "but there is an inspector who answers for him. Would you like to speak to him? Is it urgent?"

"Yes," said Marius.

A man of tall stature was standing there, behind a railing, in front of a stove. He had a square face; a thin and firm mouth; very fierce, bushy, grayish whiskers; and an eye that you might have said would turn your pockets inside out.

"What do you wish?" said he to Marius without adding monsieur.

"It is a very secret affair," said Marius, "and very urgent."

"Then speak quickly."

This man, calm and abrupt, was alarming and reassuring at the same time. He inspired both fear and confidence. Marius related his adventure. The inspector remained quiet for a moment, then answered between his teeth:

"It sounds like the Patron-Minette in this."

After a minute, he resumed:

"Number 50-52, I know the place. Impossible to hide ourselves in the interior without the artists seeing us."

Marius interrupted:

"That is well enough, but what will you do?"

The inspector merely answered:

"The lodgers have latchkeys to get in at night. Do you have yours with you?"

"Yes."

"Give it to me."

Marius took the key from his pocket and handed it to the inspector, adding:

"If you trust me, you will come in force."

The inspector plunged both hands into his pockets and took out two small steel pistols. He handed them to Marius, saying:

"Take these. Go back home. Hide yourself in your room; let them think you have gone out. You will watch. The men will come. Let them go on a little. When you think things have gone far enough and it is time to stop it, fire off a pistol. Not too soon. The rest is my business. A pistol shot in the air, into the ceiling, no matter where. Above all, not too soon."

Marius took the pistols and, as he placed his hand on the latch to go out, the inspector called to him:

"By the way, if you need me between now and then, come or send here. You will ask for Inspector Javert."

Marius returned to No. 50-52 with rapid strides and quickly climbed the stairs. The hall, as it may be remembered, was lined with rooms, which were all empty and for rent. Madame Burgon left the doors open. As Marius passed by one of the doors, he thought he saw four motionless heads made dimly visible by a ray of daylight falling through the little window. He got to his room without being seen and without any noise. A moment later he heard Madame Burgon leaving the house.

Justice Coming

Marius sat down on his bed. It might have been half past five o'clock. Only a half hour separated him from what was to come. He heard his arteries beat as one hears the ticking of a watch in the dark. He was not afraid. To him the day seemed but a dream. To reassure himself, he felt the chill of the two pistols in his pockets.

There was a light in the Jondrette den. Marius saw

the hole in the partition shine with a red gleam. He took off his boots and pushed them under his bed.

Some minutes passed. The lower door turned on its hinges; a heavy quick step ascended the stairs and passed along the corridor. The latch of the room opened and Jondrette came in.

Several voices were heard immediately. The whole family was in the room. They kept silent in the absence of the master, like cubs in the absence of the wolf.

A moment afterward, Marius heard the sound of the bare feet of the two young girls in the corridor and the voice of Jondrette calling after them:

"Pay attention now! One toward the barrier, the other at the corner of the street. And if you see the least thing, come here immediately! You have a key to come in with."

There were now in the house only Marius and the Jondrette couple, and perhaps the mysterious figures of whom Marius had caught a glimpse. He judged it was now time to resume his place at his observatory. In a twinkling, and with the agility of his age, he was at the hole in the partition. He looked in.

The entire den was illuminated by the reflection of a large sheet-iron furnace in the fireplace. It was filled with lighted charcoal which was burning red-hot. In a corner near the door, arranged as if for anticipated use, were two heaps of old iron and ropes.

Jondrette had lighted his pipe, had sat down on a chair, and was listening to his wife, who was speaking in a low tone. Suddenly, he raised his voice:

"By the way, now I think of it, in such weather he will come in a carriage. Light the lantern and take it down. Stay there behind the lower door. The moment you hear the carriage stop, open up immediately. He will come up, and when he does, you will go down again immediately, pay the driver, and send the carriage away." Fumbling in his trousers, Jondrette handed her five francs.

"What is that?" she asked.

"It is the money our neighbor gave this morning. And here is the lantern. Go quickly."

She hastily obeyed, and Jondrette was left alone. In a moment, he drew the table drawer out quickly and took out a long carving knife which was hidden there and tried its edge on his nail. This done, he put the knife back into the drawer and shut it.

Marius, for his part, grasped the pistol in his right pocket, took it out, and cocked it.

The pistol gave a little clear, sharp sound.

Jondrette jumped and half rose from his chair.

"Who is there?" he cried.

Marius held his breath. Jondrette listened for a moment, then began to laugh.

"What a fool I am! It is just the partition cracking," he said aloud to himself.

Marius kept the pistol in his hand.

Marius's Chairs Face Each Other

Six o'clock struck on the clock.

Jondrette marked each stroke with a nod of his head. At the sixth stroke, he snuffed the candle with his fingers. Then he began to pace, listen in the hall, and walk again. "Provided he comes!" he muttered; then he returned to his chair.

He had hardly sat down when the door opened. The mother Jondrette said: "Walk in."

"Walk in, my benefactor," repeated Jondrette, rising precipitately.

Monsieur Leblanc entered. He had an air of serenity which made him particularly venerable.

He laid four louis on the table. "This is for you and your urgent needs. We will see about the rest."

"God reward you," said Jondrette, glancing meaningfully at his wife, who slipped away out the door and returned a moment later.

The snow which had fallen since the morning was so deep they had not heard the carriage arrive, and they did not hear it go away.

Meanwhile Monsieur Leblanc had taken a seat, and Jondrette sat opposite him.

Marius, invisible and alert, lost no word or movement. The pistol was in his grasp. He felt horror but not fear. As he clasped the butt of the pistol, he felt reassured. "I shall stop this wretch when I please," he thought. He knew the police were somewhere nearby in ambush, awaiting the signal agreed upon, and all ready to stretch out their arms.

Dark Corners

As Jondrette was talking to Monsieur Leblanc, Marius raised his eyes and saw at the back of the room somebody he had not seen before. A man had entered so noiselessly that nobody had heard the door turn on its hinges. This man had a knit woolen coat of a violet color, old, torn, and stained. He wore full trousers of cotton velvet, socks on his feet, no shirt, his neck bare, arms bare and tattooed, and his face stained black. He sat down on the nearest bed and was distinguishable only with difficulty.

The kind of instinct that warns the eye made Monsieur Leblanc turn almost at the same time as Marius. He could not help a movement of surprise.

"Who is that man?" he asked.

"That man?" said Jondrette. "That is a neighbor. Pay no attention to him."

Jondrette, leaning his elbows on the table and gazing at Monsieur Leblanc with fixed and tender eyes like those of a boa constrictor, continued: "As I was saying, monsieur and dear patron, I have a picture to sell."

A slight noise was made at the door. A second man entered and sat down beside the female Jondrette. He had bare arms like the first, and he wore a mask of ink or soot. Although he had literally slipped into the room, Monsieur Leblanc had seen him.

"Do not mind them," said Jondrette. "They are people of the house. I was telling you, monsieur, that I have a valuable painting left. Here, monsieur, look."

"What is it?" asked Monsieur Leblanc.

"A painting by a master, a picture of great value. I cling to it as I cling to my two daughters. It calls up memories to me!   But I am so unfortunate that I would part with it."

Whether by chance or whether there was some beginning of distrust, while examining the picture, Monsieur Leblanc glanced toward the back of the room. There were now four men there, three seated on the bed and one standing near the door casing. All four were bare-armed, motionless, and with blackened faces. None of them had shoes on; those who did not have socks were barefooted.

"They are friends. They live nearby," said Jondrette. "They are dark because they work in charcoal. They are chimney doctors. Do not occupy your mind with them, my benefactor, but buy my picture. Take pity on my misery. How much do you estimate it to be worth?"

"But," said Monsieur Leblanc, looking Jondrette full in the face like a man who puts himself on guard, "this is a tavern sign and is worth about three francs."

Jondrette answered calmly:

"Have you your pocketbook here? I would be satisfied with a thousand crowns."

Monsieur Leblanc rose to his feet, placed his back to the wall, and ran his eye around the room. He had Jondrette at his left toward the window and Jondrette's wife and the four men at his right toward the door. Nobody moved.

Jondrette began to talk again in a plaintive tone and with eyes wild. Monsieur Leblanc's look was fixed on Jondrette, and Jondrette's eye was upon the door. Marius's breathless attention went from one to the other.

Suddenly Jondrette's dull eye lighted up with a hideous glare. The little man straightened up and became horrifying. He took a step toward Monsieur Leblanc and cried in a voice of thunder:

"But all this is not the question! Do you know me?"

The Ambush

The door of the room was suddenly flung open to reveal three men in blue shirts with black paper masks. The first was thin and held a long ironbound club; the second was a giant and held a butcher's ax; the third, broad-shouldered and of a build between the two others, held in his clenched fist an enormous key stolen from some prison door.

Jondrette seemed to have been awaiting the arrival of these men.

"Is everything ready?"

"Yes," answered the thin man.

"Then where is Montparnasse?"

"He stopped to chat with your daughter."

"Which one?"

"The elder."

"Is there a carriage below?"

"Yes."

"The wagon is ready?"

"Ready."

"With two good horses?"

"Excellent."

"Waiting where I said it should wait?"

"Yes."

"Good."

Monsieur Leblanc was very pale. He looked over everything in the room like a man who understands what he has fallen into. There was nothing in his manner that resembled fear.

Three of the men Jondrette had described as chimney doctors had taken from the heap of old iron a large pair of shears, a bar, and a hammer. They had placed themselves before the door without saying a word.

Marius thought that in a few seconds the time would come to interfere, and he raised his right hand toward the ceiling, in the direction of the hall, ready to let off his pistol shot.

Jondrette, after his conversation with the thin man, turned again toward Monsieur Leblanc and repeated his question:

"You do not recognize me then?"

Monsieur Leblanc looked him in the face and answered: "No."

Jondrette came up to the table. He leaned over the candle and pushed his angular and ferocious jaw toward the calm face of Monsieur Leblanc. In that posture, like a wild beast about to strike, he cried:

"My name is not Jondrette; my name is Thénardier! I am the innkeeper of Montfermeil! Do you understand me? Thénardier! Now do you know me?"

A slight flush passed over Monsieur Leblanc's forehead, and he answered without a tremor or elevation of voice:

"No more than before."

Marius did not hear this answer. He was haggard, astounded, and thunderstruck. When he had heard Jondrette say the name Thénardier, Marius had trembled in every limb, and he supported himself against the wall. His right arm, ready to fire, dropped slowly, and his nervous fingers almost dropped the pistol. Jondrette, in revealing who he was, had not moved Monsieur Leblanc, but he had completely unnerved Marius. That name he had worn on his heart, written in his father's will! He had mingled it with the name of his father in his worship. What! Here was Thénardier, here was that innkeeper for whom he had so vainly sought! He had found him at last, and how? The savior of his father was a bandit! What a mockery! How could he be bound to any gratitude toward such a wretch? He felt that he had gone mad. His knees gave way beneath him. The scene before him rushed forward. It was like a whirling wind carrying him away. He was on the verge of fainting.

Thénardier was walking to and fro in a sort of frenzied triumph.

"Ha!" he cried. "I have found you again at last! Monsieur Philanthropist![2] Monsieur Threadbare Millionaire! Ha! You don't know me? It was not you who came to my inn Christmas night eight years ago? It was not you who took away Fantine's child from my house? The Lark! It was not you who had a yellow coat? No! Zounds! You made a mock of me once! You are the cause of all my misfortunes. For fifteen hun-

---

2. **philanthropist** one who does good for mankind, especially by giving money

dred francs you got a girl that I had, who already had brought me in a good deal of money, and from whom I ought to have gotten enough to live on all my life. But now the trumps are in my hand. You are skunked! Go on, I have gotten you! I licked your paws this morning, but I will gnaw your heart out tonight."

Monsieur Leblanc did not interrupt, but said, when Thénardier stopped:

"I do not know what you mean. You are mistaken. I am a very poor man. I do not know you; you mistake me for another."

"Ha!" screamed Thénardier. "You are in a fog, my old boy! Ah! You do not remember! You do not see who I am!"

"Pardon me," said Monsieur Leblanc with a tone of politeness which, at that moment, had a peculiar effect: "I see you are a bandit."

Thénardier went berserk, letting out a string of complaints about the wretchedness of his life. He finally stopped to take a breath and asked:

"What have you to say before we begin to dance with you?"

Monsieur Leblanc said nothing. In the midst of the silence, a hoarse voice threw in:

"If there is any wood to split, I am on hand!"

One of the Patron-Minette had removed his mask, revealing a huge face that was bristly and dirty and with fangs instead of teeth. It was the man with the ax.

"Why have you taken off your mask?" cried Thénardier furiously.

"To laugh," replied the man.

Monsieur Leblanc took advantage of this diversion to push away the chair with his foot and the table with his hand. With one leap, before Thénardier had time to turn around, he was at the window. He was half way outside when six strong hands seized him and pulled him forcibly back into the room. The three "chimney doctors" had thrown themselves upon him. At the same time, Madame Thénardier had grabbed him by the hair.

At this, the other bandits ran in from the hall. A Herculean struggle commenced. Monsieur Leblanc finally disappeared under the horrible group of bandits. They succeeded in throwing him upon the bed and held him there. He made no resistance when the bandits bound him. When the last knot was tied, Thénardier took a chair and came to sit tranquilly, nearly in front of Monsieur Leblanc.

"Monsieur, you were wrong in trying to jump out the window. You might have broken your leg. Now, if you please, we will talk quietly. I noticed you did not make the least outcry. I make you compliments for that, monsieur, and I will tell you what I conclude from it. When a man cries out, who is it that comes? The police. And after the police? Justice. Well! You did not cry out. You are no more anxious than we to see justice and police come. It is because—I suspected as much long ago—you have some interest in concealing something. We have the same interest. Now we come to an understanding.

"I said I wanted a great deal of money, an immense amount. My God, rich as you are, you have expenses, too. Who does not? I do not want to ruin you. Here, I am willing to go halfway and make some sacrifice. I need only two hundred thousand francs. You will say 'I do not have two hundred thousand francs with me.' Oh! I do not require that. I ask only one thing. Have the goodness to write what I dictate."

"How do you expect me to write? I am tied."

"True," said Thénardier. "You are quite right."

When the prisoner's right hand was freed, Thénardier dipped the pen in ink and handed it to him. Then he began to dictate:

"My daughter—"

The prisoner shuddered but wrote the words.

Thénardier continued: "Come immediately. I have critical need of you. The person who will give you this note is directed to bring you to me. I am waiting. Come with confidence." Thénardier added: "Put on the address."

The prisoner thought for a moment, then wrote:

Mademoiselle Fabre, at Monsieur Urbain Fabre's, rue Saint Dominique d'Enfer, No. 17.

Thénardier gave the letter to his wife:

"Here. You know what you have to do. There is the carriage below. Go right away and come back immediately."

There were now only five bandits left in the den with Thénardier and the prisoner. An hour passed until the woman returned red-faced and breathless.

"False address!" she cried. The bandit with the ax, who had gone with her, now appeared behind her in the doorway.

Thénardier sat on the table and swung his leg, without speaking. At last he said:

"A false address! What did you hope to accomplish by that?"

"Time!" cried the prisoner. And with that, he shook off his bonds which were cut. Before the seven men had time to recover, he had bent over to the fireplace, and reached his hand toward the furnace. The group beheld him holding above his head a chisel which glowed from its hours in the furnace. He now raised his voice.

"You cannot make me write what I do not wish to write, nor say what I do not wish to say—"

With that he extended his arm and laid the red-hot chisel upon his naked flesh. They heard the hissing and smelled the odor peculiar to chambers of torture.

And drawing the chisel out of the wound, he threw it though the window, which was still open. The horrible tool disappeared whirling into the night.

"Now, do with me what you will," the prisoner resumed.

"There is only one thing to do."

"To kill him."

"That is it."

It was the husband and wife exchanging counsel.

Thénardier went to the table and took out the knife.

Marius was tormenting the trigger of the pistol he still held. Suddenly he saw something.

At his feet a clear ray of moonlight illuminated the sheet of paper on which the elder of the Thénardier girls had written: "The Cognes are here." He knelt down, caught up the sheet of paper, pulled off a bit of plaster from the partition, wrapped it in the paper, and threw the whole into the middle of the den.

The woman sprang to pick up the plaster wrapped in paper. "Egad! This must have come in the window."

Thénardier read the note quickly.

"It is Eponine's writing. The devil! Quick! The ladder! Clear the camp!"

"Without cutting his throat?" asked the woman.

"We have no time."

The bandits struggled to fix the ladder, and they began to argue over who would go out first.

Meanwhile the prisoner paid no attention to what was going on. He seemed to be dreaming or praying.

"Are you fools?" exclaimed Thénardier. "Write our names! Put them in a cap—"

"Would you like my hat?" asked a voice from the door.

They all turned. It was Javert. He had his hat in his hand and was holding it out, smiling.

The Victims Should Be Bound

A squad of policemen rushed in at Javert's call.

"Handcuffs on all," cried Javert.

Madame Thénardier had entrenched herself in one corner of the window. She had thrown off her shawl. Her husband had crouched down behind her, and she covered him with her body. She held a paving stone over her head and yelled:

"Take care!"

Javert advanced on her. She threw the stone wildly at his head. Javert bent, and the stone passed over his head. As the stone rolled back to Javert's heels, he reached the couple and put one of his huge hands on each shoulder. "The handcuffs," he cried.

The police acted quickly, and soon all were manacled. Javert passed the six bandits in review and, as he passed each man, greeted him by name: the "chimney doctors" Bigrenaille, Brujon, Deux Milliards; the three masks Gueulemer, Babet, Claquesous.

Just then he noticed the prisoner of the bandits, who had not uttered a word since the arrival of the police and who held his head down.

"Untie monsieur," said Javert, "and let no one leave."

This said, he sat down and began writing notes for his report. When he had written the first line, he said:

"Bring me the gentleman whom these gentlemen had tied up."

The officers looked around them. The prisoner, Monsieur Leblanc, had disappeared.

The door was guarded, but the window was not. An officer ran to the window and looked out. Nobody could be seen outside, but the rope ladder was still trembling.

"The devil!" said Javert. "That must have been the best one."

The Little Boy Who Had Cried

The day following these events a young boy decided to pay a visit to his mother. He sang with all his might as he walked along the streets of Paris.

He reached No. 50-52 and, finding the door locked, began to batter it with kicks. Madame Burgon arrived and recognized the boy.

"Hullo," said the child. "I have come to see my ancestors."

"There is nobody there."

"Pshaw!" said the child. "Where is my father, then?"

"At LaForce Prison."

"And my mother?"

"At Saint Lazare Prison."

"And my sisters?"

"At an orphanage."

The child scratched his head, looked at the old woman, and said:

"Oh!"

Then the boy turned on his heel and, a moment later, the old woman heard him singing in a fresh, clear voice as he disappeared under the black elms that shivered in the winter wind.

Saint Denis
and the Idyll of the Rue Plumet

1 Eponine

The Field of the Lark

Marius had watched the unfolding of the ambush for which he had tipped off Javert. Hardly had Javert left the old tenement, carrying away his prisoners in three carriages, when Marius also slipped out of the house. He went to Courfeyrac, who had moved from the Latin Quarter for the Rue de la Verrerie "for political reasons." This was the quarter where the revolts were planned these days. Marius said to Courfeyrac only: "I've come to sleep at your place." Courfeyrac drew a mattress off his bed, where there were two, laid it on the floor, and said: "There you are."

The next day, by seven o'clock, Marius went back to the tenement, paid his rent and what was due to Madame Burgon, had his belongings loaded into a handcart, and went off without leaving a forwarding address. He had no wish to be reminded of the hideousness he had seen or to be brought forward to testify against Thénardier.

When Javert came back later in the morning to question Marius about the previous evening's events, he found only Madame Burgon, who answered "moved out!" Javert thought that the young man, whose name he could not remember, had been frightened and had escaped or perhaps was not even at home at the time of the ambush. Still he made some effort to find him, without success.

A month rolled by; then another. Marius was still with Courfeyrac. He knew, through an attorney friend, that Thénardier was in solitary confinement. Every Monday Marius sent five francs to the clerk at La Force for Thénardier. Having no money of his own left, Marius borrowed the five francs from Courfeyrac. It was the first time in his life that he had borrowed money. The periodic contribution was a double enigma: to Courfeyrac who furnished it and to Thénardier who received it. "Where can it be going?" wondered Courfeyrac. "Where is it coming from?" Thénardier asked himself.

Marius had passion in his heart and night over his eyes. All had vanished except love. Even of love, he had lost the instincts and the sudden illuminations. Ordinarily this flame that consumes us also sheds a little useful light. But nothing told Marius which way to look. His whole life was a thick mist. To see her again—Her —was what he yearned for constantly; but he no longer hoped for it.

There was no more going out of the house, except to walk and dream. She—this was Marius's entire thought. He dreamed of nothing else. He felt that everything about him was wearing out, and he said to himself: "If I could only see her again before I die. Can it be that I'll never see her again?"

It happened one day that Marius's solitary walks brought him to a spot near the pond. That day there was a rare pedestrian on the walk. Marius asked the traveler: "What is the name of this place?"

The traveler answered, "It is the Field of the Lark."

In the depths of Marius's melancholy, he heard only the word "lark."

"Yes," he said, "this is her field. Here I shall learn where she lives."

It was absurd but irresistable. Every day he returned.

Early Formation of Crimes

Javert's triumph at the Gorbeau house was not complete. In the first place, he had not made the prisoner prisoner. The victim who slips away is always suspect. It was likely that this person, a precious captive to the bandits, would be no less a valuable prize to the authorities.

And then, Montparnasse had escaped Javert. He would have to wait for another occasion to lay his hands on that "devilish dandy." In fact, Montparnasse had met Eponine, who was standing guard on the boulevard, and had led her away. Well for him that he did. He was free. As for Eponine, Javert nabbed her, and she joined Azelma at Les Madelonnettes.

Finally, on the trip to La Force, one of the principal prisoners, Claquesous, had been lost. Nobody knew how it happened; he seemed to have changed into vapor, slid out of the handcuffs, and slipped through the cracks in the carriage floor.

As for Marius, "that dolt of a lawyer," who was "probably frightened," Javert did not worry much about him. Besides, he was a lawyer and lawyers always seem to turn up.

The inquiry began.

An Apparition to Father Mabeuf

Marius no longer visited anybody, but sometimes he happened to meet Father Mabeuf.

Sometimes, when M. Mabeuf went to the Jardin des Plantes,[1] the old man and the young man would meet on the Boulevard de l'Hopital. They did not speak but sadly nodded their heads. It is a bitter thing that there should be a moment when misery separates! They had been two friends; now they were two passersby.

His friend the bookseller had died. Monsieur Mabeuf now had only his books, his garden, and his indigo plants. It was enough to live on. He worked all day on his indigo bed and at night went back home to water his garden and read his books. M. Mabeuf was now nearly eighty years old.

One night he saw a strange apparition.

Twilight was beginning to whiten everything above and blacken everything below. As he read, M. Mabeuf was looking across the book in his hand at his plants. Among them was a magnificent rhododendron, which was one of his consolations. There had been four days of drought, wind, and sun, without a drop of rain. The stalks were wilted, the buds hung down, the leaves were falling; they all needed to be watered.

M. Mabeuf got up, put his books on the bench, and walked, bent over and with tottering steps, to the well. But when he grasped the chain, he could not even draw it far enough to unhook it. He looked up. The night promised to be as dry as the day had been.

He tried again to unhook the well chain, but he could not.

At that moment he heard a voice which said: "Father Mabeuf, would you like to have me water your garden?"

---

1. **Jardin des Plantes** a park in Paris

At the same time he heard a sound and saw springing out of the shrubbery a sort of tall, slender girl who came and stood before him. She had less the appearance of a human being than of a form just born of the twilight.

Before Father Mabeuf could say a word, this being had unhooked the chain, plunged in and drawn out the bucket, and filled the watering pot. The good man saw the apparition with bare feet and ragged skirt running along the beds, distributing life around her. The sound of water on the leaves filled Father Mabeuf's soul with joy. It seemed to him that the rhododendron was happy.

When she finished, Father Mabeuf approached her with tears in his eyes and touched her forehead.

"God will bless you," he said. "You are an angel."

"No," she answered, "I'm the devil, but that's all the same to me."

Without waiting for or hearing her answer, the old man exclaimed: "What a pity I am so unfortunate and cannot do anything for you."

"You can do something," she said.

"What?"

"Tell me where Monsieur Marius lives."

"What Monsieur Marius?" the old man asked, confused. He fumbled in his memory and then exclaimed: "Wait a minute! Monsieur Marius—the Baron Marius Pontmercy. Yes! I remember now. I don't know where he lives! He walks along the boulevard and goes toward the Field of the Lark. Go there. He isn't hard to find."

When Monsieur Mabeuf stood up, there was nobody there. The girl had vanished.

An Apparition to Marius

A few days later—it was a Monday, the day Marius

borrowed the hundred-sous piece from Courfeyrac for Thénardier. Marius had put the money in his pocket. Before taking it to the prison, he had gone for a little walk, hoping it would enable him to work on his return. He had gone to the Field of the Lark. He was thinking of "Her"! The birds were chattering and singing in the elms.

All at once, in the midst of his reverie, he heard a familiar voice say, "Ah, there he is!"

He looked up and recognized the elder of the Thénardier girls, Eponine; he now knew her name.

She had stopped in front of Marius, an expression of pleasure on her face, and something close to a smile. For a few seconds, she stood there and did not speak.

"I've found you, then?" she said at last. "Father Mabeuf was right. How I've looked for you! Did you know that I've been in the jug? Two weeks! They let me go, seeing there was nothing against me. And I'm still a minor. Two months to go! How I've looked for you! Six weeks! You don't live down there anymore?"

"No," said Marius.

"Oh, I understand. Because of the ruckus. You've moved. D'you know that father Mabeuf calls you Baron Marius? It's true you're a baron?"

Marius did not answer.

She looked straight into Marius's eyes and said: "I have the address."

Marius turned pale. All the blood flowed back into his heart. "What address?"

"The address you asked me to get."

She added, as if she were making an effort: "The young lady's." Having pronounced the words, she sighed deeply.

Marius sprang off the wall where he was sitting and grabbed her hand wildly.

"Come! Show me the way! Tell me! Ask me for anything you like! Where is it?"

"Come with me," she answered. "I'm not sure of the street and the number, but I know the house very well. I'll show you."

She went a few steps with Marius following and then stopped: "By the way, you know you've promised me something?"

Marius fumbled in his pockets and found the five-franc piece intended for Thénardier. He put it in Eponine's hand.

She opened her fingers and let the coin drop. Looking at him glumly, she said: "I don't want your money."

2 The House on the Rue Plumet

The Secret House

Toward the middle of the last century, a velvet-capped presiding judge of the High Judicial Court of Paris who had a mistress had a little house built in the deserted Rue Plumet.

This was a detached two-story house which was fronted by a garden with a large iron gate opening onto the street. The garden covered about an acre. It was all that the passersby could see, but in back of the house there was a small yard with a low building at the far end. That building was intended to house a child and a nurse in case of need. Through a secret door at the rear, this building opened onto a long paved passage—winding, open to the sky, cleverly hidden between two high walls. This passage came to an end at another door, also hidden, that opened a third of a mile away, almost in another quarter of Paris, onto the unbuilt end of Rue de Babylone.

In October 1829, a man of a certain age had appeared and rented the house as it stood, including of course the building at the rear and the passage that ran out to the Rue de Babylone. He had the secret openings of the doors repaired, as well as some other small things. Finally he came and settled in with a young girl and an old servant. The neighbors did not talk about them; there were no neighbors.

This new tenant was Jean Valjean; the young girl was Cosette. The servant was an old maid named

Toussaint. Jean Valjean had rented the house under the name of Fauchelevent, gentleman.

Why had Jean Valjean left the convent? What had happened?

Cosette's education was almost complete, and old Fauchelevent died.

Jean Valjean requested an audience with the reverend prioress, and he told her of a small inheritance he had received on the death of his brother, which would allow him to live without working. He would leave the service of the convent and take his daughter. But since it was not fair that Cosette had been educated freely, he humbly begged the reverend prioress to allow him to offer the community the sum of five thousand francs.

On leaving the convent, he took in his own hands—and would entrust to no assistant—the little box whose key he always had with him. This box puzzled Cosette because of the smell of embalming that it gave off.

Let us say that this box never left him again. He always had it in his room. It was the first and sometimes the only thing he carried away when he changed residence. Cosette laughed about it and called the box "the inseparable," saying, "I'm jealous of it."

Jean Valjean did not appear openly in the city again without deep concern.

He discovered the house on the Rue Plumet and buried himself in it. From then on, he used the name Ultimus Fauchelevent.

At the same time, he rented two other lodgings in Paris in order to attract less attention than if he always stayed in the same neighborhood. These two apartments were both very simple and shabby, in two neighborhoods far apart from each other. One was in the Rue de l'Ouest; the other was in the Rue de l'Homme-Armé. From time to time, he would go off, either to one or to the other, to spend a month or six weeks with Cosette.

This man of lofty virtue had three addresses in Paris in order to escape from the police.

Jean Valjean went out every day for a walk with Cosette in remote paths of the Luxembourg Gardens and every Sunday to mass at Saint Jacques-du-Haut-Pas. As that is a very poor neighborhood, he gave a great deal of alms there, and the unfortunate would surround him in the church. However, neither Jean Valjean nor Cosette nor Toussaint ever came or went except by the gate on the Rue de Babylone. Unless one were to see them through the bars of the garden gate, it would have been difficult to guess that they lived on the Rue Plumet. That gate was always shut, and the garden had been left untended so it would not attract attention.

Perhaps he was mistaken in that.

Change of Grating

On leaving the convent, Cosette could have found nothing sweeter and more dangerous than the house on the Rue Plumet. It was a continuation of the solitude with the beginning of liberty; an enclosed garden but a rich and fertile nature; the same dreams as in the convent, but with glimpses of young men; a grating, but onto the street.

Cosette loved her father—that is to say, Jean Valjean—with all her heart. He had given her the untended garden, saying, "Do with it whatever you like." He was a reader and he had come to talk very well. He had the secret wealth and eloquence of a humble and earnest intellect. He had retained just enough roughness to add to his goodness. At the Luxembourg Gardens, in their conversations, he gave long explanations of everything, drawing on what he had read as well as on what he had suffered. In other words, this simple man was enough for Cosette's thoughts. She adored the good man.

Cosette had only vague memories of her childhood. She prayed for her mother, whom she had not known. The Thénardiers were two hideous faces out of some nightmare. It seemed she had begun life in a pit and Jean Valjean had lifted her out of it. Since she had no clear memory of being Jean Valjean's daughter, she imagined that her mother's soul had passed into this good man and had come to live with her.

When he sat down, she would rest her cheek on his white hair and silently shed a tear, saying to herself, "This is perhaps my mother, this man!"

The Rose Discovers She Is an Instrument of War

One day Cosette happened to look in the mirror, and she said to herself, "Well, now!" It almost seemed to her that she was pretty. Up to that moment, she had never thought of her face. She had seen herself in a mirror, but she had not looked at herself. And she had often been told she was homely. Jean Valjean alone would quietly say, "Not at all! Not at all!"

Cosette had been beautiful for some time before she noticed it. From the day after the one on which she had said, "Really, I am beautiful!" Cosette gave attention to her clothing. In less than a month, little Cosette was not only one of the prettiest women in Paris, which is something, but also one of the best dressed, which is much more. The truth is that she was ravishing on all scores.

Jean Valjean watched these changes with anxiety.

He noticed that Cosette, who previously was always asking to stay in, was now asking to go out. He also noticed that Cosette no longer had the same preference for the backyard. She now preferred to stay in the garden, not even avoiding the iron gate.

In learning she was beautiful, Cosette lost the grace of not knowing it. But what she lost in grace she gained in serious charm.

It was at this time that Marius, after the lapse of six months, saw her again at the Luxembourg Gardens.

The spirit of the convent, in which she had been steeped for five years, was slowly evaporating from Cosette. She did not know what love was, but she began to think of Marius as something charming, luminous, and impossible.

Every day she waited impatiently for the hour to take their walk. When she saw Marius, she felt inexpressively happy. She honestly thought she was telling everything that was on her mind when she said to Jean Valjean: "What a delightful garden the Luxembourg is!"

Marius and Cosette were in the dark in regard to each other. They did not speak; they did not exchange greetings—they saw each other and they lived by gazing at each other.

To Sadness, Sadness and a Half

Every condition has its instinct. Nature warned Jean Valjean of Marius's presence. Marius, in an attempt to hide himself from the "father," took on a suspicious caution and an awkward boldness. He no longer came near them; he would sit some distance away and remain there in ecstasy. He had a book which he pretended to read, but why pretend? He used to wear his old suit, but now he wore his new suit every day. It was not entirely certain that he did not curl his hair. He had strange eyes, he wore gloves. In short, Jean Valjean detested the young man.

He never opened his mouth to Cosette about the unknown man. One day, however, he could not contain himself, and he said to her, "What a prim manner that young man has!"

Cosette merely answered, "That young man?" as if she were seeing him for the first time.

"How stupid I am," thought Jean Valjean. "She hadn't even noticed him. I've shown him to her myself."

Cosette behaved with such apparent unconcern that Jean Valjean came to this conclusion: "This booby is madly in love with Cosette, but Cosette doesn't know he exists!"

We know the rest. Marius's madness continued. One day he followed Cosette to the house on the Rue de l'Ouest. Jean Valjean cast a meaningful glance at Marius, which he never noticed. He took to watching the house. Finally he spoke with the porter, and the porter in turn told Jean Valjean that there had been a curious young man looking for him.

A week later, Jean Valjean moved. He resolved never to set foot again either in the Luxembourg or in the Rue de l'Ouest. He returned to the Rue Plumet.

Cosette pined. She suffered from Marius's absences, just as she had rejoiced in his presence. Still she did not let Jean Valjean see a thing except her pallor. This, however, was more than enough to make Jean Valjean anxious. Sometimes he would ask, "What's the matter?"

She would answer, "Nothing."

And after a pause, because she felt he was sad, too,

she would add, "And you, father, isn't something the matter with you?"

"Me? Nothing."

These two beings, who loved each other so exclusively and with so touching a love, were now suffering beside each other and through each other. Without speaking of it, without harsh feeling, and smiling all the while.

3 Aid from Below or from Above

Wound Outside, Cure Within

Thus their life together grew darker.

Only one distraction was left to them, and this had formerly been a pleasure. They would take bread to those who were hungry and clothing to those who were cold. In these visits to the poor, they found some remains of their former happiness. Sometimes, when they had had a good day, Cosette was a bit cheerful. It was during one of these times that she had gone with Jean Valjean to visit the Jondrettes.

Cosette knew nothing of the events at the Gorbeau House except that the day after that visit Jean Valjean had appeared with a very large wound on his left arm. It was very much inflamed and infected and looked very much like a burn, which he explained away. This wound kept him indoors for a month with fever. He would not see a doctor.

Cosette tended the wound day and night with such grace and angelic pleasure in being useful that Jean Valjean felt all his happiness return.

Seeing that her father was sick, Cosette deserted the house for the little lodge in the backyard where he lived. She spent all her time there with Jean Valjean and read to him from books he liked. Jean Valjean was coming alive again, his happiness revived. The Luxembourg, Cosette's distant behavior, all the clouds over his soul faded away.

As for Cosette, Jean Valjean's wound had been a

diversion. When she saw that her father was suffering less, that he was getting well, and that he seemed happy, she felt content.

It was spring; the days were growing longer and winter was leaving. Then came April, the beginning of summer. Cosette was still too young for April joy not to find its way into her heart. She was not very sad now. That is the way things stood, but she did not notice it. One morning she managed to entice her father into the garden for a short walk. While she was walking in the sun and supporting his wounded arm, she did not notice that she was constantly laughing and that she was happy.

An End Unlike the Beginning

Solitude

One day she suddenly thought of Marius. "Well, now," she said, "I don't think of him anymore."

That very week she noticed, as he went past the iron garden gate, a very handsome officer of the lancers. Fair hair, full blue eyes, plump and vain, he was the very opposite of Marius. Cosette thought he undoubtedly belonged to the regiment in barracks on the Rue de Babylone. The next day she saw him pass again, and after that—was it chance?—she saw him pass almost every day.

The officer's comrades noted that there was, in this badly kept garden, a pretty creature that almost always was there when the handsome lieutenant passed. This latter is not entirely unknown to the reader; his name was Théodule Gillenormand.

It was at this very moment when Marius was sinking gradually toward death and saying, "If I could only see her again before I die!" If Marius had seen Cosette at that moment looking at a lancer, he would have died from grief.

Whose fault was it? Nobody's.

Marius had one of those personalities that sinks into grief and remains there; Cosette was the sort that plunges in and comes out again.

Cosette's Fears

In early April, Jean Valjean went on a trip. He went

away from time to time for one or two days at the most. No one knew where he went—not even Cosette. This time he was to be gone three days.

While he was away a strange incident occurred.

Near ten o'clock on the first evening Jean Valjean was gone, Cosette was alone in the sitting room, playing the piano.

All at once it seemed to her that she heard footsteps in the garden. She went to the window shutter, which was closed, and listened. It sounded like a man's step and that he was walking very softly.

She immediately ran upstairs and into her room, opened a slide in the blind, and looked into the garden. The moon was full. She could see as plain as daylight.

There was nobody there.

She opened the window. The garden was deserted, as was the street.

Cosette decided she had been mistaken. She thought no more about it.

The next day, not so late, she was walking in the garden. Suddenly she heard the same sound as the evening before; it was as if someone were walking under the trees. But she told herself it was the rustling of two tree limbs, and she paid no attention to it. Besides, she could see nothing.

She left the trees and began to cross the green plot of grass to reach the steps.

Cosette stood still, terrified. Beside her shadow on the grass, the moon was projecting a second shadow— strangely frightening, a shadow with a round hat. For a moment she was unable to speak, cry out, stir, or even turn her head.

At last she summoned all her courage and turned. There was nobody there. She looked up and told herself it was a figure produced by a stovepipe with a cap that rose above a neighboring roof.

The following night, just at sunset, Cosette made a tour of the garden and went to sit down on the bench. Just then she noticed a rather large stone that had not been there some moments before.

She lifted the stone and saw something underneath that looked like an envelope. There was no name on one side and no seal on the other. But the envelope was not empty. Inside there were sheets of paper.

She took out the sheets, and this is what she read:

The reduction of the universe to a single being, the expansion of a single being into God; this is love.

How sad the soul when it is sad from love!

Separated lovers find a host of mysterious ways to correspond. They exchange the song of the birds, the perfume of the flowers, the sunlight, the sighs of the wind. Love is powerful enough to fill all nature with its messages.

Whoever we may be, we have our living, breathing beings. If they fail us, then we die. To die for lack of love is horrible. The smothering of the soul.

The day that a woman walking past sheds a light on you as she goes, you are lost, you love. You have then only one thing left to do: to think of her so earnestly that she will be compelled to think of you.

Does she still come to the Luxembourg? No, monsieur. She hears a mass in this church, doesn't she? She no longer comes here. Does she still live in this house? She has moved away! Where has she gone to live? She did not say! What a somber thing, not to know the address of one's soul!

You who suffer because you love, love still more. To die of love is to live by it.

What a great thing, to be loved! What a greater thing still, to love. If no one loved, the sun would go out.

Cosette After the Letter

Cosette contemplated the letter. It was written in gorgeous handwriting. She had never read anything like it. It was like a hand that had opened and suddenly thrown her a handful of sunbeams.

In these lines she felt a passionate, ardent, generous, honest nature. Who could have written them? She did not hesitate for a single moment. One single man.

He!

It was he! He who had written to her! He who had been there. While she was forgetting him, he had found her again! But had she forgotten him? Never!

All day Cosette was in a sort of daze. She could hardly think.

O transforming love! O dreams!

The Elderly Are Out When Convenient

When evening came, Cosette dressed carefully and went down to the garden. Jean Valjean was not at home. Toussaint was busy in her kitchen, which looked out into the backyard, away from the garden.

Cosette walked under the branches; some were very low. She reached the bench. The stone was still there. She sat down and laid her hand on that stone as though to caress it and thank it.

All at once, she had the indefinable impression that we feel, though we see nothing, when there is someone standing behind us.

She turned her head and stood up.

It was he.

He was bareheaded. He looked pale and thin. His face was lit by the light of a dying day, and he seemed not yet a phantom but no longer a man.

His hat was lying a few steps away in the shrubbery.

Then she heard his voice murmuring, "Pardon me, I am here. My heart is bursting; I couldn't live as I was, so I've come. Have you read what I put there, on the bench? Do you recognize me at all? Don't be afraid; nobody sees me. I come to look at your windows from nearby. I walk very softly so you won't hear me, because you might be frightened. The other evening I was behind you; you turned and I fled. Once I heard you sing. I was happy. I think I am going to die. If you only knew! I adore you! Pardon me, I don't know what I'm saying to you. Perhaps I annoy you. Am I annoying you?"

"Oh!" she said.

And she collapsed.

She fell, he caught her in his arms, he held her tightly, unconscious of what he was doing.

She took his hand and laid it on her heart. He felt his letter there and stammered, "You love me, then?"

She answered in a voice so low it was no more than a breath, "Hush, you know it!"

And she hid her blushing head against the proud and dazed young man.

He fell to the seat, she by his side. There were no more words. How is it that their lips met? How is it that birds sing, that the snow melts, that the rose opens?

One kiss, and that was all.

Gradually they began to talk. The night was serene and glorious over their heads. These two beings, pure as spirits, told each other everything—their dreams, their fears, how they had adored each other, their despair when they had ceased to see each other. They confided to each other all that was most hidden and most mysterious in themselves. They told each other all that love, youth, and the remains of childhood that were theirs brought to mind. These two hearts poured themselves out to each other so that at the end of an hour it was the young man who had the young girl's soul and the young girl who had the soul of the young man.

When they finished, when they had told each other everything, she laid her head on his shoulder and asked him, "What is your name?"

"My name is Marius," he said. "And yours?"

"My name is Cosette."

5 *The Escape*

The Fortunes and Misfortunes

An escape had been concocted among Babet, Brujon, Gueulemer, and Thénardier, even though Thénardier was in solitary. Montparnasse was to help them from outside.

Having spent a month in the punishment cell, Brujon had had time—first to braid a rope and second to perfect a plan. Since he was understood to be very dangerous, he was put into Building 9. The first thing he found there was Gueulemer; the second was a nail. Gueulemer plus one nail equaled freedom.

What made this particular moment favorable for an escape attempt was that some workmen were removing and relaying part of the prison's slate roof. There were scaffoldings and ladders around—in other words, bridges and stairways to liberty.

Building 9 was the weak point of the prison. The walls were corroded, stones had become loose, and wood facings had been placed over the arches to the dormitories. It was a blunder to put hardened criminals there. Brujon and Gueulemer had been put in the same dormitory. As a precaution, they had been put on the lower floor. It happened that the heads of their beds rested against the chimney flue.

Thénardier was directly above them on the floor called the Bel-Air. The Bel-Air was an attic in Building 9 which contained four large heavily-built cages with space between them. He had been there in solitary since February 3. No one knows exactly how he managed to get his hands on a bottle of wine mixed with a narcotic.

Brujon and Gueulemer knew that Babet had escaped that very morning and was waiting for them in the street with Montparnasse. They got up from their beds quietly and began to pierce the chimney flue with the nail Brujon had found. The fragments fell onto Brujon's bed, so nobody heard them. Also, a hailstorm and thunder shook the prison doors on their hinges, making a convenient cover for the noise. Before any sound reached the watchman, the wall was pierced, the chimney was scaled, the iron trellis covering the flue was forced, and the two bandits were on the roof. The wind and rain increased; the roof was slippery.

They fastened one end of the rope Brujon had made to the stumps of the chimney bars. Then they threw the other end over the wall, cleared the gap with one leap, clung to the wall, let themselves down one after the other onto a little roof next to the bathhouse, pulled down the rope, crossed the bathhouse yard, pushed open the porter's side, opened the carriage door, and were in the street. The rope had broken off part way down as they pulled it, but that was of no matter to them.

That night Thénardier received a tip and did not go to sleep. About one in the morning he looked out to see two shadows going by on the roof, in the rain and howling wind, in front of the window opposite his cage. One of the shadows stopped for a look. It was Brujon. Thénardier recognized him immediately and understood.

Thénardier, described as an assassin, was kept under constant watch. A guard with two dogs checked his irons several times a day. Every day at four o'clock, a guard with his dogs entered the cage and placed near Thénardier's bed a plate with a two-pound loaf of black bread, a jug of water, and a thin soup with some beans floating in it. Thénardier had obtained permission to keep a small iron spike which he used to nail his bread to a crack in the wall "in order," he said, "to keep it from the rats."

At four o'clock in the morning when the relief guard came to relieve the young recruit who had been watching Thénardier, he found the young man asleep like a log near Thénardier's cage. As for Thénardier, he had disappeared.

There was a hole in the ceiling of the cage and, above that, a hole in the roof. A board was missing from his bed; a half-empty bottle containing a drugged wine was in the cell, and the young guard's bayonet was missing.

At the time of discovery, it was supposed that Thénardier was well out of reach. The reality is that he was still in great danger. On reaching the roof of Building 9, he had found the remnant of Brujon's cord hanging from the chimney, but it was much too short to use in reaching the next wall.

Dripping with sweat and soaked by the rain, his clothing in shreds, his hands and knees bleeding, Thénardier found himself three stories high above the pavement where his friends waited. Horrified at the prospect of recapture, his thoughts swung like a pendulum: "Dead if I fall, taken if I stay."

"One of us has to get up there," said Montparnasse, who considered himself to some slight extent a son-in-law of Thénardier.

"Three stories!" said Brujon.

The old plaster flue for a stove formerly used in the

shanty crept along the wall almost to the spot where they saw Thénardier. This flue was cracked and full of seams. It was very narrow.

"By that flue!" exclaimed Babet. "It would take a child!"

"Wait," said Montparnasse. "I have got the answer."

Several minutes later little Gavroche was examining the rope, the flue, the wall, and the windows. He made a disdainful sound in response to the charge he had been given. "That's all?" he said.

Just as he was about to start, Thénardier bent over the wall and Gavroche recognized him.

"Wait a minute!" he said. "That's my father! Well, never mind!"

And taking the length of good rope in his teeth, he began the ascent.

A moment later, Thénardier was in the street.

Ferocious in freedom, his first words were these: "Now, who're we going to eat?" (It is needless to explain that this frightful word meant "to kill, assassinate, plunder.")

Brujon described a job with some promise in the Rue Plumet, a deserted house on a deserted street with a rusty gate into a garden and some lone women.

"Your daughter Eponine found it," Babet explained.

"Well, she's not stupid, so it's worth a look," replied the leader.

Nobody noticed Gavroche, who had seated himself on one of the stones supporting the fence. He waited, perhaps for his father to acknowledge him; then he put on his shoes, saying, "It's all over? You have no more use for me? Well, I'm off."

And he left.

One of the men said to Thénardier, "Did you notice that kid?"

"Not much."

"Well, I don't know, but it seems to me it's your son."

"What?" said Thénardier. "You think so?"

And he left.

6   *Enchantments and Desolations*

Sunshine

The reader will remember that Marius, drawn as by the force that propels iron toward a magnet, had finally entered Cosette's garden as Romeo did Juliet's. It was even easier for him than for Romeo. Romeo had to scale a wall; he had only to push aside the bar in a decrepit gate. He was slender and easily slipped through.

As there was never anybody in the street, and as Marius entered the garden only at night, he ran no risk of being seen.

From the blessed moment when a kiss betrothed these two souls, Marius came through the gate every evening. Throughout the month of May of that year 1832, every night, in that wild garden, two human beings glowed for each other in the darkness. It seemed to Cosette that Marius had a crown and to Marius that Cosette had a halo. They touched, they gazed at each other, they clasped hands. They pressed close together, but there was a distance they did not pass. The first kiss was also the last. Since then, Marius had not gone beyond touching Cosette's hand or her scarf or her curls with his lips. What happened between these two beings? Nothing. They were adoring each other.

Love almost replaces thought. Love is a burning forgetfulness of everything else. To Cosette and Marius there was nothing in existence beyond Marius

214

and Cosette. The universe around them had fallen out of sight. They lived in a golden moment. There was nothing before, nothing after. Marius scarcely thought whether Cosette had a father. He was so dazzled his brain was wiped clean.

Marius and Cosette did not ask where this would lead them. They thought of themselves as having arrived. It is a strange pretension for men to ask that love should lead them somewhere.

Shadow Commences

Jean Valjean suspected nothing.

A little less dreamy than Marius, Cosette was cheerful, and that was enough to make Jean Valjean happy.

When two lovers have an understanding, they always get along well. Any third person who might disturb their love is kept in the darkness by a few simple precautions—always the same for all lovers. So Cosette never objected to Jean Valjean's proposals. Did he wish to stay home? Very well. Would he like to spend the evening with Cosette? She was delighted. As he always went to bed at ten o'clock, on those occasions Marius would not come to the garden till that time, when he would hear Cosette open the glass door to the steps. It goes without saying that the two never met by day. Jean Valjean never thought Marius existed. Old Toussaint, who went to bed early, thought of nothing except sleep once her work was done. She was unaware of everything, like Jean Valjean. When Marius came and went, he carefully replaced the bar of the grating in such a way that nothing looked out of order.

Courfeyrac, a practical man, had little taste for unpublished passions. He was impatient with them and would occasionally serve Marius with a summons to return to reality. He tried to get Marius to reveal the name of his beloved, but nothing could make Marius "confess." You might have torn out his nails sooner than one of the two syllables that composed that name, Cosette.

Meanwhile various complications were approaching.

One evening Marius was on his way to the rendez-vous, walking as usual with his head down, when he heard someone say very near to him, "Good evening, Monsieur Marius."

He looked up and recognized Eponine.

This produced a strange effect on him. He had reason to be grateful to the girl; he owed his present happiness to her, and yet he felt annoyed to meet her.

With some embarrassment, he answered, "Ah, you, Eponine!"

"Why do you speak to me so sternly? Have I done anything to you?"

"No," he answered.

Certainly he had nothing against her. Far from it. Except he felt that now that he had whispered to Cosette he could not do anything but speak coldly to Eponine.

As he was silent, she exclaimed, "So, tell me—."

She stopped. It seemed that words had failed this creature, once so reckless and bold. She tried to smile and could not. She began again, "Well?"

Then she was silent again and stood with her eyes cast down.

"Good evening, Monsieur Marius," she said abruptly and walked off.

A Dog in the Garden

The next day, at nightfall, Marius was following the same path with some rapturous thoughts in his heart when he spotted Eponine approaching him. Two days in a row were two much. He turned hastily, left the boulevard, changed his route, and went to the Rue Plumet from a different direction.

This caused Eponine to follow him, a thing she had not done before. She had been content until then to see him on the street without even seeking to meet him. Only on the previous evening had she tried to speak to him.

So Eponine followed him with suspicion. She saw him push aside the bar and slip into the garden. She went up to the gate, felt the bars one after another, and easily found the one Marius had removed.

She sat down on the base of the gate, close to the grating, as if she were guarding it. There was a dark nook in which Eponine was entirely hidden. She remained this way for more than an hour, without stirring.

Shortly after ten o'clock in the evening, six men, walking separately and at some distance from one another along the wall, and who might have been taken for a slightly drunk patrol, entered the Rue Plumet. The first to arrive at the garden gate stopped and waited for the others. The men began to talk in low voices.

"It's here," said one of them.

"Is there a dog in the yard?" asked another.

"I don't know. In any case I've got a bullet for him to eat."

"Do you have some tape to break the pane?"

"Yes."

"The grating is old," added a fifth man, who had a voice like a ventriloquist.

The sixth man, who had not yet spoken, began to examine the grating as Eponine had done an hour before. In this way, he came to the loosened bar. Just as he was about to lay hold of it, a hand fell on his arm, he felt himself pushed back sharply, and a roughened voice said, "There's a dog."

At the same time he saw a pale girl standing in front of him.

The man recoiled and stammered, "What is this creature?"

"Your daughter."

It was indeed Eponine who was speaking to Thénardier. At this, the five others—Claquesous, Gueulemer, Babet, Montparnasse, and Brujon—approached without a word. In their hands were tools that burglars such as they use.

"Ah, there, what are you doing here? What do you want from us? Are you crazy?" exclaimed Thénardier. "Why do you come and get in our way?"

Eponine began to laugh and threw herself at his neck. "Aren't you happy to see me, your daughter? You know very well I'm no fool. Usually you believe me. I've done you service many times. Well, I've learned about this job, and you'd expose yourselves uselessly, you see. I swear to you that there's nothing to be done in that house."

"There are lone women," said Gueulemer.

"No, the people have moved away."

"The candles haven't, anyhow!" said Babet.

And he showed Eponine a light moving about in the attic of the cottage. It was Toussaint, who had stayed up to hang out her clothes to dry.

Eponine made a final effort. She laughed derisively.

"So you want to go into that house? You can try all you like; you won't go in. There are six of you; what's that to me? You're men. Well, I'm a woman. I'm not afraid of you, not one bit. I tell you you won't go into this house because I don't like the idea. If you come near, I'll bark. I told you I'm the dog. I don't care about you. Go on about your business somewhere else, but don't come back here. I forbid it!"

She took a step forward; she was frightening. She began to laugh:

"I'll just cry out. They'll come—bang! You're six, but I'm everyone."

Thénardier took a step forward. "Don't speak so loud. We have to earn our keep. You don't love your father anymore?"

She sat down again against the gatepost, put her elbow on her knee, put her chin in her hand, and casually began to swing her foot.

The six thugs were sullen and abashed at being held in check by a girl. They moved under the protecting shade of the street lantern and conferred, their shoulders hunched in fury and humiliation.

Finally Brujon shook his head and spoke: "This morning I met two sparrows fighting; tonight I run into a woman squawking. All this is bad business. Let's go."

Eponine, who had never taken her eyes off the men, saw them turn back the way they had come. She got up and followed them as far as the boulevard. There she saw them separate and melt away in the dark.

Paradise Threatened

While Eponine was standing guard over the iron gate, Marius was with Cosette.

Never had Marius been happier, more in love, more in ecstasy. But he had found Cosette sad. She had been weeping. It was the first cloud in this wonderful dream.

"What is it?" was Marius's first greeting.

"I'll tell you. We are going away."

Marius woke up. For six weeks he had lived outside of life. The phrase "going away" brought him roughly back.

Cosette continued, "This morning my father told me to arrange all my things and be ready, that he would give me his clothes to pack, that he had to take a trip, that we were going away, that we must have a large trunk for me and a smaller one for him, to get ready within a week, and that perhaps we would go to England."

Marius asked in a feeble voice, "And when would you leave?"

"He didn't say when."

"And when would you return?"

"He didn't say when."

Marius arose and said coldly, "Cosette, are you going?"

Cosette answered in a sort of daze, "Where?"

"To England. Will you go?"

"What would you have me do?" she asked, clasping her hands.

"So you are going?"

"If my father goes."

"So you are going?"

Cosette took Marius's hand without answering. Then she smiled. "How stupid we are, Marius! I have an idea!"

"What?"

"Go if we go! I'll tell you where! Come and join me where I am!"

Marius was now entirely awake. He cried to Cosette, "Go with you? Are you mad? It takes money, and I have none! Go to England? Why, I owe now more than ten louis to Courfeyrac, one of my friends you don't know! Go to England? I can't even pay for a passport!"

He threw himself against a tree and stood like that for a long time. At last he turned. Behind him he heard a stifled sound. It was Cosette weeping.

She had been sobbing for more than two hours while Marius had been thinking.

"Cosette," Marius said, "I give you my most sacred word of honor that if you go away I will die."

There was a melancholy in his voice that produced a chill in Cosette. From the shock, she stopped crying.

"Now, listen," Marius said. "Don't expect me till the day after tomorrow."

"Oh! Why not?"

"You'll see." He added in an undertone and aside, "He is not a man who changes his habits, and he has never received any visitors until evening."

"What man are you speaking of?" inquired Cosette.

Marius went on, "It occurs to me that you have to know my address. Something may happen; we don't know what. I live with my friend Courfeyrac at No. 16, Rue de Verrerie. He took out a pen knife and wrote with the blade on the plaster wall:

16, Rue de la Verrerie.

When Marius left, the street was empty. It was the moment when Eponine was following the robbers to the boulevard.

Old Heart and Young Together

Grandfather Gillenormand had passed his ninety-first year. He still lived with Mlle. Gillenormand, Rue des Filles-du-Calvaire, No. 6, in his old house. He no longer beat the servants, and he struck his cane with less animation on the top doorstep. The fact is, the old man was dejected. For four years he had been waiting for Marius to ring his door some day or another. Now, when he was gloomy, he thought that perhaps he would never see Marius again. The idea chilled him.

He admitted no fault on his side, but he thought of Marius only with a deep tenderness that he was unable to show.

Mlle. Gillenormand had attempted to substitute her favorite, Théodule, officer of the lancers.[1] But the effort had failed miserably. The old man wearied the lancer and the lancer shocked the old man. M. Gillenormand had tired of hearing him brag of all the favors he had won in the neighborhood of his barracks. Finally Grandfather Gillenormand said to his daughter, "I've had enough of your Théodule. I have little taste for warriors in peace. Entertain him yourself, if you like."

One evening—it was June 4, which did not prevent M. Gillenormand from having a blazing fire—he had said goodnight to his daughter and was alone in his room. He was just explaining to himself that now there was no longer any reason for Marius to return, that he must give him up. His bald head had fallen on his chest and he was in a reverie when his old servant, Basque, came in and asked, "Can Monsieur receive Monsieur Marius?"

The old man straightened up, and all the blood flowed back into his heart. He faltered. "Monsieur Marius what?"

"I don't know," answered Basque, disconcerted about his master's appearance. "I have not seen him. Nicolette just told me that there is a young man here and to say that it is Monsieur Marius."

M. Gillenormand stammered out a whisper, "Show

---

1. **lancers** an army regiment

him in." And he remained, his head shaking, staring at the door. It opened. A young man entered. It was Marius.

At last! After all these years! He looked him over. He thought him beautiful, noble, striking, adult, a mature man with a graceful attitude and pleasing air. He would have gladly opened his arms, called him, rushed to him. Indeed all his tenderness rose to his lips, but through the contrast that was his nature, harsh words came out. He said abruptly, "What has brought you here?"

Marius was embarrassed.

M. Gillenormand would have liked Marius to throw himself in his arms. He was displeased with Marius and with himself. He felt that he was rough and Marius was cold.

The old man went on sternly, "Have you come to ask my pardon? Have you seen the error of your ways?"

Marius shuddered. He was being asked, he felt, to disavow his father. He looked down and answered, "No, monsieur."

"Well, then," the old man exclaimed with a grief that was bitter and angry, "what do you want from me?"

"Monsieur," said Marius, "I know that my presence is displeasing to you, but I have come only to ask one thing of you and then I will go away immediately."

"You are a fool!" said the old man. "Who is telling you to go away? You left me! Me, your grandfather. You left my house to go who knows where. And now, at the end of four years, you come to my house and have nothing to say? Let us be brief. You have, you say, come to ask for something. What is it? Speak up!"

"Monsieur," said Marius, with the look of a man

who feels he is about to fall into an abyss, "I have come to ask your permission to get married."

"You marry! At twenty-one! You have nothing but a permission to ask? Sit down, monsieur. So you want to marry? Whom? Can the question be asked without being indiscreet?"

He stopped, but before Marius could answer he added violently, "Come now, you have a business. Your fortune made? How much do you earn at your lawyer's trade?"

"Nothing."

"Then I understand the girl is rich?"

"As I am."

"What? No dowry?"

"No."

"What is the father?"

"I do not know."

"What is her name?"

"Mademoiselle Fauchelevent."

"Fauche-what?"

"Fauchelevent."

"Pftt!"

"Monsieur," said Marius, "I implore you, in the name of heaven, allow me to marry her!"

"Ha! The devil! Go, my boy, as you please; tie yourself down, marry your Pousselevent, your Couplevent—Never, monsieur! Never!"

"Father!"

"Never!"

At the tone the "never" was spoken, Marius lost all hope. He walked slowly to the door. M. Gillenormand followed him with his eyes and, as Marius opened the door, took four strides, seized Marius by the collar, drew him forcibly into the room, and threw him into an armchair, saying:

"Tell me about it!"

It was the single word "father," dropped by Marius, that caused the old man's turnabout.

"Father," continued Marius, "my good father, if you knew. I love her. The first time I saw her was at the Luxembourg. I don't know how it happened; I fell in love with her. I was wretched. Now at last I see her every day, at her own house. Her father does not know it. Just think—they are going away. We see each other in the garden every evening. Her father wants to take her away to England, so I said to myself: 'I'll go and see my grandfather and tell him about it.' I could go crazy, I'd die, I'd get sick, I'd throw myself in the river. I absolutely have to marry her because I'd go crazy. Now, that's the whole truth; I don't believe I've forgotten anything. She lives in a garden where there is an iron gate, in the Rue Plumet."

Grandfather Gillenormand, radiant with joy, had sat down by Marius's side. At the words "Rue Plumet," he sat up straight.

"Rue Plumet! You say Rue Plumet! Let's see now. There are some barracks down there. Your cousin Théodule has told me about her. The lancer, the officer. Yes! It comes back to me now. I have heard about this little girl of the gate on the Rue Plumet. In a garden. They say she's nice. Between ourselves, I think that ninny of a lancer paid her a little attention. I don't know how far he got! Marius! I think it is all well and good to be in love. As for the little girl, she receives you unknown to papa? That's all right. I've had such adventures myself. More than one. But do you know what we do? We don't marry them. You ninny! Make her your mistress."

Marius turned pale. He had understood nothing of what his grandfather said of the lancer, of the barracks.

None of this had to do with Cosette, who was a lily. But the old man's wandering led up to a deadly insult to Cosette. The phrase "make her your mistress" entered the heart of the pure young man like a sword.

He rose, picked up his hat from the floor, and strode firmly toward the door. There he turned, bowed low to his grandfather, raised his head again, and said: "Five years ago you outraged my father; today you have outraged my wife. I ask nothing more of you. Adieu."

Grandfather Gillenormand was astounded. He attempted to rise, but before he could say a word, the door closed and Marius had disappeared.

For a few moments, the old man could not move, breathe, or speak. At last he tore himself from the chair and ran to the door crying, "Help, help!"

His daughter and then the servants appeared. "Run after him! Catch him! What have I done to him? He's mad! He's going! Oh! My God! Oh! My God! This time he won't come back!"

He ran to the window, hung halfway out while Basque and Nicolette held onto him, and cried, "Marius! Marius! Marius!"

But Marius was already out of hearing.

The old man raised his hands to his temples two or three times in anguish, drew back tottering, and sank into a chair, pulseless, voiceless, tearless, shaking his head and moving his lips, stunned. There was nothing more left in his eyes than something deep and mournful, resembling night.

7 Where Are They Going?

Jean Valjean

Jean Valjean had decided to leave Paris and even France and to cross over to England. He had told that to Cosette. He wanted to be gone in less than a week. He was sitting on a bank in the park mulling over a variety of things: Thénardier, the police, the journey, and the difficulty of procuring a passport. He was anxious on all points.

Finally, an inexplicable and alarming discovery had put him even more on alert. That very morning he had come upon this line scratched on the wall, probably with a nail:

16, Rue de la Verrerie.

What was it? An address? A signal? A warning for him? In any case, it was clear that the garden had been entered, that strangers had been there. He took care not to mention the writing to Cosette for fear of frightening her.

Suddenly he noticed that somebody had stopped on the bank just behind him. He was about to turn when a sheet of folded paper fell onto his knee. He took the paper and read on it the following, in large letters written with a pencil: Move!

Jean Valjean rose hastily; there was nobody on the embankment. He saw only a creature larger than a child, smaller than a man, who jumped over a bridge and slid into the gully.

Jean Valjean returned home immediately, deep in thought.

Marius

Marius had left his grandfather's house desolated. He had entered with very little hope; he came out with immense despair.

He walked the streets, went home to Courfeyrac's, and slept until broad daylight. When he awoke, he saw Courfeyrac, Enjolras, Feuilly, and Combeferre standing in the room, hats on their heads. Courfeyrac said to him, "Are you coming to General Lamarque's funeral?"

Marius looked at Courfeyrac as if he were speaking Chinese.

He went out some time after them. He was going to see Cosette. He took with him the pistols Javert had given to him for the adventure of February 3. It is not clear what obscure thought prompted him to take them.

At intervals, as he walked, he seemed to hear strange sounds in Paris. He roused himself and thought, "Are they fighting?"

Marius approached the gate on the Rue Plumet, moved the bar, and hurried into the garden. Cosette was not at the spot where she usually waited for him. He looked up at the house and saw that the shutters were closed. He went to the house and, mad with love, grief, and anxiety, rapped on the shutters. He rapped and rapped again. "Cosette!" he cried. There was no answer. It was all over. Nobody in the garden. Nobody in the house.

Suddenly he heard a voice which seemed to come from the street, hollering through the trees, "Monsieur Marius!"

He stood up. "What?" he said.

"Monsieur Marius, is it you?"

"Yes."

"Monsieur Marius," added the voice, "your friends are expecting you at the barricade on the Rue de la Chanvrerie."

The voice was not entirely unknown to him. It was something like Eponine's hoarse voice. Marius ran to the gate, pushed aside the bar, poked his head through, and saw somebody who looked like a young man disappearing in the twilight.

Monsieur Mabeuf's Descent

Monsieur Mabeuf had come on hard times. The experiments with indigo were unsuccessful, and he had been compelled to sell the printing plates of his book on plants. A coppersmith had made saucepans of them. He had nothing left of his whole life's work.

He had given up the two eggs and beef that he occasionally would eat. He dined on bread and potatoes. He had sold his last furniture, then all his spare bedding and clothing. He had only his most precious books, several of which were extremely rare.

One day, Mother Plutarch said to him, "I have nothing to buy dinner with."

M. Mabeuf went to his bookcase, took one of his books, put it under his arm, and went out. He returned two hours later, laid thirty sous on the table, and said, "Buy something for dinner."

From that day on there was over the old man's face a dark veil that never lifted.

The next day, the day after, every day, M. Mabeuf went out with a book and came back with a little money. Volume by volume, his library disappeared.

The next day there was no dinner.

Weeks went by. Mother Plutarch fell ill. The doctor prescribed an expensive potion. Then the illness grew worse and a nurse was needed. M. Mabeuf opened his bookcase; there was nothing left.

The next day at dawn, he was sitting on the stone post that lay in the garden. His head was bowed down, and he was staring vaguely at the withered beets. Occasionally he wept without knowing it.

In the afternoon, unusual noises broke out. They sounded like musket shots and the noise of a mob.

Father Mabeuf raised his head. He saw a gardener going by and asked: "What is that?"

"It's a riot."

"What, a riot?"

"Yes. They are fighting."

"What are they fighting about?"

"No idea!" said the gardener.

"Where is it?" asked M. Mabeuf.

"Near the Arsenal."

Father Mabeuf went into the house, automatically looked for a book to put under his arm, did not find any, and said, "Oh, yes, I forgot."

8 June 5, 1832

A Burial and Rebirth

What actually makes up a revolt? Nothing and everything. A spark gradually released, a flame suddenly
leaping out, a drifting force, a passing breeze. This
wind touches heads that think, minds that dream,
souls that suffer, passions that burn, and miseries that
howl, and it sweeps them away.

To where?

Almost anywhere. Across the country, across laws.

Irritated convictions, sharpened enthusiasms, noble
impulses, young courage, curiosity, a taste for change,
vague hatreds, disappointments, frustrated ambitions,
empty dreams—and finally, at the bottom, the rabble—such are the elements of a riot.

In the spring of 1832, although for three months an
epidemic of cholera had chilled all hearts and damp-
ened agitations, Paris was ready for a riot. The great
city is like a piece of artillery. When it is loaded, one
spark is enough to send the shot off. In June, 1832,
the spark was the death of General Lamarque.

Lamarque was a man of renown and action. Under
the Empire[1] and under the Restoration,[2] he had
shown two forms of bravery: bravery on the battle-

---

1. **Empire** period from 1804 to 1815, when Napoleon
   Bonaparte was emperor
2. **Restoration** period from 1815 to 1830 during which
   France was ruled by two kings, Louis XVIII and Charles X

field and bravery on the specter's stand. He was as
eloquent as he had been valiant; men felt a sword in
his speech. After upholding command, he upheld liberty. He was loved by the people because he accepted
the chances of the future, and he was loved by the
masses because he had served the Emperor well.
Napoleon had died pronouncing the word *armée;*[3]
Lamarque had died pronouncing the word *patrie.*[4] His
death, which was expected, was dreaded—by the people as a loss, by the government as a pretext for something. His death brought a mourning. Like
everything bitter, mourning may turn into revolt.
That is what happened.

On the evening and the morning of the 5th of June,
the day of the funeral, the Faubourg[5] Saint-Antoine—
which the procession was to go around—took on an
intimidating air. The streets were teeming with
rumors. Men armed themselves as best they could.
Carpenters carried their bench claws "to smash in the
doors." One of them had made a dagger out of a but-
tonhook by breaking off the tip and sharpening the
end. In the fever "to attack," another had slept fully
dressed for three nights.

On the 5th of June, a day of mixed rain and sunshine, General Lamarque's procession passed through
Paris. The coffin was escorted by two battalions,
drums muffled and muskets reversed; ten thousand
National Guardsmen, their sabers at their sides; and
batteries of the National Guard. The officers of the
Invalides[6] followed, carrying laurel branches. Then

---

3. **armée** army
4. **patrie** country, fatherland
5. **Faubourg** district
6. **Invalides** home for retired or disabled soldiers

came the agitated multitude: the Friends of the People, the law school, the medical school, refugees from every nation, every possible group's banner, children waving branches, stonecutters, as well as carpenters who were on strike at that moment, and printers—walking two by two, three by three, uttering cries and brandishing clubs, without order and yet with a single soul. On the cross alleys of the boulevards were swarms of men, women, and children; their eyes were filled with anxiety. An armed multitude was passing, and a terrified multitude looked on.

The government looked on, too. It observed with a hand on the hilt of its sword. One might have seen troops all along the route: at one place, ready to march, with full cartridge boxes, guns, and muskets loaded, four squadrons of riflemen saddled up; at another place, the Municipal Guard in formation; here a squadron of dragoons, there the 12th Light Brigade and the 6th dragoons; the Court of the Louvre was full of artillery. The rest of the troops were stationed in the barracks, and some were in the outskirts of Paris. An anxious government authority had ready, suspended over the multitude, twenty-four thousand soldiers in the city and thirty thousand in the suburbs.

The hearse passed the Bastille, followed the canal, crossed the little bridge, and reached the entrance to the Bridge of Austerlitz. There it stopped. A circle was formed around the hearse, and the vast crowd was silent. Lafayette[7] spoke and bade farewell to Lamarque. It was a touching and august moment; all hearts throbbed. Suddenly a man on horseback,

---

7. **Lafayette** the Marquis de Lafayette, general and statesman

dressed in black, appeared in the midst of the throng with a red flag. Some people said it was a pike with a red cap atop it. Lafayette looked away.

This red flag raised a storm; shouts and cheers arose, and some young men harnassed themselves and began to draw the general's hearse over the Bridge of Austerlitz and Lafayette in a carriage along the Quai Morland.

Meanwhile, on the left bank of the river, the municipal cavalry had just barred the bridge. On the right bank, dragoons began to deploy, advancing at a walk, in silence, pistols in their holsters, sabers sheathed, muskets at rest. At two hundred paces from the little bridge they halted. They opened ranks to let Lafayette's carriage pass; then they closed ranks again. At that moment, the dragoons and the multitude came together. The women fled in terror.

What took place at that fatal moment? Nobody could tell for sure. The fact is that three shots were suddenly fired. The first killed the chief of squadron, Cholet; the second killed an old deaf woman closing her window; the third grazed the shoulder of an officer. A woman shouted, "They are beginning too soon!" All at once there could be seen, from the side opposite the Quai Morland, a squadron of dragoons coming from the barracks at a gallop, with swords drawn and sweeping everything before them.

Outburst of Former Times

Nothing is more extraordinary than the first swarming of a popular uprising. Everything bursts out everywhere at once. Was it foreseen? Yes. Was it prepared? No. From where did it spring? From the streets. From where did it fall? From the clouds.

A quarter hour had not passed, and here is what

had taken place nearly at the same time at twenty different points in Paris.

Right bank, left bank, on the quays, on the boulevards, in the Latin Quarter, in the market region, breathless men, workingmen, students read proclamations and cried: "To arms!" They broke street lamps, unharnessed wagons, tore up the pavement, broke in the doors of houses, uprooted trees, ransacked cellars, rolled hogsheads, heaped up paving stones and pebbles and pieces of furniture and boards to make barricades.

In less than three hours, like a train of powder which catches fire, the insurgents had invaded and occupied many buildings in the city. At five o'clock in the afternoon, they were masters of the Bastille, the Lingerie, the Blancs Manteaux, the Place des Victoires, and the Hotel des Postes. A third of Paris was in the *revolt*. At six o'clock, the Arcade du Saumon became a battlefield. The *revolt* was at one end, the troops at the opposite. They fired from one grating to the other. The drums beat the long roll; the National Guard dressed and armed themselves hastily and left their barracks. For their part, the insurgents placed pickets at the street corners and boldly sent patrols out from the barricades. They kept watch on both sides. The government, with an army in its hand, hesitated. Their tactics were lost in the wrath of the people. The wind of revolution is not tractable.

Night fell. Anxiety was widespread; there was a certain nervousness little known to Paris. The city seemed lit by the ominous flame of uprising.

Solitude reigned at the Tuileries.[8] Louis Philippe[9] was full of serenity.

---

8. **Tuileries** the royal palace in Paris
9. **Louis Philippe** King of France from 1830 until 1848

9

The Atom Fraternizes
with the Hurricane

A Child and an Old Man

A ragged child came down the street carrying a branch of flowers in bloom. He caught sight of an old horse pistol before a secondhand shop. He threw the flowering branch on the pavement and cried:

"Mother What's-your-name, I'll borrow your machine."

And he ran off with the pistol.

It was little Gavroche going to war.

On the boulevard, he noticed that the pistol had no hammer. Nonetheless he continued on his way.

At the Saint Jean market where the guard was already disarmed, he joined up with Enjolras, Courfeyrac, Combeferre, and Feuilly. They were almost armed. Bahorel and Jean Prouvaire had joined them, enlarging the group. Among them they had two pistols, a long musket, a short musket, a carbine rifle, a walking cane containing a sword, and a saber.

"Where are we going?" asked Gavroche calmly.

"Come on!" said Courfeyrac.

Behind Feuilly and Bahorel came a throng of students, artists, workingmen, rivermen. A few had pistols thrust in their waistbands. A man, who appeared very old, was marching with this band. He was not armed and was hurrying so that he would not be left behind; he had a thoughtful expression.

"Who's that?" asked Gavroche of Courfeyrac.

"That is an old man."

It was Monsieur Mabeuf.

He advanced almost to the front of the column, with the motion of a man who is walking and the appearance of a man who is asleep.

Recruits

The band increased at every moment. Toward the rue de Billettes, they were joined by a tall man who was turning gray, whom Courfeyrac, Enjolras, and Combeferre noticed but whom none of them knew.

It happened that they passed Courfeyrac's door.

"This is lucky," said Courfeyrac. "I have forgotten my wallet, and I have lost my hat." He left the company and went up to his room, four steps at a time. He took, besides his hat and wallet, a large square box which was hidden among his clothes. As he was running down the stairs again, the cleaning woman hailed him:

"There is somebody who wishes to speak to you."

A sort of young workingman, thin, pale, freckled, and who had rather the appearance of a girl in boy's clothing, came out and said to Courfeyrac in a voice which was not the least like a woman's voice:

"Monsieur Marius—is he in?"

"He is not."

"Will he be in this evening?"

"I don't know anything about it." And Courfeyrac added, "As for myself, I shall not be in."

The young man looked fixedly at him and asked:

"Why not?"

"I am going to the barricades."

"Do you want me to carry your box?"

Courfeyrac did not answer but ran off to rejoin his friends. He gave the box to one of them to carry. It was not until a quarter hour afterward that he noticed that the young man had in fact followed them.

10 *Corinth*

A History of Corinth

Corinth, the wineshop, was one of the meeting places, if not rallying points, of Courfeyrac and his friends. They drank there, they ate there, they shouted there, they paid little, they paid poorly, they did not pay at all, they were always welcome. Father Hucheloup, the landlord, was a good man.

Perhaps Father Hucheloup was a born chemist; he was certainly a cook. People not only drank at his bistro[1] but also ate there. Hucheloup had invented an excellent dish found only at his house; it was a stuffed carp. People came there from great distances to eat his food and enjoy his company.

His wife, Mother Hucheloup, was a bearded creature, very ugly.

Around 1830, Father Hucheloup died. With him went the secret of the stuffed carp, although his wife kept up the bistro. The kitchen deteriorated; the wine, which was always bad, became frightful. Courfeyrac and his friends continued to go to Corinth, however, "out of pity," said Bossuet.

Two servants, called Chowder and Soufflé, and for whom nobody ever knew any other names, helped Mother Hucheloup put the food on the tables.

Before entering the restaurant room, you might

---

1. bistro a bar or wineshop that may serve food

read on the door this line written in chalk by
Courfeyrac:
Feast if you can, and eat if you dare.

Preliminary Gaiety

Laigle de Meaux, as we know, lived more with Joly
than elsewhere. He had a place to lay his head, as
the bird has a branch. The two friends shared everything. One morning, the 5th of June, they went to
breakfast at Corinth. Joly's head was stopped up with
a bad cold. They went in the door about nine o'clock in
the morning, and they went up to the second floor
restaurant room.

Chowder and Soufflé received them. "Oysters,
cheese, and ham," said Laigle.

And they sat down at a table. The room was empty;
only the two of them were there.

As they were eating their first oysters, a head
appeared at the stairs and a voice said, "I was passing
by, and in the street I smelled the delicious odor of
ripe cheese. I have come in."

It was Grantaire. He took a stool and sat down at
the table.

"Grantaire," asked Laigle, "have you just come from
the boulevard?"

"No."

"We saw the head of the procession go by, Joly
and I."

"It was a marvelous spectacle," said Joly.

"How quiet the street is!" exclaimed Laigle. "Who
would suspect that Paris is all topsy-turvy?"

"Speaking of topsy-turvy," said Joly, "it appears that
Marius is decidedly in love."

"Does anyone know who she is?" inquired Laigle.

"No."

"No?"

"No! I tell you."

"Marius's loves!" exclaimed Grantaire. "I see them now. Marius is in a fog. He is of the poets' race. He who says 'poet' says 'fool.'"

Grantaire was continuing when a new actor emerged from the square hole of the stairway. It was a small boy of less than ten years—ragged and very small, a mug of a face, a keen eye, monstrous long hair, wet to the skin, a calm look.

The boy, choosing without hesitation among the three men although he knew none of them, addressed himself to Laigle de Meaux.

"Are you Monsieur Bossuet?" he asked.

"That is my nickname," answered Laigle. "What do you want?"

"This is it. A big fellow with blond hair said to me on the boulevard: 'Do you know Mother Hucheloup?' I said, 'Yes, Rue de la Chanvrerie, the old man's widow.' He said to me, 'Go there. You'll find Monsieur Bossuet there, and you'll tell him from me: A B C.' It's a joke somebody's playing on you, isn't it? He gave me ten sous."

"What's your name?" asked Laigle.

"Navet, Gavroche's friend."

"Stay with us," said Laigle.

"Have breakfast with us," said Grantaire.

"I can't," the child said. "I am with the procession."

And, dragging his foot in a long scrape behind him, the most respectful of all bows, he went off.

Meanwhile Laigle was meditating. He said in an undertone, "a b c, meaning Lamarque's funeral."

"The big blond man," observed Grantaire, "is Enjolras, who sent to let you know."

"Shall we go?" asked Bossuet.

"It's raining," said Joly. "I swore to go through fire, not water. I don't want to catch cold."

"I'm staying here," said Grantaire. "I prefer breakfast to a funeral."

"Agreed. We stay," continued Laigle. "Let's drink then. Besides, we can miss the funeral without missing the riot.

"Ah! The riot—I'm in for that!" exclaimed Joly.

Bossuet sat in the open window, wetting his back with the rain, gazing at his two friends. Suddenly there was a tumult behind him, hurried steps, and cries of "To arms!" He turned and at the end of the street caught sight of Enjolras going by, carbine in hand; and Gavroche with his pistol; Feuilly with his saber; Courfeyrac with his sword; Jean Prouvaire, Combeferre, and Bahorel with their muskets; and all the armed and stormy gathering that was following them.

Bossuet improvised a speaking trumpet with his two hands and shouted, "Courfeyrac! Ahoy!"

Courfeyrac heard the call, saw Bossuet, and came a few steps into the street, crying, "What do you want?" just as Bossuet called, "Where are you going?"

"To make a barricade," answered Courfeyrac.

"Well, then, here! This is a good place! Make it here!"

"That's true, Laigle," said Courfeyrac.

And at a sign from Courfeyrac, the band rushed into the Rue de la Chanvrerie.

Night Begins to Gather

The place was indeed admirably chosen. The entrance to the street was wide, and the far end narrowed like a cul-de-sac,[2] with the Corinth choking it off. No attack

---

2. **cul-de-sac** a place with no exit

was possible except from the Rue Saint-Denis, that is from the front and without cover.

As the mob burst in, the whole street was seized with terror. Pedestrians vanished; shops and stalls were closed from the ground to the rooftops. One frightened old woman attached a mattress in front of her window, a shield against bullets. Only the bistro stayed open, and that because the mob had rushed into it. "Oh, my God!" sighed Madame Hucheloup.

In a few minutes, twenty iron bars were wrested from the grated front of the wineshop, twenty yards of pavement were torn up, Gavroche and Bahorel had seized and tipped over the horse cart that belonged to a merchant named Anceau, and its lime barrels had been placed under the paving stones; Enjolras had opened the trapdoor of the cellar, and all of Madame Hucheloup's empty vats had been lined up next to the lime barrels. Two massive heaps of rubble buttressed the barrels. Shoring beams from a neighboring house were pulled down and laid across the barrels. When Bossuet and Courfeyrac looked back, half the street was already barred by a rampart larger than a man.

Chowder and Soufflé had joined the laborers, going back and forth with rubbish. Mother Hucheloup had taken refuge on the second floor of the Corinth. Her eyes were glazed, and she cried in a whisper. Her shrieks of horror did not leave her throat.

"It's the end of the world," she murmured.

The Recruits at Work

The rain had let up. Recruits had arrived. Enjolras, Combeferre, and Courfeyrac directed everything. Two barricades were being built at the same time. Both touched the Corinth and made a right angle. The larger one closed the Rue de la Chanvrerie; the other closed the Rue Mondétour. This one was very narrow and was constructed only of casks and paving stones. There were about fifty laborers there, some thirty armed with muskets because—on their way—they had effected a wholesale loan from a gun shop.

The tall man whom Courfeyrac, Combeferre, and Enjolras had noticed when he joined the company at the Rue des Billettes was working on the little barricade and making himself useful there. Gavroche worked on the large one. As for the thin young man who had asked for Marius, he seemed to have disappeared. Gavroche, completely carried away and radiant, had taken responsibility for getting everything ready. He came and went, upstairs and down, up again. He was a whirlwind. Perpetual motion was in his little arms, and perpetual clamor was in his lungs.

"More paving stones! More barrels! Where can we get some machines? A basket of plaster to stop up that hole. It's too small, your barricade. It has to go higher. Pile on everything, brace it. Break up the house."

The Preparations

The journals of the time said that the barricade at Rue de la Chanvrerie was three stories high. In fact it did not exceed an average height of six or seven feet. It was built so that the combatants could, at will, either look over it or disappear. The front of the barricade on the outside was composed of paving stones and barrels bound together by timbers and boards interlocked in the wheels of the Anseau cart and an overturned bus. There was an opening wide enough for a man to pass through so that sorties would be possible. Overhead, a red flag flew from the pole of the bus.

All this was accomplished in less than an hour. The few merchants who still ventured out at this point in the revolt glanced down the street, saw the barricade, and hurried on.

The barricades finished, a table was dragged out of the wineshop, and Courfeyrac climbed on it. Enjolras brought the square box, and Courfeyrac opened it. The box was filled with bullets. Courfeyrac distributed them with a smile.

Each man received thirty bullets. Many had powder and set about making more bullets with the balls they were molding. As for the keg of powder, it was on a table by itself near the door and was being held in reserve.

Finally, posts were assigned, muskets were loaded, lookouts were placed along the streets where there were no more pedestrians. The shadows of night were beginning to fall and, through the silence, they felt the advance of something possibly tragic and terrifying. Isolated, armed, determined, tranquil, they waited.

The Man from the Rue des Billettes

By now night had closed in; nothing was coming. There were only confused sounds and, at intervals, musket volleys that were poorly sustained and distant. It was a sign that the government was taking its time and massing its forces. These fifty men were waiting for sixty thousand.

Enjolras went to find Gavroche, who had set himself to making bullets in the lower room. At that moment, Gavroche was very busy, although not exactly with his bullets.

The man who had joined the group at the Rue des Billettes had just entered the room and taken a seat at the table with the least light. A large infantry musket had fallen to him, and he held it between his knees. Gavroche, previously distracted by a hundred things, had not even seen the man. Now he followed the man with his eyes, admiring the musket; then suddenly when the man sat down the boy got up. Had anyone watched the man before now, he would have seen him observe everything with keen attention; but since he had come into the room, he had fallen into a kind of meditation and appeared to see nothing that was going on. The boy approached and began to tiptoe around the man the way someone walks near someone he does not want to awaken. At the same time, over his childish face came a frown that said, "Oh, no! Impossible! I'm seeing things!" Gavroche was both uncertain and convinced. Every part of him was at work—the instinct that scents and the intellect that combines. It was clear that an event had occurred for Gavroche.

It was at that moment that Enjolras approached him.

"You're small," said Enjolras. "Nobody will see you. Go outside of the barricades, slip along the houses, look around the streets a little, and come tell me what's going on."

Gavroche straightened up.

"Little folks are good for something, then! I'll go! Meantime, trust the little folks, distrust the big—." And Gavroche, raising his head and lowering his voice, added, "You see that big fellow over there?" pointing to the man of the Rue des Billettes.

"Well?"

"He's a spy."

"Are you sure?"

"Not two weeks ago he pulled me by the ear as I was out taking some air."

Enjolras hastily left the boy and murmured a few words to a workingman nearby. The workingman left the room and returned almost immediately with three others.

Then Enjolras approached the man at the table and asked him, "Who are you?"

At this abrupt question, the man jumped. He looked straight to the depths of Enjolras's frank eyes and smiled a smile that was the most disdainful, energetic, and resolute imaginable and answered with a haughty seriousness, "I see how it is—"

"You're an informer?"

"I am a government officer."

"Your name is?"

"Javert."

Enjolras made a sign to the four men. In a twinkling, before Javert had time to turn around, he was grabbed, thrown down, bound, and searched.

They found on him a little round card framed between two pieces of glass and bearing the legend

Javert, Inspector of police, aged fifty-two

and the signature of the police commissioner of the time, M. Gisquet. In his watch they found a folded sheet of paper, which Enjolras opened and on which he read these lines written in the commissioner's handwriting:

As soon as his political mission is fulfilled, Inspector Javert will ascertain, by a special examination, whether it is true that evildoers have something going on the right bank of the Seine, near the Iéna Bridge.

They stood Javert up, tied his arms behind his back, and tied him to the post in the middle of the room.

Gavroche, who had witnessed the entire scene and approved the whole by silent nods of the head, approached Javert and said to him, "The mouse has caught the cat."

All this had happened so quickly that it was finished as it was noticed in the wineshop. Seeing Javert tied to the post, Joly, Bossuet, Combeferre, Courfeyrac, and others ran in.

Backed up against the post and tied so he could make no movement, Javert held his head with the confidence of the man who has never lied.

"He's a spy," said Enjolras.

And turning to Javert, he added, "You will be shot ten minutes before the barricade is taken."

Javert replied in his most imperious tone, "Why not immediately?"

"We're economizing on powder."

"Then do it with a knife."

"Spy," said the handsome Enjolras, "we are judges, not assassins."

Then he called Gavroche.

"You! Go on about your business! Do what I told you!"

"I'm going," cried Gavroche.

And pausing just as he was leaving, he said, "By the way, you'll give me his musket?"

Then, giving a military salute, he sprang through the opening in the large barricade.

The whole insurgent group was so distracted by the incident that they did not see in the barricade the small youth who had called for Marius at Courfeyrac's house that morning.

The boy, who had a bold and reckless air, had come at night to join the insurgents.

11 *Marius Enters the Shadow*

From the Rue Plumet to Saint-Denis

The voice that had called Marius to the barricade at the Rue de la Chanvrerie sounded to him like the voice of destiny. He wanted to die; the opportunity had presented itself. Marius pushed aside the bar that had let him pass so many times, came out of the garden, and said, "Let's go!"

Mad with grief, no longer feeling anything fixed or solid in his brain, he now had one desire: to make a quick end to it.

He began to walk quickly. It happened that he was armed, having Javert's pistols with him.

In the streets, he lost sight of the young man he thought he had seen.

As Marius left the Rue Plumet and walked toward the Rue de Rivoli, shops were open and the gas lamps were burning under the arches. Once he entered the Rue Saint-Honoré, the shops were closed but the merchants were chatting in front of the shops and the street lamps burned. There was cavalry in sight. Finally, at the entrance of the Rue des Prouvaires, the throng no longer moved. It was a resisting, massive, solid, almost impenetrable block of people, heaped together and talking in whispers. There could be seen rifles in stacks, bayonets moving, and troops getting situated. The curious did not pass this boundary. Here, traffic came to a halt. Here, the crowd ended and the army began.

Marius had the will of a man who no longer hopes. He had been called; he had to go. He found a way to pass through the crowd and through the troops, avoiding patrols and sentries. Past the outer fringe of troops, he found himself in the midst of something terrible. Not a pedestrian, not a soldier, not a light, nothing. Solitude, silence, night. A mysterious chill gripped him.

He continued on. The whole route was like a descent down a flight of dark stairs. He went on nonetheless.

Finally Marius reached Les Halles. From there he could see a red glare, which was the reflection of the torch blazing in the barricade of the Corinth. Marius walked toward that glare.

Soon he saw a portion of the bistro, a kind of shapeless wall, and men crouching with muskets on their knees. All this was twenty yards from him. It was the interior of the barricade.

The houses on the right hid the rest of the bistro, the large barricade, and the flag.

The Limit

Marius had only one more step to take.

Then, the unhappy young man sat down on a stone, crossed his arms, and thought of his father.

He thought of that heroic Colonel Pontmercy who had been such a brave soldier. He said to himself that his day had come, too—that like his father, he too was to be brave, bold, and intrepid; to face the bullets; to seek the enemy and death.

He began to weep bitterly.

It was horrible. But what could he do? Live without Cosette? He could not. Since she had gone away, he must surely die. He had given his word of honor.

She had gone away knowing that; therefore it did not matter to her that he would die.   It was clear she no longer loved him, since she had gone away like that. What use life, and why live any longer?   And then to have come so far and recoil?   To have approached the danger and fled!   To have seen the barricade and slinked away!   To abandon his friends who were expecting him, who needed him perhaps!   To fail in all things at the same time: in his love, in friendship, in his word!   If his father's ghost were there in the shadow and saw him recoil, he would strike him with the flat of his sword and cry out, "Advance, coward!"

Marius stood up.

12 *The Grandeur of Despair*

The Flag: Act One

The clock had struck ten. Nothing had happened yet. Enjolras and Combeferre sat down, carbines in hand, near the opening of the large barricade. They were not talking; they were listening, seeking to catch even the faintest, most distant sound of marching.

Suddenly in the midst of this calm a clear, young, cheerful voice began to sing.

The two men grasped each other by the hand.

"It's Gavroche," said Enjolras.

"He's warning us," said Combeferre.

A headlong run startled the empty street. They saw a nimble creature climb over the bus, and Gavroche bounded into the barricade out of breath, saying, "My musket! Here they come."

An electric thrill went through the whole barricade, and a moving of hands was heard as all reached for their muskets.

"Do you want my carbine?" asked Enjolras.

"No, I want the big musket," answered the boy.

And he took Javert's musket.

Every man took up his post for the fight.

Forty-three insurgents—among them Enjolras, Combeferre, Courfeyrac, Bossuet, Joly, Bahorel, and Gavroche—were on their knees in the large barricade. Their heads were even with the crest of the wall; the barrels of their guns pointed over the paving stones as through loopholes—watchful, silent, ready to fire.

Six other men, commanded by Feuilly, were stationed in the windows of the two upper floors of the Corinth.

A few more minutes elapsed; then the sound of footsteps, measured and heavy, many, was clearly heard. The sound, at first faint, then distinct, then heavy and resounding, approached slowly but without halt or interruption. Nothing but its tranquil and terrible continuity could be heard.

There was a pause, as if on both sides they were waiting. Suddenly, from the shadows, a voice cried, "Who goes there?"

At the same time was the click of leveled muskets heard.

Enjolras answered in a strong voice:

"The French Revolution!"

"Fire!" said the voice.

Crimson flashed along the street as if the door of a furnace had been opened and abruptly closed.

A fearful explosion burst over the barricade. The red flag fell. The volley was so heavy that it had sheared off the pole. Some bullets ricocheted off the houses, entered the barricade, and wounded several men.

The burst created a chilling impression. It was evident they were dealing with a whole regiment at least.

"Comrades," cried Courfeyrac, "don't waste powder. Let's wait until they come down the street."

"And," said Enjolras, "let's hoist the flag again!"

They heard the rattling of ramrods reloading muskets outside.

Enjolras continued, "Who is there who has courage here? Who is going to raise the flag on the barricade?"

Nobody answered. To climb up onto the barricade at that moment was certain death. Enjolras himself shuddered.

The Flag: Act Two

When everybody had gone to take a place for combat, there remained in the lower room only Javert—tied to the post—an insurgent with a drawn saber watching Javert, and Father Mabeuf. Some hours before the barricade was attacked, M. Mabeuf had assumed a pose that he had not left since. The old man was sitting with his hands on his knees and his head bent forward as if looking into an abyss. At the moment of the attack, the physical shock reached the old man and somehow woke him up. He suddenly got to his feet, crossed the room, and at the instant that Enjolras repeated his appeal, appeared in the doorway of the wineshop.

He walked straight to Enjolras, he snatched the flag from him, and then, nobody daring to stop him or aid him, this old man of eighty, with shaking head but firm foot, began to climb slowly up the stairway of paving stones built into the barricade.

When he reached the top of the last step, when this trembling and terrible phantom was standing on that mound of rubbish before twelve hundred invisible muskets, when he rose up into the face of death as if he were stronger than it, the whole barricade in the darkness seemed a supernatural colossal image.

There was a silence that occurs only in the presence of wonders.

In the midst of the silence, the old man waved the red flag and cried: "Long live the Revolution! Long live the Republic! Fraternity! Equality! And death!"

The same voice they had heard before called, "Who goes there? Disperse!"

M. Mabeuf, pale and haggard, his eyes illuminated from the mournful fires of insanity, raised the flag above his head and repeated, "Long live the Republic!"

"Fire!" said the voice.

A second discharge beat against the barricade.

The old man fell to his knees; then he rose up, let go of the flag, and fell heavily backward onto the pavement inside the barricade, with his arms outstretched like a cross.

During the time that the men in the barricade stood stunned by the action of M. Mabeuf, little Gavroche had stayed on watch. He thought he saw some men stealing toward the barricade. He cried, "Watch out!" with only a moment to spare. They caught sight of an expanse of bayonets moving above the barricade. Tall Municipal Guards were penetrating the barricade, some through the opening and others by climbing over the wall.

Bahorel sprang at the first soldier and killed him point blank. The second killed Bahorel with his bayonet. Another had injured Courfeyrac, who shouted for help. The largest of all marched on Gavroche with bayonet fixed. The boy did not retreat. He took Javert's musket, aimed it, and pulled the trigger. Nothing happened. Javert had not loaded it. The Guard laughed and raised his bayonet over the boy.

Before the bayonet touched Gavroche, a ball struck the Guard in the middle of his forehead. A second ball struck the Guard who had attacked Courfeyrac.

It was Marius who had just entered the barricade.

Powder Keg

Marius had rushed into the conflict, his pistols in hand. With the first shot he saved Gavroche, and with the second he freed Courfeyrac. Now he had no weapon. He had thrown down the discharged pistols, but he noticed the powder keg in the low room near the door.

As he half turned, looking in that direction, a soldier aimed at him. As the man was ready to fire at Marius, a hand was laid on the muzzle and stopped it. It was a young workingman with corduroy trousers. The shot went off and passed through the hand and perhaps the young man himself as he fell, but the ball did not reach Marius.

The most determined of the insurgents now openly faced the ranks of soldiers climbing over the barricade.

"Surrender!" shouted an officer.

"Fire!" said Enjolras.

When the smoke cleared, combatants on both sides were thinned out but still in the same places, reloading weapons in silence.

Suddenly a voice cried, "Get back, or I'll blow up the barricade!"

Everyone turned in the direction of the voice.

Marius had entered the ground-floor room, taken the powder keg and, under cover of the smoke, slipped along the barricade to the nearest torch. Everyone — National Guards, Municipal Guards, officers, soldiers—looked at him in horror. He stood, his foot on the stones, the torch in his hand, his face lit by deadly resolution.

"Blow up the barricade," said a sergeant, "and yourself, too."

Marius answered, "And myself, too."

And he brought the torch down toward the powder keg.

It was a rout. The soldiers left their dead and wounded and fled to the far end of the street.

The barricade was cleared.

Everyone flocked around Marius.

"Where's the leader?" inquired Marius.

"You're the leader," said Enjolras.

The Agony of Death and of Life

The whole attention of the insurgents was on the large barricade, where the struggle would inevitably resume. Marius, however, thought about the small barricade and went to inspect it. As he was leaving, he heard his name spoken faintly in the darkness.

"Monsieur Marius!"

He recognized the voice that had called him two hours before through the gate in the Rue Plumet. Only now, the voice seemed no more than a breath.

He looked about him and saw nobody.

"At your feet," said the voice.

He stooped and saw in the shadows a form, dragging itself toward him. By the lantern he could just make out torn corduroy trousers, bare feet, and what seemed to be a pool of blood. Marius caught a glimpse of a pale face that rose toward him and said, "Don't you know me?"

"No."

"Eponine."

Marius bent quickly. It was indeed Eponine. She was dressed as a man.

"How did you get here? What are you doing?"

"I'm dying," she said.

She raised her hand to Marius, and in the center of that hand Marius saw a black hole.

"Did you see a musket aimed at you?"

"Yes, and a hand that stopped it."

"That was mine."

Marius shuddered.

"What madness! Poor child! But that's not so bad. We'll take care of you; people don't die from a shot in the hand."

"The bullet went through my hand, and it also went

through my back. It's no use moving me from here. Sit beside me."

Marius obeyed. She laid her head on Marius's knees and stayed still for a moment. Then she looked at him.

"How odd it is! You are lost! Nobody will get out of the barricade. It was I who led you into this. I wanted to die before you. When the bullet hit me, I dragged myself over here. I waited for you. Oh! I'm so happy! We're all going to die!"

At that moment the singing of little Gavroche sounded through the barricade. Eponine raised herself and listened, murmuring, "There he is!"

Turning toward Marius, she said, "My brother's here. He mustn't see me. He'd scold me."

Marius started.

"Listen. I don't want to deceive you. I have a letter in my pocket for you. I was told to mail it. I kept it. I didn't want it to reach you. Take your letter."

She put Marius's hand into the pocket of her blouse, and he took out the letter.

"Promise me," Eponine said. "Promise to kiss me on the forehead when I'm dead. I'll feel it."

She let her head fall back, and her eyes closed. Just when Marius supposed her forever asleep, she opened her eyes, smiled, and said to him with an accent whose sweetness seemed to come from another world, "Do you know, Monsieur Marius, I believe I was a little in love with you."

She tried to smile again and died.

Gavroche the Messenger

Marius kept his promise. He kissed the forehead of Eponine in thoughtful, gentle farewell to an unhappy soul. Then he took the letter to the lower room of the Corinth.

He broke the seal and read:

> To M. Marius Pontmercy, care of M.
> Courfeyrac, Rue de la Verrerie, No. 16
>
> My beloved, alas! My father wants us to
> leave immediately. Tonight we will be at
> Rue de l'Homme-Armé, No. 7. In a week,
> we will be in England.
>
> Cosette
June 4th

What had happened was simple. Eponine had done it all. After June 3rd, she had thwarted the efforts of her father's band and tried to separate Cosette from Marius. It was she who had dropped the note "MOVE" with Jean Valjean, which had prompted that man to announce their departure for England. Cosette hastily wrote the lines to Marius, and she gave the letter to Eponine, whom she thought was a "young workingman," to deliver. Eponine pocketed the letter, and the next day she asked Courfeyrac about Marius. She was not sure she would deliver the letter. When Courfeyrac said he was going to the barricades, Eponine had an idea—to throw herself into that death and to push Marius into it. She followed Courfeyrac and then went back to the Rue Plumet to wait for Marius. She counted on his despair when he did not find Cosette, and she urged him to the barricades.

Marius knew that nothing was fated to change. "She's going away. Her father is taking her to England, and my grandfather refuses to consent to the marriage." He thought that there were two duties for him to fulfill: to inform Cosette of his death and send her a last farewell and to save from imminent death the boy who was Eponine's brother and Thénardier's son.

He had a pocket notebook with him. He tore out a leaf and wrote:

> Our marriage is impossible. I have asked my grandfather, and he has refused. I have no funds, nor do you. I ran to your house; I did not find you. You know the promise I made to you? I am keeping it. I will die. I love you. When you read this, my soul will be near you and will smile upon you.

Marius called Gavroche. The boy ran up with a joyful and devoted expression.

"Take this letter. Go out of the barricade immediately"—a worried Gavroche began to scratch his ear—"and tomorrow morning you will carry it to its address, to Mademoiselle Cosette, at M. Fauchelevent's, Rue de l'Homme-Armé, No. 7."

The heroic boy answered, "Ah, well, but meanwhile they'll take the barricade, and I won't be here."

"The barricade will not be attacked again before daybreak, and it won't be taken before noon."

"Well," said Gavroche, "suppose I go and carry your letter in the morning."

"It will be too late. You won't be able to get out. Go now, right away!"

Gavroche had nothing more to say. He had an idea, but he did not tell it for fear that Marius would object. The idea was this:

"It's hardly midnight, the address is not far. I'll take the letter there right away, and I'll be back in time."

13 *The Rue de l'Homme-Armé*

The Blotter Talks

On the night of that same day, June 5th, Jean Valjean, with Cosette and Toussaint, had moved into the house on the Rue de l'Homme-Armé.

Cosette had not left the Rue Plumet willingly. For the first time since they had been together, Cosette's will and Jean Valjean's came into conflict. They arrived at the new address without speaking. Neither noticed the other's anxiety.

In the flight from the Rue Plumet, Jean Valjean took nothing except the little embalmed case which Cosette called "the inseparable." Full trunks would have required porters, and porters are witnesses.

It was only with great difficulty that Toussaint got permission to pack a little linen and clothing and a few toilet articles. Cosette herself carried only her writing case and blotter. Since they had not left the house until nightfall, she had had time to write her note to Marius.

They went to bed in silence.

Jean Valjean slept well. He woke up almost cheerful. He noticed the bundles Toussaint had brought, and he saw through an opening in one his National Guard uniform.

As for Cosette, she had Toussaint bring soup to her room and did not appear until evening. At dinner time, out of deference to her father, Cosette consented to nibble on some cold chicken. This done, on the pretext of a severe headache, Cosette said "good night" and shut herself in her bedroom.

Jean Valjean heard Toussaint's comment about some "rows and fighting in Paris," but he paid no attention to it. He walked from the window to the door of the dining room, growing calmer and calmer.

While he was walking, his eyes suddenly fell on something strange. Facing him he saw, in the mirror above the sideboard, the clear lines that follow:

> My beloved, alas! My father wants us to leave immediately. Tonight we will be at Rue de l'Homme-Armé, No. 7. In a week, we will be in England.
>
> Cosette
June 4th

Jean Valjean was aghast. He was reading the lines from Cosette's blotter, which sat atop the writing case, which she had left wide open.

The discovery was simple and devastating. Until that moment, Jean Valjean had never in his life been defeated when put to the test. But the supreme ordeal is the loss of a beloved being.

Except for Cosette, Jean Valjean had, in all his long life, known nothing of those things a man can love. He was a father to her, a father who adored her and to whom that young woman was light, family, homeland, paradise. When he saw that she was escaping him, that it was positively ended, his grief surpassed the possible. To have done all he had done and to come to this! He felt a shudder of revolt from head to toe. He felt the awakening of selfishness, and the self howled in his soul.

His instinct did not hesitate. He put together certain circumstances, certain dates, certain of Cosette's blushes, and he said to himself, "He's the one." With his first guess, he hit Marius. He recognized the unknown prowler of the Luxembourg, that seeker of flirtations, that idler, that imbecile, that coward—for it is cowardice to make eyes at girls who are beside a father who loves them. He did not know the name, but he found the man at once. The young man was at the bottom of this state of affairs, and everything stemmed from him. Jean Valjean looked within himself and saw a specter—Hatred.

A few minutes later, Jean Valjean found himself in the street. He was bareheaded, seated on the stone block by the door of his house. He seemed to be listening for something.

An Enemy of Light

The street was empty. However, almost at that very moment, there was a sharp explosion in the direction of Les Halles. He raised his eyes. Somebody was walking down the street. By the light of a lamp, he saw a pale face, young and radiant.

Gavroche had reached the Rue de l'Homme-Armé.

He was searching for something. He saw Jean Valjean perfectly well, but he took no notice of him.

Jean Valjean went up to Gavroche.

"Poor devil," he said in an undertone, "he's hungry." And he put a hundred-sous piece in the boy's hand.

"You're a fine fellow," said Gavroche, putting the coin in his pocket. His confidence increasing, he added, "Do you belong to this street?"

"Yes. Why?"

"Could you show me number seven?"

"What do you want with number seven?"

Here the boy stopped; he feared he had said too

much, and he merely answered, "Ah, that's it."

An idea crossed Jean Valjean's mind. He said to the boy, "Are you the one who's bringing me the letter I'm waiting for?"

"You?" said Gavroche. "You're not a young lady."

"The letter is for Mademoiselle Cosette, isn't it?"

"Cosette?" muttered Gavroche. "Yes. I think it's that funny name."

"Well," said Jean Valjean, "I'm to deliver it to her."

"Then you must know I'm sent from the barricade?"

"Of course," said Jean Valjean.

Gavroche thrust his hand into another pocket and drew out a folded paper. Then he gave a military salute and handed over the paper to Jean Valjean.

"Is it to Saint-Merry that the answer should be sent?" Jean Valjean asked.

"If you do, you would make one of those things commonly called a blunder. That letter comes from the barricade in the Rue de la Chanvrerie, and I'm going back there. Good night, citizen."

This said, Gavroche went away.

While Cosette and Toussaint Sleep

Jean Valjean went inside with Marius's letter. In the note, he only saw these words:

> — I will die . . . When you read this, my soul
> will be near you.

He looked at Marius's note with a sort of drunken surprise. He had before his eyes that marvel: the death of the hated being.

He uttered a hideous cry of inward joy. So, it was finished. The end was coming sooner than he had

dared to hope. Perhaps he was already dead. No. He
was not dead yet, but he was caught in the net of the
war—he was lost. "I merely have to let things take
their course. The man cannot escape. If he is not
dead yet, he soon will be. How fortunate!"

Then he went down and awakened the doorkeeper.
About an hour later, Jean Valjean went out in the full
dress of a National Guard and armed. The doorkeeper
had easily found what was necessary to complete his
equipment. He had a loaded musket and a full box of
cartridges. He headed toward Les Halles.

Jean Valjean

1 *War Between Four Walls*

Saint-Merry and Saint-Denis

The insurgents used the night to their advantage. The barricade was not only repaired but also enlarged. They raised it two feet. Iron bars planted in the paving stones were like lances at rest. All sorts of rubbish were added and brought from all sides. It was skillfully made over into a wall inside and a thicket outside.

They rebuilt the stairway of paving stones, which allowed them to climb up, as on a fortress wall.

They put the barricade in order, cleared up the lower room of the Corinth, took over the kitchen for a hospital, completed the dressing of wounds, gathered up powder scattered over the floor and tables, made bullets and cartridges, cleaned up debris, and carried away the corpses.

Around two o'clock in the morning, they took a count. There were thirty-seven of them left.

Enjolras had gone to get information on the enemy. He went out by the little Rue Mondétour, creeping next to the houses.

The insurgents, we must say, were full of hope. They had no more doubt about their success than they did of their cause. Moreover, help was evidently about to come. They counted on it.

They heard the bells of Saint-Merry, proof that the other large barricade was still holding out. All these hopes were communicated from one to another in a sort of cheerful yet terrible whisper, like the buzz of a hive of bees at war.

Enjolras reappeared. He listened to all this joy with his arms crossed; then he said, "The whole army of Paris is fighting. A third of that army is drawn up against the barricade where you are. Besides the National Guard, I can make out the shakos[1] of the Fifth of the line and the colors of the Sixth Legion. You will be attacked in an hour. As for the people, they were boiling yesterday, but this morning they are not moving. Nothing to wait for, nothing to hope for. You are abandoned."

These words fell on the buzzing of the groups and struck them dumb. There was a moment of indescribable silence.

The moment was brief.

A voice cried out to Enjolras, "All right then. Let's make the barricade twenty feet high, and let's all stand by it. Citizens, let's offer a protest of corpses. Let's show them that, even if the people abandon the republicans, the republicans do not abandon the people."

This resolution so filled the air of June 6, 1832, that at almost the same moment, in the barricade at Saint-Merry, the insurgents raised this cry which has come down in history: "Let them come to our aid or let them not come; what does it matter? Let us die here to the last man."

As we see, the two barricades, though essentially cut off from each other, communicated.

---

1. **shakos** military hats

Five Less, One More

Enjolras touched Combeferre's shoulder, and they both went into the lower room. They came back a moment later. Enjolras held out in his hands the four uniforms he had kept in reserve. Combeferre followed him, bringing the crossbelts[2] and shakos.

"With this uniform," Enjolras said, "you can mingle with the ranks and escape. Here are uniforms for four."

And he threw them onto the unpaved ground.

Marius added his voice: "There are some among you who have families: mothers, sisters, wives, children. Let them leave the ranks."

Nobody stirred.

"Married men and supporters of families, out of the ranks!" repeated Marius.

His authority was great. Enjolras was indeed the leader of the barricade, but Marius was its savior.

"I order it," cried Enjolras.

"I beg you," said Marius.

They obeyed. In a few minutes five were unanimously chosen and left the ranks.

"There are five!" exclaimed Marius.

There were only four uniforms.

"Well," said the five, "one of us must stay."

It was a question of who should leave and who should find reasons why the others should leave. The generous quarrel started up.

"You have a wife who loves you." "But you have an old mother." "You have neither a father nor a mother; what will become of your three little brothers?"

---

2. **crossbelt** belt in two parts that crosses across the chest and supports a pack on the back

"You're the father of five children." "But you're only seventeen; you have a right to live; it's too soon."

Somebody of the group cried out to Marius, "You choose which one has to stay."

"Yes," said the five. "You choose. We'll obey you."

At this moment, a fifth uniform dropped, as if from heaven, onto the four others. The fifth man was saved.

Marius looked up and saw M. Fauchelevent.

At the moment when Jean Valjean entered the area, nobody had noticed him, all eyes being fixed on the five chosen men and the four uniforms. Jean Valjean saw and understood, and silently he stripped off his coat and threw it on the pile with the others.

"Who is this man?" asked Bossuet.

"He," answered Courfeyrac, "is a man who saves others."

Marius added in a serious voice, "I know him."

This assurance was enough for all.

Enjolras turned to Jean Valjean. "Citizen, you are welcome."

And he added, "You know that we are going to die."

Without answering, Jean Valjean helped the insurgent he was saving put on his uniform.

He did not look at Marius; he did not speak to him or even seem to hear when Marius said "I know him."

The five men left the barricade by the little Rue Mondétour; they looked like the National Guards. One of them went away weeping; all embraced those who remained.

When the five sent away to life had gone, Enjolras remembered the one condemned to death. He went into the lower room. Javert was still tied to the pillar.

"Do you need anything?" Enjolras asked him.

"I'm uncomfortable at this post," answered Javert. "It wasn't thoughtful to leave me to spend the night here. Tie me as you like, but please lay me on a table. Like the other."

With a nod, he indicated the body of M. Mabeuf.

At Enjolras's order, four insurgents untied Javert from the post. They walked him to the table at the back of the room, on which they stretched him out, tightly bound about the middle of his body.

While they were retying Javert, a man on the threshhold of the door was gazing at him with singular attention. The shadow this man cast made Javert turn his head. He raised his eyes and recognized Jean Valjean. He did not jump; he haughtily lowered his eyelids and merely said, "Of course."

The Situation Grows Serious

It was rapidly growing light. Although the insurgents saw nothing, they could hear a mysterious movement taking place some distance away. It was clear that the critical moment was at hand.

They did not have long to wait. Activity started up, but it was not like the first attack. A rattle of chains, a clicking of brass rolling over the pavement, a kind of uproar warned that an ominous mass of iron was approaching. A piece of artillery appeared.

The gunners were pushing the piece forward; the carriage was set for firing. The front wheels had been removed. Two supported the carriage; four were at the wheels; others followed with the caisson.[3]

A moment later, placed squarely in the middle of the street, astride the gutter, the gun was in position. Its formidable mouth was open toward the barricade.

"Come on; be quick!" shouted Courfeyrac. "There's

---

3. **caisson** two-wheeled cart used to pull large guns or cannons

the brute. The army is stretching out its big paw to us. The barricade is going to be seriously shaken."

"It's a bronze eight-pounder, new model," added Combeferre. "Sometimes those pieces burst if they go over ten parts tin to a hundred parts copper."

"Load arms," said Enjolras.

How was the front of the barricade going to behave under fire? Would the shot breach the wall? That was the question. While the insurgents loaded their muskets, the gunners loaded the cannon.

The gun went off; the detonation burst.

"Present!" called a cheerful voice.

At the same moment that the cannonball hit the outside of the barricade, Gavroche tumbled into the inside.

The Gunners Are Taken More Seriously

Gavroche produced a greater effect than the cannonball, which was lost in the rubble. At the most, it broke a wheel of the bus and finished off the old Anceau cart. Seeing this, the barricade began to laugh.

"Proceed," called Bossuet to the gunners.

They surrounded Gavroche.

But he had no time to tell anything. Marius took him aside.

"Who told you to come back? Did you at least deliver my letter to its address?"

Gavroche felt a little remorse about the letter. In his haste to return to the barricade, he had gotten rid of it rather than delivered it. He had entrusted it to a stranger whose face he could not even make out. To get himself out of trouble, he took the simplest course: he lied abominably.

"Citizen, I carried the letter to the doorkeeper. The lady was asleep. She'll get the letter when she wakes up."

Marius had planned both to save Gavroche and to say farewell to Cosette. He had to be content with half of what he intended. However, sending the letter had coincided with M. Fauchelevent's arrival in the barricade. He pointed out the man to Gavroche.

"Do you know that man?"

"No," said Gavroche. In fact, Gavroche had seen Jean Valjean only in the dark.

Marius pondered this response, but his suspicions were dispelled. Meanwhile, Gavroche was already at the other end of the barricade, shouting, "My musket!"

Courfeyrac ordered it given to him.

Gavroche warned his "comrades," as he called them, that the barricade was surrounded. He had had great difficulty getting through. On one side was a battalion of the line; on the other the municipal guard. In front, they had the bulk of the army.

This information given, Gavroche added, "I authorize you to give them a dose of pills."

Meanwhile Enjolras, on his battlement, was watching and listening intently. He thought he detected the particular sound that is made when canisters of grapeshot[4] are taken from the caisson, and he saw the gunner change aim and incline the piece slightly to the left. Then the cannoneers began to load.

"Heads down; keep close to the wall!" cried Enjolras. "And on your knees along the barricade!"

The insurgents who had left their stations on Gavroche's arrival rushed pell-mell toward the barricade. But before Enjolras's order was executed, the gun went off with a rattle like grapeshot.

---

4. **grapeshot** ammunition that is a cluster of small cannonballs

The shot ricocheted off the wall, and the terrible ricochet killed two men and wounded three.

If that continued, the barricade was no longer tenable. It could not hold out against grapeshot.

"Let's prevent the second shot at any rate," said Enjolras. And, lowering his carbine, he aimed at the gunner who, at that moment, was leaning over the breech of the gun to correct its aim.

This gunner was a fine-looking sergeant of artillery, quite young, blond, with a nice face.

"What a pity!" said Combeferre. "He's well educated; he has a father and mother; he's in love, probably; he's twenty-five at most; he might be your brother."

"He is," Enjolras replied.

"Yes," said Combeferre, "and mine, too. Let's not kill him."

"Leave me alone. We do what we must." And a tear rolled down Enjolras's marble cheek.

At that same time he pressed the trigger of the carbine. The flash burst out. The artillery sergeant turned twice around, his arms raised out in front of him and his head raised as if to drink the air; then he fell over sideways onto the gun and lay there motionless. His back could be seen, from the center of which a stream of blood gushed upward. The bullet had entered his breast and passed through his body. He was dead.

They had to carry him away and replace him. It gave those defending the barricade a few extra minutes.

The Infallible Shot

Opinions flew back and forth in the barricade. The gun was about to fire again. They could not hold out fifteen minutes in that storm of grapeshot. It was absolutely necessary to deaden the blows.

Enjolras threw out his command: "We must put a mattress there."

"We don't have any," said Combeferre. "The wounded are on them."

Jean Valjean, seated out of the way on a block, his musket between his knees, had up to that moment taken no part in what was going on.

At Enjolras's order, he got up.

It will be remembered that on the arrival of the company in the Rue de la Chanvrerie, an old woman, foreseeing bullets, had put her mattress up across her window. This window, an attic window, was on the roof of a house six stories high and standing a little outside the barricade. The mattress, placed crosswise, was resting at the bottom on two laundry poles and was held up at the top by two ropes which were attached to nails driven into the window casing. The two ropes stood out clearly against the sky.

"Can somebody lend me a double-barreled carbine?" asked Jean Valjean.

Enjolras, who had just reloaded his, handed it to him.

Jean Valjean aimed at the window and fired.

One of the two mattress ropes was severed. The mattress was now hanging by only one thread.

Jean Valjean fired the second barrel. The second rope whipped the glass of the window. The mattress slid down between the two poles and fell to the street.

The barricade applauded. They all shouted, "There's a mattress."

"Yes," said Combeferre, "but who'll go out after it?"

Jean Valjean went out into the street through the opening, crossed through a hail of bullets, went to the mattress, picked it up, put it on his back, and returned to the barricade.

He shoved the mattress into the opening himself. He secured it against the wall in such a way that the artillery men did not see it.

This done, they waited for the blast of grapeshot. They did not have long to wait.

With a roar, the canon vomited its package of shot. But there was no ricochet. The pellets miscarried against the mattress. The desired effect was obtained. The barricade was saved.

"Citizen," said Enjolras to Jean Valjean, "the Republic thanks you."

The Shot That Misses Nothing and Kills Nobody

The barrage kept up. The musket fire and grapeshot alternated without causing much damage.

With each platoon's volley, Gavroche poked out his cheek with his tongue, a sign of lofty disdain.

"That's right," he said. "Tear up the cloth. We need lint.[5]"

Courfeyrac taunted the grapeshot about its lack of effect and said to the cannon, "You're stretching yourself thin, my good man."

Suddenly the insurgents noticed a helmet shining in the sun on a neighboring roof. A soldier was standing against a tall chimney and seemed to be there as a lookout.

Jean Valjean had returned the carbine to Enjolras, but he still had his musket. Without saying a word, he aimed at the lookout, and a second later the helmet fell clattering to the street. The startled soldier disappeared in a hurry.

A second observer took his place. It was an officer. Jean Valjean, who had reloaded his musket, aimed at

---

5. lint particles of cloth used to cover wounds

the newcomer and sent his helmet to keep company with the soldier's. This time, the warning was understood. Nobody appeared on the roof again, and they gave up watching the barricade.

"Why didn't you kill them?" Bossuet asked of Jean Valjean.

Jean Valjean did not answer.

Bossuet murmured in Combeferre's ear, "He hasn't answered my question."

"He's a man with a kindly musket," said Combeferre.

Of the two pieces now battering the barricade in the Rue de la Chanvrerie, one fired grapeshot, the other cannonballs.

The gun that hurled cannonballs was elevated a little, and the range was calculated so that the ball struck the extreme edge of the upper ridge of the barricade, notched it, and crumbled the paving stones over the insurgent in showers. This technique was intended to force the insurgents from the summit and drive them to crowd together in the interior. In other words, it anticipated the assault. Once the combatants were driven from the summit and the windows, the attacking columns could venture into the streets without being watched, suddenly scale the barricade as they had the evening before, and—who knows?—take it by surprise.

"We absolutely must reduce the inconvenience of those pieces," said Enjolras. He cried, "Fire on the cannoneers!"

Everyone was ready. The barricade, silent for so long, opened fire desperately. Seven or eight volleys succeeded one another with a kind of fury and joy. The street was filled with a blinding smoke. The fire slacked.

"This works well," said Bossuet to Enjolras.

"Success!"

Enjolras shook his head and answered, "Fifteen more minutes of this success and there won't be ten cartridges left in the barricade."

It seems that Gavroche heard this remark.

Gavroche Outside

Courfeyrac suddenly noticed somebody at the foot of the barricade, outside in the street, under the line of fire.

Gavroche had taken a basket from the wineshop, had gone out the opening, and was quietly occupied in emptying into his basket the full cartridge boxes of the National Guards who had been killed on the slopes of the barricade.

"What are you doing there?" asked Courfeyrac.

Gavroche looked up.

"Citizen, I'm filling my basket."

"But don't you see the grapeshot?"

Gavroche answered, "So, it's raining. So what?"

Courfeyrac cried out, "Come back!"

"In a bit," said Gavroche.

And he went deeper into the street.

Some twenty dead lay scattered along the length of the street on the pavement. Twenty cartridge boxes for Gavroche, a supply for the barricade.

The smoke in the street was like a dense fog, useful to Gavroche. He emptied the first seven or eight cartridge boxes without much danger. He crawled on his belly, ran on this hands and feet, held the basket in his teeth, twisted, slid, writhed, wormed his way from one body to another, and emptied the cartridge boxes as a monkey opens a nut.

Just as Gavroche was relieving a sergeant of his cartridges, a ball struck the body.

"There they go," said Gavroche, "killing my dead for me."

A second bullet splintered the pavement beside him. A third upset his basket. Gavroche looked and saw that it came from the sharpshooters from the suburbs.

He stood up straight—on his feet, his hair in the wind, his hands on his hips, his eye on the National Guards who were firing—and he sang a verse at the top of his lungs.

Then he picked up his basket, put back in all the cartridges that had fallen out, and advanced toward the barricade, stopping to empty another cartridge box. There a fourth bullet just missed him. Gavroche sang another verse. A fifth bullet only managed to draw a third verse from him. This went on for some time. The sight was fascinating. Gavroche, under fire, was mocking the bullets. He seemed very much amused. They aimed at him incessantly; they always missed. The National Guards and the soldiers laughed as they aimed at him. He lay down, then stood up, hid in a doorway, then sprang out, disappeared, reappeared, escaped, returned, answered the volleys by thumbing his nose, meanwhile stealing cartridges and cartridge boxes and filling his basket. The insurgents held their breath and followed him with their eyes. He was playing a terrible game of hide-and-seek with death.

One bullet, better aimed than the others, finally reached the child. They saw Gavroche totter and fall. The whole barricade let out a cry. But Gavroche had fallen only to rise again. He sat up, a long stream of blood streaking his face, raised both arms in the air, looked in the direction of the shot, and began to sing his verse.

He did not finish. A second bullet from the same

marksman cut him short. This time he fell face down on the pavement and did not stir again. The great little soul had taken flight.

Marius had sprung out of the barricade. Combeferre followed him. But it was too late. Gavroche was dead. Combeferre brought back the basket of cartridges; Marius brought back the child.

Just as he had stooped down to pick up the boy, a bullet had grazed his skull; he did not notice it.

They laid Gavroche on the same table as Mabeuf, and they stretched the black shawl over the two bodies. It was large enough for the old man and the young boy.

Courfeyrac distributed the cartridges from the basket. This gave each man fifteen shots.

Jean Valjean was still at the same place, motionless. When Combeferre presented him with his fifteen cartridges, he shook his head.

"That is a strange man," said Combeferre softly to Enjolras. "He finds a way not to fight in this barricade."

"Which does not prevent him from defending it," answered Enjolras.

"Heroism has its originals," replied Combeferre.

The Vulture Becomes Prey

Because the defenders of a barricade must always hoard their ammunition and the besiegers know that, the besiegers make their preparations with a kind of provoking slowness. They expose themselves to fire ahead of time and relax, more in appearance than reality. The preparations for an attack are always made with a methodical slowness, after which comes the thunderbolt.

This slowness gave Enjolras time to review the

whole picture and to perfect it. He felt that if such men were to die, it should be a masterpiece.

He had the door to the kitchen, which we remember was the hospital, nailed up. He ordered the second floor ready to cut the staircase away. He counted the men.

"Good. There are twenty-six of us left on our feet. How many muskets?"

"Thirty-four."

"Eight extra. Keep those eight muskets loaded like the rest and at hand. Swords and pistols in your belts. Twenty men to the barricade. Six in ambush at the small windows and at the second-floor window to fire down on the attackers through the paving stones. There can't be a single wasted movement. The moment the drum beats the charge, the twenty downstairs must rush to the barricade. The first there will get the best places."

With these orders given, he turned to Javert and said, "I won't forget you."

And, laying a pistol on the table, he added, "The last man to leave this room will blow out this spy's brains!"

At this point, Jean Valjean appeared. He stepped forward and said to Enjolras, "You thanked me just now."

"In the name of the Republic. The barricade has two saviors, Marius Pontmercy and you."

"Well, I have a reward to ask of you."

"What?"

"To blow out that man's brains myself."

Javert raised his head, saw Jean Valjean, made a slight movement, and said, "That is appropriate."

As for Enjolras, he glanced around him: "No objection." And turning to Jean Valjean: "Take the spy."

Jean Valjean sat at the end of Javert's table. He took up the pistol, and a slight click indicated he had cocked it.

At that very moment, they heard a flourish of trumpets.

"Here they come!" shouted Marius from the top of the barricade.

As the insurgents sprang forward, they got in the back a final word from Javert: "We'll meet again soon!"

Jean Valjean Takes His Revenge

When Jean Valjean was alone with Javert, he untied the rope holding the prisoner around the middle. Then he motioned him to get up.

Javert obeyed, with an undefinable smile of superiority.

Jean Valjean took Javert out of the bistro slowly, for his legs were still tied.

The insurgents, prepared for the coming attack, were looking the other way. Only Marius, positioned at the far end of the wall, saw them go by.

With some difficulty, Jean Valjean made him climb the small barricade. No one could see them now. The corner of the house hid them. A few steps away, the corpses made a terrible mound. Among the dead, they saw a flowing head of hair, a wounded hand, and a woman's chest. It was Eponine. Javert glanced at this body and, perfectly calm, said, "It seems to me I know that girl."

Then he turned to Jean Valjean, who put the pistol under his arm and glared at Javert.

"Take your revenge," Javert answered the look.

Jean Valjean took out a knife from his pocket and cut the ropes on Javert's hands and feet. Standing up, he said to him, "You are free."

Javert was not easily surprised. Still, he could not avoid an emotion. He was astonished and motionless.

Jean Valjean continued, "I don't expect to leave this place. Still, if by any chance I do, I live under the name of Fauchelevent, in the Rue de l'Homme-Armé, Number Seven."

Javert scowled like a tiger, half opening the corner of his mouth, and he muttered between his teeth, "Be careful." And he repeated the address Jean Valjean had given to him. He did not notice that his tone had become more respectful toward Jean Valjean.

"Go away," said Jean Valjean.

Meanwhile, at the barricade, Marius had had a sudden memory. When he had seen Jean Valjean with the spy in broad daylight, he had recognized him. He had said to himself: "Isn't that the police inspector who told me his name was Javert?"

"Enjolras," he called, "what's that man's name?"

"Who?"

"The police officer. Do you know his name?"

"Javert."

Marius jumped up.

At that second, they heard the pistol shot.

Jean Valjean reappeared and called out, "Done."

A dreary chill passed through Marius's heart.

The Heroes

The drum beat the charge. Fury was now skill. A powerful column of infantry, joined by the National Guards and Municipal Guards and supported by masses heard but unseen, turned into the street at quick step. Drums beating, trumpets sounding, bayonets fixed, and sabers at their heads, they came straight at the barricade.

The wall held well.

Enjolras was at one end of the barricade and Marius was at the other. Enjolras, who carried the whole barricade in his head, sheltered and reserved himself. Marius fought without shelter. There is no man more fearsome in battle than a dreamer. He was terrible and pensive, in the battle as in a dream. One would have thought him a phantom firing a musket.

The assaults came one after another. The horror increased and then burst out over this pile of paving stone. The barricade was ten times approached, assaulted, scaled, and not taken.

They fought hand to hand, tooth and nail, foot to foot, with pistols, with sabers, with fists, at a distance, close up, from above, from below, from everywhere. The front of the Corinth was half demolished. Bossuet was killed; Feuilly was killed; Courfeyrac was killed; Joly was killed; Combeferre died as he was pierced by three bayonets in the chest. Marius, still fighting, was covered with bloody wounds. Enjolras alone was untouched. When his weapon failed, he reached left or right, and an insurgent put whatever weapon he could into his grasp.

A final assault was attempted, and this one succeeded. This time it was over. The group of insurgents, who defended the center of the redoubt,[6] fell back. Enjolras and Marius, with seven or eight others, sprang forward to protect them. Enjolras shouted to the soldiers, "Keep back!" An officer, not obeying, was killed by Enjolras. Covering his men with his body, he ordered them through the door into the wineshop. Enjolras, using his carbine like a cane to beat off the nightmare of bayonets all around him, entered last of all. The door closed with such violence that it cut off

---

6. redoubt a small area being defended

the fingers and thumb of a soldier who had caught hold of it. The siege of the Corinth was now beginning.

Marius had stayed outside. A shot had broken his shoulder; he felt himself fainting, that he was falling. At the moment his eyes closed, he felt the shock of a hand grabbing him, and he lost consciousness.

Step By Step

Climbing on one another's shoulders, pulling themselves up the remains of the staircase, hanging to the ceiling, some twenty soldiers and guards—most of them blinded by the blood from their wounds—burst furiously into the second-floor room. There was now only one man on his feet—Enjolras. Without ammunition, without a sword, he held in his hand the remains of his carbine. He had retreated to the corner of the room and from there was so formidable that a large space was left around him. A cry went up—"This is their leader. Let him stay there. Let's shoot him on the spot."

"Shoot me," said Enjolras. And he threw away the stump of the carbine and crossed his arms, presenting his chest.

Twelve men formed in platoon in the corner opposite Enjolras and readied their muskets in silence.

Then a sergeant cried, "Take aim!"

An officer intervened and addressed Enjolras, "Do you wish your eyes bandaged?"

"No."

Pierced by eight bullets, Enjolras remained backed up against the wall as if the bullets had nailed him there. Except that his head was tilted.

Prisoner

Marius was also a prisoner. Prisoner of Jean Valjean.

The hand that had seized him from behind as he lost consciousness was Jean Valjean's.

Jean Valjean had taken no part in the combat other than to expose himself. He had defended the barricade, seen to the wounded, and at intervals repaired the redoubt. But nothing like a personal defense came from him. He was silent and gave aid. Moreover, he had only a few scratches. The bullets seemed to want no part of him.

In the dense cloud of combat, Jean Valjean did not appear to see Marius. The fact is he never took his eyes off him. When the shot struck Marius down, Jean Valjean leaped with the agility of a tiger, dropped down on him as upon a prey, and carried him away.

The whirlwind of the attack concentrated so fiercely on Enjolras and the door of the Corinth that nobody saw Jean Valjean cross the unpaved field of the barricade, holding the unconscious Marius in his arms, and disappear behind the corner of the house.

Once out of sight, Jean Valjean dropped Marius to the ground and cast his eyes about him. The situation was dreadful. The stretch of wall on which he leaned was a shelter only for two or three minutes, perhaps. How to escape the massacre? He had to decide instantly. He looked at the barricade beside him, at the house in front of him, at the ground—in desperation, as if he wanted to bore a hole in it with his eyes.

A few steps away, he noticed an iron grating laid flat and level with the ground. The frame that secured it had been torn up, and it was unsecured. Through the bars, there was a glimpse of something like the flue of a chimney or the pipe of a cistern. Jean Valjean sprang forward. To remove the stones, to lift the grating, to load up Marius (who was as limp as a corpse), to climb down into this kind of well, to drop back over his head the iron trapdoor on which the stones he had moved rolled back again, to find a foothold on the surface ten feet below the ground—these things were executed with the strength of a giant and the speed of an eagle. It took hardly a minute or two.

Jean Valjean found himself, with Marius still unconscious, in a sort of long underground passage.

He could hear overhead the awesome noise of the wineshop being overrun by the assault.

The impression he had formerly felt in falling from the street into a convent came back to him. Only now he was not carrying Cosette; it was Marius.

2 *Mire, but Soul*

The Sewer's Surprises

Jean Valjean found himself in the Paris sewer. And he did not know whether the burden he was carrying was dead or alive.

His first sensation was blindness. Suddenly he could not see anything. He reached out first one hand and then the other, touched the wall on each side, and realized that the passageway was narrow. He slipped and realized that the pavement was wet. He put one foot forward cautiously, fearing some kind of hole or pit; he made sure the stone pavement continued. It was the foul odor that told him where he was.

After a few moments, he was able to distinguish something. The passage in which he had landed was walled up behind him. It was a cul-de-sac called a branchment. In front was another wall, this one a wall of night. Ten or twelve paces from where Jean Valjean stood, the darkness was terrible; to enter it seemed to be swallowed up. He could force himself into that wall, and he had to. He even had to hurry. There was not a moment to lose. He had laid Marius on the ground; he picked him up again onto his shoulders, and he began to walk.

After fifty paces, he had to stop. A question arose. The passage ended in another which crossed it. Two roads were offered. Which way to go—left or right? To follow the descending road was to go to the river.

Jean Valjean understood that at once. He might come out near some gathering of people. Imagine the amazement of pedestrians at seeing two bloody people emerge from the ground at their feet. The police would be called, and he would be seized before he got out. Better to trust the darkness and rely on Providence for the outcome.

He chose the right and ascended. The light from the airhole vanished, and he was once again in darkness. He went as fast as he could. Marius's arms were around his neck, and his feet hung down. With one hand Jean Valjean held both arms, and he felt for the wall with the other. Marius's cheek touched his and stuck to it, being bloody. He felt a moist warmth at his ear, which touched the wounded man's mouth; that indicated breathing and consequently life.

He continued anxiously but calmly, seeing nothing, swallowed up in chance, that is to say Providence. He invented his route as he went. In this unknown region, each step could be his last. How would he get out? Would he find an outlet? Would he find it in time? Would Marius die of hemorrhage and he of hunger? Would they both perish here and become two skeletons in some corner of this night? He did not know.

Suddenly he was surprised. At a most unexpected moment, he discovered he was no longer climbing. The water lapped at his heels instead of the top of his feet. The sewer was now headed downward. Why? Would he then soon reach the Seine? While this danger was great, the peril of retreating was greater. He continued on.

Jean Valjean was making his way toward the belt sewer; he was on the right path. But he knew nothing of that.

Whenever he came to a branch, he felt the walls and, if he found the opening was not as wide as the corridor he was on, he did not enter.

Eventually he was getting further and further away from the Paris of the revolt and entering the Paris that was alive and normal. Above his head he could hear a sound like thunder, distant but steady. It was the rumbling of carriages overhead.

He had been walking for about half an hour by his calculation, and he had not yet thought of resting. The darkness was deeper than ever, but this depth reassured him.

Suddenly he saw his shadow in front of him. It was outlined by a faint red glow. Amazed, he turned around. Behind him appeared some sort of horrible star that appeared to be searching for him.

It was the pale star of the police rising in the sewer.

Behind the star, moving in disorder, were eight or ten black forms, straight and terrible.

Explanation

During the day of the 6th of June, a search of the sewers had been ordered. It was feared that the defeated insurgents would take refuge there. Three platoons of officers and sewer men explored the subterranean streets of Paris. They were armed with carbines, clubs, swords, and daggers.

What was at that moment headed toward Jean Valjean was a lantern of the patrol assigned to the right bank of the Seine.

This was an indescribable moment for Jean Valjean.

Luckily the lantern could not see him well. It was light and he was shadow. He drew close to the wall and stopped.

He did not realize what he was seeing. He saw a staring flame and around it ghosts.

The men of the patrol listened and heard nothing. They looked and saw nothing. They consulted.

The sergeant gave the order to go left toward the Seine. If they had thought of splitting up into two sections and going in both directions, Jean Valjean would have been caught.

Before going away, the sergeant fired his carbine into the direction they were abandoning, toward Jean Valjean. The detonation rolled and echoed in the cave. Some plaster that fell into the stream made Jean Valjean aware that the ball had struck the arch above his head.

Jean Valjean, not yet daring to move, stood for a long time with his back to the wall, watching the vanishing phantom patrol.

The Stalker and the Stalked

Something occurred in the afternoon of the 6th of June beside the Seine, on the shore of the right bank.

That place has changed, but on that bank two men seemed to be watching each other, one avoiding the other. The one trying to escape had a slight build and a sickly look; the one trying to capture was a tall individual with a tough look.

The reader might recognize these two men if they could be seen up close. What was the purpose of the second man?

If he was allowing the other to go on his way, it was probably with the hope of seeing him rendezvous with some other prizes. This operation is called "spinning."

What makes this conjecture probable is that the tall man, noticing a carriage driving along the empty bank, beckoned to the driver. The driver understood, obviously recognized the man, and turned his horse around to follow the direction of the two men.

One of the instructions given by the police to officers contains this note: "Always have a vehicle within call, in case of need."

It seemed as if the first man would attempt an escape into the Champs-Elysées boulevard, it being decorated with trees. However, to the great surprise of the second man, the man did not take that ramp. He continued down the shore.

The man reached a little hill and doubled around it so that he was out of sight. The second man, taking advantage of not being seen himself, advanced very rapidly and reached the mound. There he stopped in amazement. The man he was hunting was gone.

The tall man, in his closely buttoned coat, paused a moment, his fists clenched and his eyes darting. Then he slapped his forehead. He had just noticed, at the place where the water began, a wide, low iron grate, arched, with a heavy lock and three massive hinges. A blackish stream flowed from beneath it and emptied into the Seine.

The man crossed his arms and stared at the grating. He shook it; it resisted firmly. It had been opened, though no sound had been made, and then closed again. The one for whom this door had so recently opened had used not a hook but a key.

"Well! Well! Well! Well!" expressed the man ironically.

So saying, hoping who knows what, he posted himself on watch behind the mound with all the patience of a watchdog.

He Also Bears His Cross

Jean Valjean had continued to walk and had not stopped again.

His progress became more and more laborious. He was compelled to bend so that Marius's head would not hit the top of the arches; he had to stoop over and then rise to feel for the walls. The slime on the floor gave little support for hand or foot. He was hungry and thirsty; thirsty particularly—the place, like the sea, being full of water you cannot drink. He was growing tired, and his strength was diminishing. He could feel the scurrying of rats between his legs. One was so frightened it bit him. From time to time, through the aprons of the sewer openings came a breath of fresh air, which revived him.

It might have been three o'clock in the afternoon when he arrived at the belt sewer.

He was astonished at its sudden widening. The Great Sewer is in fact eight feet wide and seven high.

The old question came back. Left or right, up or down? He knew the situation was urgent and that he must now reach the Seine. In other words, descend. He turned left.

Well for him that he did. Although he did not know it, the other direction terminates upstream in a cul-de-sac. His instinct served him well.

A little beyond the branching, he stopped. He was very tired, and a large air hole produced an almost vivid light. Jean Valjean laid Marius down on the side bank of the sewer. Marius's eyes were closed, his hair stuck to his temple like brushes in red paint, his hands hung lifelessly, his arms and legs were cold, there was coagulated blood in the corners of his mouth. A clot of blood had gathered in the knot of his tie, and his shirt was dried into the wounds of his chest. Jean Valjean removed the garment with the tips of his fingers and felt that his heart was still beating. He tore up his shirt and bandaged the wounds as best he could. Then, bending over Marius, who was still unconscious, he looked at him with hatred.

In going through Marius's clothes, he had found two things: the bread that had been forgotten there since the day before and Marius's notebook. On the first page there were four lines written by Marius:

My name is Marius Pontmercy.
Carry my corpse to my grandfather's.
M. Gillenormand,
Rue des Filles du Calvaire, No. 6, in the Marais.

Jean Valjean replaced the notebook in Marius's pocket, put Marius on his back again, laying his head carefully on his right shoulder, and began to walk down the six miles of the Great Sewer.

He walked desperately and with supreme effort. Once he sat down on the curb to change Marius's position, and he thought to stay there. He got to his feet again and went on.

Finally he reached a bend in the sewer and bumped into the wall, as he was walking with his head down. He looked up and saw, at the far end of the passage, far, far away, a light. It was the clear white light of day.

Jean Valjean reached the outlet. It might have been half past eight in the evening. The daylight was fading.

He laid Marius down and checked the bars of the grating with both hands. The gate did not move. Not a bar would budge. The obstacle was invincible. No means of opening the door. Chance had unsealed the grating by which they had entered. He had only succeeded in escaping into a prison. It was over. All that Jean Valjean had done was useless. God refused him.

He dropped onto the pavement beside the still motionless Marius, and his head dropped to his knees. No exit. He did not think of himself or of Marius. He thought of Cosette.

The Torn Coat

A hand was laid on his shoulder, and a low voice said, "Go halves."

Jean Valjean thought he was dreaming. He had heard no footsteps. He raised his eyes.

The man in front of him was barefoot; he had evidently taken off his shoes to be able to approach Jean Valjean without being heard.

Jean Valjean did not hesitate a moment. This man was known to him; it was Thénardier.

Jean Valjean recognized immediately that Thénardier did not recognize him.

Thénardier said, "How do you plan to get out? It is impossible to pick the lock."

"That's true," said Jean Valjean calmly. "What do you have in mind?"

"Well, you've killed this man. Very well. As for me, I have a key."

Jean Valjean began to understand. Thénardier took him for a murderer.

Thénardier went on, "I don't know your name, and I can't see your face, but you'd do wrong to think that I don't know who you are and what you want. It's understood. You've bashed this gentleman; now you want to tuck him somewhere. You need the river to get rid of him. I'm going to get you out of this scrape.

To help a good fellow in trouble, that suits me fine. So, let's finish it. Here's my key; let's see your money."

Jean Valjean felt in his pockets. On putting on his National Guard coat, he had forgotten to take his wallet with him. He had only some coins with him. He turned out his pocket for Thénardier.

Thénardier was feeling Marius's pockets and found a means, without attracting Jean Valjean's attention, to tear off a strip, which he hid under his shirt. He probably thought that this scrap of cloth might help him later to identify the assassin or the victim. He found, however, only thirty francs.

"It's true," he said. "Both together, you have no more."

Forgetting his words, "go halves," he took it all.

True to his word, Thénardier helped Jean Valjean get Marius to the gate. There he put the key in the lock. The bolt slid and the door swung without a creaking or grinding sound. It was clear that this grating and its hinges were oiled with care and opened more often than anyone supposed.

Thénardier opened the gate, left an opening for Jean Valjean and his burden, closed the grating again, turned the key twice in the lock, and went back inside noiselessly.

Jean Valjean was outside.

Marius Seems Dead to Someone Who Is a Good Judge

He let Marius down on the shore and looked up. All about him was silence. Night was coming. The sky extended on all sides with an enormous calm. For a few seconds Jean Valjean was overcome with this calm and serenity. Then, as if feeling a duty, he bent over Marius and, dipping some water into his hands, he threw a few drops onto Marius's face. Marius's eyelids did not open, but his half-open mouth was breathing.

Jean Valjean was plunging his hand into the river again when suddenly he felt an uneasiness such as we feel when someone is behind us even though we do not see him.

He turned around.

A tall man in a long overcoat, with crossed arms and in his right hand a club, stood erect a few steps away.

Jean Valjean recognized Javert.

The reader had doubtless guessed that Thénardier's pursuer had been none other than Javert. The reader might also have guessed that, by opening the gate for Jean Valjean, Thénardier had been clever. Feeling that Javert was still close by, he had thrown Jean Valjean to him. Here was a scapegoat, an assassin! Putting Jean Valjean out instead of himself, Thénardier had given a victim to the police and thrown them off his track.

Javert did not recognize Jean Valjean. Keeping his arms crossed, with the club secure in his grasp, he said in a curt, calm voice, "Who are you?"

"Jean Valjean."

Javert put the club between his teeth, bent down, laid two powerful hands on Jean Valjean's shoulders, examined him, and recognized him. Their faces almost touched. Javert's look was fearsome.

"Inspector Javert," said Jean Valjean, "you have me. Since this morning, I have considered myself your prisoner. I did not give you my address to escape you. Take me. Only grant me one thing. It is about him. Dispose of me as you like; but first help me carry him home. I ask only that of you."

Javert's face contorted. Still he did not say no. He

stooped and took from his pocket a handkerchief, which he dipped into the water and used to wipe Marius's bloodied forehead.

"This man was in the barricade," he said in an undertone. "This is the one they called Marius." He took Marius's hand and tried to find a pulse.

"He is wounded," said Jean Valjean.

"He is dead," said Javert.

Jean Valjean answered, "Not yet."

And he reached into Marius's pocket and took out the notebook with its message from Marius. "He lives in the Marais, at his grandfather's—I forget the name."

Javert looked at the page and then put the notebook in his own pocket. He cried, "Driver!"

A moment later, the carriage was on the beach. Marius was laid on the back seat, and Javert sat beside Jean Valjean on the front seat. The carriage moved off.

The Prodigal Son

It was after dark when the carriage arrived at No. 6, Rue des Filles du Calvaire. Everyone was asleep.

Jean Valjean and the driver carried Marius to the door. Javert called out to the doorkeeper in a tone that befits a government man.

"Somebody whose name is Gillenormand?"

"He is here. What do you want with him?"

"His son is brought home."

"His son?" said the porter in amazement.

"He is dead."

Jean Valjean, ragged and dirty behind Javert, motioned with his head that this was not true.

Javert continued, "He has been to the barricade, and here he is."

The porter woke up Basque. Basque woke up Nicolette. Nicolette woke up Aunt Gillenormand. As for the grandfather, they let him sleep, thinking he would know soon enough in any event.

They took Marius up to the second floor and laid him on a couch in M. Gillenormand's anteroom. Basque went for the doctor, and Nicolette opened the linen closets. Jean Valjean felt Javert's hand on his shoulder. He understood, and they went downstairs.

In the carriage, Jean Valjean said, "Inspector, grant me one thing more."

"What?" demanded Javert roughly.

"Let me go home a moment. Then you may do with me whatever you like."

Javert was silent for a few seconds, his chin in the collar of his coat; then he let down the window in front.

"Driver," he said, "Rue de l'Homme Armé, No. Seven."

Shaking Up the Absolute

They did not say a word for the whole distance.

What did Jean Valjean want? To finish what he had begun: to inform Cosette, to tell her where Marius was, to give her some useful other information, to make some final dispositions? As for himself, it was all over. He had been seized by Javert and did not resist.

They reached the Rue de l'Homme Armé, which was too narrow for the carriage. Javert and Jean Valjean got out, and they entered the empty street. They found No. Seven. Jean Valjean rapped. The door opened.

"Very well," said Javert, "go on up."

And with a strange expression on his face and as

though it required great effort for him to speak, he continued, "I'll wait for you here."

On reaching the second floor, he paused. Either for some fresh air or automatically, Jean Valjean looked out the window. He leaned over into the street. He was dumbfounded. There was nobody on the street.

Javert had gone away.

The Grandfather

The doctor examined Marius and established that there was a steady pulse and there were no serious chest wounds, the blood at the corners of his lips coming from his nasal cavities. The long walk underground had finished dislocating the shoulder blade, and there were no serious problems there. His arms had sword cuts, but no scars disfigured him. The hemorrhage had exhausted him, but from the waist down, he had been protected by the barricade.

As the doctor was wiping the face and touching the closed eyelids, a door opened at the end of the room and a pale figure approached.

M. Gillenormand's room was next door and, in spite of the precautions, the noise had awakened him. He was bent forward and shaking.

He noticed the bed and murmured, "Marius!"

"Monsieur," said Basque, "he has been at the barricade. He has just been brought home—"

"He is dead! He is dead! He got himself killed at the barricade! Out of hatred for me! It is against me that he did this! This is the way he comes back to me! Misery of my life! You knew very well that you had only to come in and say 'Here I am' and you would be master of this house, that I would obey you, and that you could do whatever you liked with this fool of a grandfather. You knew it, but you went to the barricades and got yourself killed out of spite! Go to bed, then, and sleep quietly!"

He approached Marius, who was still motionless, and began to wring his hands. He spoke again:

"Go on; he is dead. Stone dead. You are wasting your time, idiot doctor. And as you have no pity for getting yourself killed like that, I will have no grief for your death. Do you understand?"

At that moment, Marius slowly opened his eyes, and his gaze rested on M. Gillenormand.

"Marius!" cried the old man. "Marius! My darling Marius! My child! My son! You are alive; you are looking at me, thank you!" And he fainted.

3 *Javert off the Track*

Final Decision

Javert walked slowly away from the Rue de l'Homme Armé. He walked with his head down and, for the first time in his life, with his hands behind his back. But he kept to one direction.

He took the shortest route to the Seine, at the place where there is a kind of square lake crossed by rapids. This point of the river is dreaded by sailors because of its dangerous current. The two bridges, so close to each other, increase the danger, and the water races strongly under the arches. It rolls on with wide folds; it gathers in and rolls up; the torrent strains at the pilings as if to tear them out. Men who fall in there are never seen again; the best swimmers drown.

Javert was tormented.

Before him he saw two roads, and that terrified him—he who had never in his life known anything but one straight line. His situation was difficult to describe.

One thing that astonished him was that Jean Valjean had spared his life; and one thing that terrified him was that he, Javert, had spared Jean Valjean.

Where was he? He could no longer find the person he knew as himself.

What he had just done made him shudder. He had decided, against all police regulations, against the whole social and judicial organization, against the entire code, in favor of a release. Every time he faced this nameless act he had committed, he trembled from head to toe. How could he resolve this? Only one act remained: to return immediately to the Rue de l'Homme Armé and arrest Jean Valjean. It was clear what he must do. He could not. Something barred him from that direction.

Jean Valjean confused him.

A compassionate convict, kind, helpful, returning good for evil, returning pardon for hatred, loving pity rather than vengeance, preferring to destroy himself rather than destroy his enemy, nearer angels than men. Javert was compelled to acknowledge that this monster existed.

This could not go on.

His reflections turned onto himself and, beside an exalted Jean Valjean, he saw himself degraded. A convict was his benefactor! He was compelled to recognize the existence of kindness. This convict had been kind. And he, himself—he had just been kind. Therefore he had become depraved. He thought himself cowardly. He was a horror to himself.

Javert's ideal was not to be humane, to be great or sublime. His ideal was to be irreproachable. Now he had failed.

He was emptied, useless, broken off from his past life, dissolved. Authority was dead in him. He had no further reason for being.

Terrible situation! Moved to emotion. It was unendurable. Unnatural state, if ever there was one. Only two ways out. One, to go to Jean Valjean and return the convict to the dungeon. The other . . . .

The place where Javert stood, it will be remembered, was situated directly over the rapids, where the frightening whirlpool knots and unknots itself like an endless liquid corkscrew.

Javert leaned out and looked. Everything was black. He could not make out anything. He heard the gurgling sound of the water, but he could not see the river.

For some minutes, he remained still, gazing into that darkness. Suddenly he removed his hat and placed it on the edge of the bank.

A moment later, a tall black form, which from the distance a pedestrian might have taken for a ghost, appeared on the bridge, bent toward the river, leaped up, and then fell straight into the darkness. There was a dull splash, and only the night knows what agonies transpired with that form which disappeared under the water.

4 *Grandson and Grandfather*

We See the Tree with the Zinc Plate Once More

Monsieur Boulatruelle, it may be remembered, was the road laborer from Montfermeil who saw mysterious events in the forest near the highway where he worked. He believed in treasures buried in the forest of Montfermeil.

One morning before daybreak, on the lookout, he saw among the branches a man, whose back was not altogether unfamiliar. He could not remember where he had seen the man, except that it looked like a man he vaguely remembered.

Boulatruelle thought of the treasure. Very possibly it was the same man. While he was thinking, he had bowed his head, which was not very smart. When he raised it again the man was gone.

Doing his best to follow the path the man must have taken, he hurried off through the thicket. He faced holly, nettles, hawthorns, thistles, brambles.[1] He was quite scratched. Finally he came to a stream to be crossed.

Forty minutes later, he reached a glade, sweating, soaked, breathless, and torn.

Nobody there.

Boulatruelle ran to the pile of stones. It was in place.

---

1. **holly ... brambles** shrubs and bushes which have sharp ends that cut and scratch

As for the man, he had vanished. And—a worse thing—in front of the tree with the zinc plate were fresh earth that had been dug, a pickax, and a hole.

The hole was empty.

"Robber!" cried Boulatruelle, shaking his fists at the horizon.

Marius Prepares for Domestic War

On the 7th of September, three months after the night they had brought him home to his grandfather, the doctor declared Marius was out of danger.

Convalescence began.

M. Gillenormand had spent every night with the young man. He had his large armchair brought to the bedside, and he supervised all the dressings. Nothing was as touching as to see his old trembling hand offer a cup of herbal tea to the wounded young man.

When the doctor declared Marius out of danger, the good man was delirious. He danced, snapped his fingers, and sang.

As for Marius, while he let them all care for him, he had one thought: Cosette.

Since the delirium had left, he had not uttered the name, and they supposed he no longer thought of it. He only held his peace and waited for the proper time.

He did not know what had become of Cosette. Shadows in his memory, indistinct, floated: Eponine, Gavroche, Mabeuf. The Thénardiers and all his friends mingled with the smoke of the barricade. A strange fleeting appearance of M. Fauchelevent puzzled him. He did not know how, or by whom, he had been saved, and nobody around him knew. All they could tell him is that a carriage arrived by night.

His past, present, and future seemed the mist of a vague idea. But within this, there was a granite-hard idea: to find Cosette again.

Marius was not won over by all the tenderness of his grandfather. In the first place, he was not aware of most of it. Then, he distrusted this gentleness as a strange new thing whose aim was to subdue him. Marius said to himself that it was all right as long as he did not offer any resistance but that, when the question of Cosette was raised, his grandfather's real attitude would be revealed.

He was determined that if his grandfather refused he would tear off his bandages, dislocate his shoulder, lay bare all his other wounds, and refuse all nourishment. His wounds would be his ammunition. To have Cosette or die. He waited for the favorable moment with patience.

The moment came.

Marius Attacks

One day, M. Gillenormand leaned over Marius and said in his tenderest voice, "You see, my dear Marius, in your place I would eat meat now rather than fish. Sole is excellent to begin a convalescence, but to put a sick man back on his legs, it takes a good cutlet."

Marius, who had regained almost all his strength, gathered it up, sat up in bed, rested clenched fists on the sheets, looked his grandfather in the face, and said, "This leads me to say something to you."

"What is it?"

"It is that I wish to marry."

"Understood," said the grandfather. And he burst out laughing.

"What do you mean, understood?"

"Yes, understood. You will have her."

Marius was astounded and overwhelmed by the burst of happiness.

M. Gillenormand continued, "Yes, you will marry her, your handsome, pretty girl. She comes every day in the person of an old gentleman to inquire after you. Since you were wounded, she has spent her time weeping and making lint for your bandages. I have made inquiries. She lives in the Rue de l'Homme Armé, Number Seven. So, that surprises you! You had arranged your little plot. I'm sly, too. She is charming; she is modest; the thing about the lancer is not true; she has made heaps of lint; she is a jewel; she worships you. If you had died, there would have been three of us. Well, at any rate, let us not discuss it any more. It is settled and done. Marry her. Be so kind as to get married. Be happy, my dear child."

So saying the old man burst into sobs. He took Marius's head and hugged it in both arms, and they both began to weep. Weeping can be one of the forms of supreme happiness.

"Father!" exclaimed Marius.

"You do love me then!" said the old man.

Marius released his head from the old man's arms and said gently, "Father, now that I am well, it seems to me I could see her."

"Well, all right. You have called me 'Father'; it is well worth that. I will see to it. She will be brought to you."

Something Under the Arm of Monsieur Fauchelevent

Cosette and Marius saw each other again. The whole family, including Basque and Nicolette, was assembled in Marius's room when Cosette entered.

She was as frightened as one can be by happiness. She stammered, quite pale and quite red, wanting to throw herself in Marius's arms and not daring to in front of all those people.

With Cosette and behind her was "Monsieur Fauchelevent"; this was Jean Valjean. He was very well dressed, in a new black suit and a white necktie.

In the room, he stayed near the door, as if apart. He had under his arm a package similar to a book, wrapped in paper. The paper was greenish and seemed moldy.

"Does the gentleman always have a book under his arm like that?" asked Mlle. Gillenormand, who did not like books, softly to Nicolette.

"Well," answered M. Gillenormand, who had heard her, "he is a scholar. What then? Is it his fault?"

And bowing, he said in a loud voice, "Monsieur Tranchelevent—"

Father Gillenormand did not do this on purpose. Rather, inattention to proper names was a way he had.

"I have the honor of asking you for my grandson, Monsieur the Baron Marius Pontmercy, for the hand of mademoiselle."

Monsieur Tranchelevent bowed in response.

"It is done," said the grandfather.

And, turning to Marius and Cosette, with arms extended, he cried, "Permission to adore each other."

He sat down near them and took their four hands in his old wrinkled ones. "She is exquisite, this darling. She is a masterpiece, this Cosette! My children, love each other. Be foolish about it. Love is the foolishness of men and the wisdom of God. Adore each other. Only," he added, suddenly darkening, "what a misfortune! Now that I think of it! More than half of what I have is in annuity; as long as I live, it's all well enough, but after my death, twenty or more years from now, my poor children, you will not have a penny."

"Mademoiselle Euphrasie Fauchelevent has six hundred thousand francs."

It was the voice of Jean Valjean.

Since he had entered he had not said a word. Nobody seemed to remember he was there, and he stood erect and motionless behind all these happy people.

"Mademoiselle Euphrasie?" asked the grandfather, startled.

"That's I," answered Cosette.

"Six hundred thousand francs!" continued M. Gillenormand.

"Less some thousands," said Jean Valjean.

And he placed on the table the package he had held. It was a bundle of banknotes. They counted them. In all five hundred and eighty-four thousand francs.

"Now there's a good book!" said M. Gillenormand.

"Five hundred eighty-four thousand francs!" murmured Mlle. Gillenormand in an undertone. "You might as well say six hundred thousand!"

Deposit Your Money in a Forest Rather Than Some Bank

The reader has no doubt figured out that Jean Valjean, thanks to his first escape after the Champmathieu affair, had come to Paris to withdraw from Lafitte's the money he had earned under the name of Monsieur Madeleine and that he had buried it in the forest at Montfermeil. The money, six hundred and thirty thousand francs, all in banknotes, was contained in an oaken chest full of chestnut shavings. In the same chest he had put the bishop's candlesticks. The man that Boulatruelle had seen the first time in the evening was Jean Valjean. Afterward, whenever he needed money, he would go to the forest for it. Hence his unexplained absences. When he saw that Marius was convalescing, he had sensed that the time was approaching when the money would be useful. He had gone to the forest and was again seen by Boulatruelle, but this time in the morning.

The real sum was five hundred and eighty-four thousand five hundred francs. Jean Valjean took out only five hundred for himself. "After that, we will see," he thought.

Two Old Men Do What They Can to Make Cosette Happy
All the preparations were made for the wedding. The doctor said that it could take place in February. This was December. Some weeks of happiness went by.

Not the least happy was Marius's grandfather. He remained for long periods of time gazing at Cosette.

Jean Valjean did everything he could to smooth things. He hurried toward Cosette's happiness with as much eagerness and joy as Cosette herself.

As he had been a mayor, he knew how to solve a problem, the secret he alone knew. To be blunt about her origins— who knows what could happen? It might prevent the marriage. So he took Cosette out of any difficulty. He arranged a family of dead people for her. Cosette became what remained of an extinct family; she was not his daughter, but the daughter of another Fauchelevent.

If Cosette had learned at another time that she was not the daughter of that man whom she had so long called father, it might have broken her heart. But now it was only a little shadow. She had Marius. The young man came; the good old man faded away. Such was life.

She continued, however, to say "father" when she spoke to Jean Valjean.

Cosette adored Grandfather Gillenormand. He

loaded her with songs and gifts. While Jean Valjean was building an identity acceptable to society for Cosette, M. Gillenormand concentrated on the wedding presents. Nothing amused him as much as being magnanimous. Every day a new offering arrived from the grandfather to Cosette.

As for Aunt Gillenormand, she took it all in stride. Within five or six months, she had had a number of emotions. Marius returned, Marius brought back bleeding, Marius from the barricade, Marius dead, Marius alive, Marius reconciled with his grandfather, Marius engaged, Marius marrying a pauper, Marius marrying a millionaire. She went regularly to church, said her prayers, and saw everyone else as shadows.

It was arranged that the couple would live with the grandfather. M. Gillenormand insisted that they have his room, which was the finest in the house. His library became Marius's law office, as the rules required.

Dreams Mingled with Happiness

The couple saw each other every day. Cosette came to the house with M. Fauchelevent, reversing the usual order of things partly out of consideration for Marius's condition.

Marius and M. Fauchelevent saw each other but did not speak. That seemed to be understood. Every girl needs a chaperone. Cosette could not have come to the house without M. Fauchelevent. To Marius, the man was the condition on which he got Cosette.

At times, Marius's recollections would overcome him. But in his memory there was a gap, a pit scooped out by four months of agony. Many things were lost in it. He asked himself if it were really true that he had seen M. Fauchelevent at the barricade. The past often crossed the twilight that filled his brain. He would see Mabeuf fall, would hear Gavroche singing under the hale of bullets. He felt again the chill of Eponine's brow against his lips; all his friends—Enjolras, Courfeyrac, Prouvaire, Combeferre, Bossuet, Grantaire—would rise up in front of him and then fade away. All these beings— were they dreams? Had they really existed? The revolt had covered everything in smoke. Was it true they were all dead? Everything except himself was gone. It seemed that he had passed into a tomb, that he had gone into it black and come out white. And in this tomb the others remained.

M. Fauchelevent almost had a place among the vanished. But Marius could not believe that the Fauchelevent of the barricade was the same as this man seated near Cosette. But each of their two natures showed a closed face to the other, and no question was possible from Marius to M. Fauchelevent. The idea did not even occur to him.

Two men have a common secret and they do not exchange a word on the subject; such a situation is less rare than one would think.

Two Men Impossible to Find

Marius's enchantment did not erase some other preoccupations from his mind. There was Thénardier and the unknown man who had brought him home.

None of the agents Marius hired was able to find any trace of Thénardier and his daughter Anzelma, the only two remaining members of that family. And as for the unknown man, the search stopped short. Marius learned only that the carriage had brought him on the orders of a policeman and that that policeman had paid him and then taken away another man, whom he did not remember.

There was a man whom Marius was seeking. But of this man, who was his savior, nothing. No trace, not the least hint.

5   *The White Night*

February 16, 1833

The day of February 16 of 1833 was a blessed day. The heavens were open; it was the wedding day of Marius and Cosette.

The previous evening, Jean Valjean had handed to Marius, in the presence of M. Gillenormand, the dowry money for Cosette. And since he had no further need for Toussaint, Cosette inherited her as lady's maid.

As for Jean Valjean, there was a beautiful room in the house furnished expressly for him, and Cosette had said to him so irresistibly, "Father, I beg you," that she had almost made him promise to come and stay in it.

A few days before the wedding, an accident happened to Jean Valjean; he slightly crushed the thumb of his right hand. It was not serious, but he allowed nobody to bandage or touch it—not even Cosette. It forced him, however, to wrap the hand in a bandage and carry his arm in a sling. He was unable to sign anything; M. Gillenormand, as Cosette's temporary guardian, took his place.

The Arm Still in a Sling

The wedding took place at the church of Saint-Paul and the reception at M. Gillenormand's.

Cosette was luminous and touching. Marius's hair was gleaming, and only here and there could be glimpsed under the locks the pale scars from his wounds. The grandfather was superb, his head held

high, taking the place of Jean Valjean who, his arm
still in the sling, could not give his arm to the bride.
Jean Valjean, dressed in black, followed and smiled.

People stopped in front of the church to see,
through the carriage window, the orange blossoms
trembling on Cosette's head.

Then they returned to Rue des Filles du Calvaire,
to their home. Marius and Cosette, radiant and tri-
umphant, climbed the staircase Marius had been carried up while dying. There were flowers everywhere.

A good number of old friends of the Gillenormands
had been invited. They surrounded Cosette and vied
with one another to call her Madame the Baronne.

The officer Théodule Gillenormand had come from
Chartres to attend the wedding of his cousin
Pontmercy. Cosette did not recognize him.

Cosette exhaled love and kindness like a perfume.
The truly happy wish everyone happiness.

She spoke to Jean Valjean in the tone of her childhood. She caressed him with smiles. In the anteroom,
three violins and a flute played softly some Haydn
quartets.

Jean Valjean sat in a chair in the drawing room,
which folded back on him so as almost to hide him.
Basque came to announce dinner. The guests, preced-
ed by M. Gillenormand, giving his arm to Cosette,
entered the dining room and took their places around
the table. Two armchairs were placed to the right and
left of the bride, the first for M. Gillenormand and the
second for Jean Valjean. M. Gillenormand took his
seat. The other remained empty.

All eyes sought "Monsieur Fauchelevent."

"Monsieur," said Basque, "M. Fauchelevent asked
me to say that he was suffering a little from his sore
hand and could not dine with Monsieur the Baron and

Madame the Baronne. He begged that they excuse him, that he would come tomorrow morning. He has just left."

For a moment, his absence chilled the enthusiasm of the wedding dinner. But if one "father" was absent, the other was beaming enough for two. He quickly suggested that Marius take the empty chair, to applause of the whole table. Cosette, at first saddened by Jean Valjean's absence, was finally satisfied with it. On that day, Cosette could be forgiven for thinking only of Marius.

The evening was delightful. The good humor of the grandfather set the mood for the whole gathering. They danced a little; they laughed a great deal. It was a fine wedding.

The Inseparable

What had become of Jean Valjean?

Jean Valjean went home. He lit his candle and went upstairs. The apartment was empty. He went to Cosette's room. There remained only the heavy furniture and the four walls.

Then he found his own room. Only a single bed was made and waiting for him. He had released his arm from the sling, and he was using his right hand with no effort. He went to the bed, and his eye fell on the little case, on the inseparable of which Cosette had been jealous, on the thing that never left him. From his pocket he took a key, and he opened the case.

Slowly he took out the clothes in which, ten years before, Cosette had left Montfermeil. First the little dress, then the knitted petticoat, then the apron with pockets, then the wool stockings. As he lifted them out of the case, he placed them carefully on the bed. He was thinking. He was remembering.

Then his venerable white head fell on the bed; his stoic heart broke. Anyone who had passed along the staircase at that moment would have heard terrible sobbing.

The Last Struggle

How should Jean Valjean behave in regard to the happiness of Marius and Cosette? It was he who had willed the happiness; it was he who had made it possible. He had driven it into his own heart.

Cosette had Marius; Marius possessed Cosette. They had everything, even riches. And he had seen to it.

But, now that this happiness existed, what was he to do with it—he, Jean Valjean? Should he impose himself on this happiness? Should he treat it as belonging to him? Should he introduce himself quietly into Cosette's house? Should he present himself there as if he had a right to take a seat at that hearth? Should he place at that peaceful hearth the feet that dragged after them the infamous shadow of the law? Should he continue to be quiet?

Cosette was the raft of this shipwreck. Should he hang on or let go?

If he clung to it, he escaped disaster, he was saved, he lived. If he let go? The pit.

At last, Jean Valjean entered the calm of despair.

What solution did he come to? What door did he decide to open? Which side of his life did he decide to close and to condemn? What extremity did he accept?

His whirling thoughts continued all night.

He remained there until dawn, in the same position, doubled over on the bed and arms outstretched. He stayed there for twelve hours, chilled, without lifting his head, without uttering a word. To see him like this, one would have thought him dead. Suddenly he moved, and he kissed little Cosette's garments; then one saw that he was alive.

What *one*—since Jean Valjean was alone and there was nobody else there?

6 *The Last Drop in the Chalice*

Revelation

The day after the wedding, it was a little after noon when Basque heard a light rap on the door. He opened it and saw M. Fauchelevent, whom he led into the drawing room.

"Oh, monsieur," observed Basque, "we are waking up late."

"Is your master up?" inquired Jean Valjean.

"How is monsieur's arm?" inquired Basque.

"Better. Is your new master up?"

"Monsieur the Baron?" said Basque, drawing himself up to his height. One is a baron to his servants above all. "I will go and see. I will tell him Monsieur Fauchelevent is here."

"No. Do not tell him it is I. Tell him that somebody would like to speak with him in private, and do not give any name."

"Ah!" said Basque, and he went off.

Jean Valjean did not move from the spot where Basque left him. He was very pale. His eyes were so sunken from lack of sleep that they could barely be seen.

Marius entered, head up, his mouth smiling.

"It is you, Father!" he exclaimed. That idiot of a Basque with his mysterious air! But you are too early. It is still only twelve twenty. Cosette is asleep."

Marius had used the word "father." He had reached the level of happiness where the barrier between the two men was falling and M. Fauchelevent was to him, as to Cosette, a father. He continued, "How glad I am to see you! If you knew how we missed you yesterday! How is your hand? Better, I hope?"

Satisfied with the reply he had made himself, he went on, "We have talked about you a great deal. Cosette loves you so much! You will not forget your room is here. Come and settle in today. Or you will have to deal with Cosette. She intends to lead us all by the nose, I warn you. I believe there is a little case you treasure. I have selected a place of honor for it. You have won over my grandfather. You will take Cosette out for a walk on my court days. You'll give her your arm as you used to at the Luxembourg. We have positively decided to be very happy. And you are part of our happiness. Do you understand, Father?"

"Monsieur," said Jean Valjean, "I have one thing to tell you. I am a former convict."

Marius did not hear. He did not know what had just been said to him. He was aghast.

He then noticed that the man talking to him was terrifying. He had not noticed his frightful pallor until this moment.

Jean Valjean went on, "Monsieur Pontmercy, I spent nineteen years in prison. For robbery. Then I was sentenced for life. I escaped. At this moment, I am illegally free."

"Tell me everything!" Marius cried. "You are Cosette's father!"

"You will believe me. I, the father of Cosette? Before God, no. Monsieur Baron Pontmercy, my name is not Fauchelevent; my name is Jean Valjean. I am nothing to Cosette. Rest assured."

"I believe you," said Marius. "But what compels you to tell me this? You could have kept this secret.

You are not denounced, or pursued, or hunted. You have some reason for this revelation. Tell me the rest. What is your motive?"

"Well, yes," said Jean Valjean in a voice so low one would have said he was speaking to himself, "the motive is strange. It is from honor. You have offered me a room in this house. Cosette loves me, and your grandfather says I suit him. We will have just one roof, one table, one fire in winter, one stroll in summer; that is joy, that is happiness, that is everything. We will live as one family."

At the word "family," Jean Valjean grew wild.

"You ask what compels me to speak. Strange thing. My conscience. Yet to keep silent was very easy. I have spent the night persuading myself to do this. It was not an easy decision. To keep on being M. Fauchelevent would have smoothed the way for everything. There was joy everywhere. Except in my soul. In the presence of this cheerfulness I would have been an enigma, a darkness in your bright day. I would have looked at Cosette and answered the smile of an angel with the smile of the damned. And what for? To be happy! To be happy—I? Have I any right to be happy? I am outside of life, monsieur."

He drew a breath with difficulty and forced out these final words:

"Once, to live, I stole a loaf of bread. Today, to live, I will not steal a name."

"To live," interrupted Marius. "You don't need that name to live!"

"Ah! I know what you mean," answered Jean Valjean, nodding several times.

There was a pause. Both men were silent, each sunk in thought. Jean Valjean was pacing back and forth. Then he turned toward Marius:

"Monsieur, picture this. I have taken my place in your house. We all are happy, we are together, you suppose me an equal. We are chatting and laughing, and suddenly you hear a voice shout: 'Jean Valjean.' And you see the appalling hand spring out of the shadows and abruptly tear off my mask!"

Marius answered with silence.

"You see I am right in not keeping quiet," Jean Valjean continued.

Marius crossed the room and stretched out a hand to Jean Valjean.

"My grandfather has friends. I will procure a pardon for you."

"That would be useless," answered Jean Valjean. "They think I am dead as it is. And besides, to do my duty is the friend I need. And I need the pardon of only one—my conscience."

"Poor Cosette!" Marius murmured. "When she finds out—"

At these words, Jean Valjean trembled. He looked at Marius, concerned.

"Cosette! Oh, yes, that's true. You will tell Cosette; that's fair. Well, I had not thought of that. Monsieur, I beg of you; don't tell her. Isn't it enough that you know? She doesn't know what this means. A convict! You would have to explain it to her, to tell her. Oh, my God!"

He sank into an armchair, and one could see from the shaking of his shoulders that he was weeping. Marius heard him murmur, "Oh, I would like to die!"

"Don't worry," said Marius. "I will keep your secret to myself."

"Thank you, monsieur," answered Jean Valjean softly.

He thought for a moment and then stammered,

"Now that you know this, do you think it is best I should not see Cosette again?"

"I think that would be best," answered Marius coldly.

Jean Valjean walked toward the door. He placed his hand on the latch, and the door began to swing. Then he stopped, shut the door, and turned toward Marius.

He was no longer pale; he was livid. His voice had regained that strange calmness.

"But, monsieur," he said, "if you are willing, I will come to see her. I assure you that I want that very much. If I had not wanted to see Cosette, I would not have made the admission I made. But wishing to continue to see Cosette, I was compelled in all honesty to tell you everything. You see my reasoning, don't you? For nine years, I have had her near me. I was her father, and she was my child. I don't know whether you understand me, Monsieur Pontmercy, but not to see her again, not to speak to her, to have nothing left—that would be hard. I will come from time to time to see Cosette. I will not come often. I will not stay long. I can be received on the ground floor. I will come as rarely as you like. Put yourself in my place; she is all I have. And then, we must be careful. If I were not to come at all, it would look strange. For instance, I can come in the evening, at nightfall."

"You will come every evening," said Marius, "and Cosette will expect you."

"You are kind, monsieur," said Jean Valjean.

Marius bowed to Jean Valjean. Happiness conducted despair to the door, and the two men separated.

7 *The Twilight Wanes*

The Basement Room

The next day, at nightfall, Jean Valjean knocked at the Gillenormand carriage gate. Basque let him in and addressed him as follows:

"Monsieur the Baron told me to ask monsieur if he prefers to go up or stay down."

"Stay down," answered Jean Valjean.

Basque, absolutely respectful, opened the door of the ground-floor room and said, "I will inform madame."

The room was damp, used as a storeroom when necessary. A fire had been lit, which seemed to indicate someone had anticipated Jean Valjean's answer.

Cosette entered the room. Jean Valjean looked at her. She was beautiful, but what he looked at was her soul.

"Well!" exclaimed Cosette. "Father, I know you are odd, but I would never have thought of this. What an idea! Marius says you wish me to receive you here."

"Yes."

"What have I done to you? I declare I am confused. You owe me amends. You will have dinner with us."

"I have already had my dinner."

"That is not true. Go up to the drawing room with me now."

"Madame, you know I am peculiar. I have my whims."

"Madame! That's new. What does this mean,

Father?"

"Don't call me father anymore."

"Why not?"

"Call me Monsieur Jean. Jean, if you like."

"I don't understand any of this. It's all nonsense. I'll ask my husband's permission for you to be Monsieur Jean. I hope he won't agree to it. I am furious. Since yesterday you all make me rage. I don't understand. I arrange a room nicely for you. If I could have put the good Lord into it, I would have. You leave me with the room. And my father, Fauchelevent, wants me to call him Monsieur Jean and to receive him in a moldy, hideous old cellar. What do you have against me?"

And, growing very serious, she looked fixedly at Jean Valjean and added, "So you don't like it that I am happy?"

Jean Valjean paled. For a moment he did not answer; then, talking to himself, he murmured, "Her happiness was the aim of my life. Cosette, you are happy; my time is done."

"You called me Cosette!" she exclaimed and threw her arms around his neck.

"Thank you, Father," said Cosette to him.

He gently took Cosette's arms away and took his hat.

"I will leave you, madame," he said. "They are waiting for you."

And from the door, he added, "I called you Cosette. Tell your husband that it will not happen again. Pardon me." Then he went out, leaving Cosette astounded at his farewell.

Other Backward Steps

Every succeeding evening Jean Valjean came at the

same time. He came every evening, taking Marius's words to the letter. Marius always managed to be out when Jean Valjean came.

Several weeks passed this way. A new life gradually took over Cosette. Cosette's pleasure consisted of a single one: being with Marius. Going out with him, staying at home with him—this was the great occupation of her life. It was a happiness still new to them— to go out arm in arm, in full daylight, in the open street, without hiding, all alone with each other. Cosette had one problem: Toussaint could not get along with Nicolette, so she went away. The grandfather was in good health; Marius argued a few cases now and then. Aunt Gillenormand calmly led a life separate from the new household. Jean Valjean came to see her every day.

One day, she suddenly said to him, "You were my father, you are no longer my father; you were my uncle, you are no longer my uncle; you were Monsieur Fauchelevent, you are Jean. So who are you? I don't like all that. If I didn't know you so well, I would be afraid of you."

They Remember the Garden in the Rue Plumet

To see Cosette every day satisfied Jean Valjean. His whole life was concentrated in that hour. He sat by her side in silence, or he talked to her about the past— of her childhood or the convent or her friends of those days.

One afternoon—it was an early day in April that was already warm and fresh, the season of cheerfulness in the sunshine—Marius said to Cosette, "We have said we would go to see our garden in the Rue Plumet again. Let's go." And they flew away like two swallows in the spring. When Jean Valjean arrived for his visit, Cosette was not home.

Cosette was so happy with her walk to "the garden" and so happy about having "lived a whole day in her past" that she did not speak of anything else the next day. It did not occur to her that she had not seen Jean Valjean.

"How did you get there?" Jean Valjean asked.

"We walked."

For some time, Jean Valjean had noticed the frugal life the young couple led.

He probed: "You ought to have a house of your own, servants of your own, a carriage, a box at the theater. There is nothing too good for you. Why not take advantage of your riches? Riches add to happiness."

Cosette did not answer.

One day he stayed longer than usual. The next day there was no fire in the fireplace.

"Goodness! How cold it is!" said Cosette.

"I told Basque not to make a fire," Jean Valjean said. "It is almost May."

The next day there was a fire. But the two armchairs were placed near the door. "What does that mean?" thought Jean Valjean.

As he was getting up to leave, Cosette said to him, "My husband said a funny thing yesterday."

"What was it?"

"He said, 'Cosette, we have an income of thirty thousand francs. Twenty-seven that you have, three that my grandfather gives me.' I answered, 'That makes thirty.' 'Would you have the courage to live on only three thousand?' I answered, 'Yes—on nothing. Provided it is with you. Why do you ask?' He answered, 'Just to know.'"

Jean Valjean did not say a word. He walked home racked with conjectures. Marius had perhaps discovered that this money came from him, Jean Valjean, and hesitated to take a suspicious fortune as his own, preferring to remain poor rather than to be rich with a doubtful wealth.

Beyond that, Jean Valjean was getting the impression that he was being shown the way to the door.

The next day, on entering the ground-floor room, he was shocked. The chairs had disappeared. There was not a chair of any kind.

"Ah, now," exclaimed Cosette, "no chairs! Where are the chairs?"

"I believe that Basque needed them for the salon."

Cosette shrugged. "To have the chairs taken away! The other day you had the fire put out. How strange!"

He went away overwhelmed. But he understood.

The next day he did not come.

Cosette didn't notice until the next morning, when she sent Nicolette to see if Monsieur Jean was sick. Nicolette brought back word that he was not sick. He was busy. He would come very soon. As soon as he could. However, he was going on a short trip. Cosette should not worry.

Attraction and Extinction

During the last months of the spring and the first months of the summer in 1833, an old man dressed in black, every day about the same time, at nightfall, came out of the Rue de l'Homme Armé. He walked slowly, his head forward, seeing nothing, hearing nothing, his eye fixed always on one point, always the same. It was nothing more or less than the corner of the Rue des Filles du Calvaire. As he approached the corner, his eyes lit up and he had a fascinated and soft expression. His lips moved slightly, as if he were speaking to someone whom he did not see. He smiled, and he moved as slowly as he could. You would have said that even while wanting to reach some destination he dreaded the moment when he would be near it. At last he reached the street; then he stopped. A tear, which had gathered in the corner of his eye and grown large enough to fall, slid down his cheek and sometimes stopped at his mouth. The old man tasted the bitterness. He stayed like that a few moments, then he returned by the same route and at the same pace.

Little by little, the old man stopped going as far as the corner. One day, he stopped and looked at the street from a distance. He shook his head as if refusing himself something, and he went home.

The women of the district said, "He is an innocent." But the children followed him, laughing.

Supreme Shadow, Supreme Dawn

Indulgence for the Happy

It is terrible to be happy! How all-sufficient we think it is! Being in possession of the false aim of life, happiness, we forget the true aim: duty!

We must say it would be unfair to blame Marius! Marius did what he thought necessary and just. He supposed that he had serious reasons for keeping Jean Valjean away—reasons which we have already seen and still others which we shall see later on. Having chanced to meet a former clerk of Lafitte, he had received some mysterious information which he could not probe to the bottom out of respect for the secret he had promised to keep. He believed that he had a solemn duty to make restitution of the six hundred thousand francs. In the meantime, he refrained from using it.

As for Cosette, she was in on none of the secrets, but it would be wrong to condemn her, too. It sometimes happened that Cosette spoke of Jean Valjean and wondered. Then Marius would calm her by saying, "Didn't he say he was going off on a trip?" Cosette would think, "That is true. He was in the habit of disappearing this way. But not for so long." Two or three times she sent Nicolette to ask if Monsieur Jean had returned. The word came back that he had not.

Marius had, little by little, drawn Cosette away from Jean Valjean. Cosette was passive.

Youth goes where joy is. Old age goes to its end.

They do not lose sight of each other, but the ties are loosened. We must not blame these poor children.

The Last Flickering of the Exhausted Lamp

One day Jean Valjean went downstairs, took three steps into the street, and sat down on a stone block. It was the same block where Gavroche found him on the 5th of June. He stayed there a few minutes; then he went upstairs again. The next day he did not leave his room. The day after that, he did not leave his bed.

A week elapsed, and Jean Valjean had not taken a step in his room. He was still in bed.

The concierge saw a doctor going by in the street. She took it upon herself to ask him to go up.

"It is on the third floor," she said to him. "You can simply walk in. Since the good man doesn't stir from his bed now, the key is in the door all the time."

The doctor saw Jean Valjean and spoke with him. When he came down, the old woman questioned him: "Well, doctor?"

"Your old man is very sick."

"What's the matter with him?"

"Everything and nothing. He is a man who, to all appearances, has lost some dear friend. People die of that."

The Pen Is Heavy

One evening Jean Valjean had difficulty getting up on his elbow. He felt his wrist and found no pulse. But, under some great desire, he sat up in bed and got dressed.

He opened the valise and took out Cosette's clothing. He spread it on the bed.

The bishop's candlesticks were in their place on the mantel.

Night had fallen. He drew a table and an old armchair near the fireplace, and he put on the table pen, ink, and paper.

Then he fainted. When he came to, he was thirsty. He tipped the water pitcher toward his mouth and drank a swallow.

His hand trembled. He slowly wrote a few lines:

> *Cosette, I bless you. I am going to explain something. Your husband was quite right in making me understand that I ought to leave. While there is some mistake in what he believed. . . .*

Here the pen fell from his fingers, and he gave way to one of those sobs that rose from the depths of his being.

"Oh!" he cried. "It is all over. Forever. Here I am all alone. My God! I shall never see her again."

At that moment there was a knock on the door.

The Bottle of Ink Serves to Whiten

That very day, just as Marius was leaving the table on his way to his office with a folder of papers, Basque handed him a letter, saying, "The person who wrote that letter is in the anteroom.[1]"

The scent, the mystery, revived a whole world within him. The very paper, the way of folding, the paleness of the ink— it was certainly the well-known handwriting. Above all there was the tobacco. The Jondrette garret appeared before him.

He broke the seal and read:

---

1. **anteroom** a small room outside a larger one, such as a waiting room

Monsieur Baron,— I am in possession of a secret con-
serning an individual. This individual conserns you.
I hold the secret at your disposition, desiring to have
the honor of being yuseful to you. I will give you the
simple means of drivving it from your honorable family
this individual who has no right to it.

I await in the entichamber the orders of Monsieur
the Baron. —With respect,

Thénard

Basque announced, "Monsieur Thénard."

A man entered. He was completely unknown to
Marius. He had a large nose, his chin tucked into his
tie, and green glasses with a double shade of silk over
them. His hair was gray, smooth, and slicked down.
He was dressed in black from head to toe, and he held
an old hat in his hand.

Marius's disappointment on seeing the man turned
into dislike. "What do you want?" he asked sharply.

"Monsieur Baron, please listen to me. In America,
near Panama, there is a village called Lajoya. I would
like to go there and establish myself. There are three
of us: myself, my wife, and my daughter, a beautiful
young lady. The voyage is long and expensive. I must
have a little money."

"How does that concern me?" inquired Marius.

"I will explain. I have a secret to tell you."

"Go on."

"Monsieur Baron, you have in your house a robber
and an assassin. This man has slipped into your confidence and almost into your family under a false
name. I am going to tell you his true name. And tell
it to you for nothing."

"I am listening."

"His name is Jean Valjean."

"I know that."

"I am also going to tell you, for nothing, who he is."

"Go on."

"He is a former convict."

"I know that."

"Monsieur Baron, say ten thousand francs, and I will go on."

"I repeat that you have no news to tell me. I know what you want to tell me."

"It's an extraordinary secret, I tell you. I am going to speak, Monsieur Baron. I will speak. Give me twenty francs."

"I know your extraordinary secret, just as I knew Jean Valjean's name and just as I know your name."

"That is not difficult, Monsieur Baron. I have had the honor of giving it to you in writing and telling it to you. It is Thénard."

"Dier."

"Eh?"

"Thénardier."

"Who is that?"

Marius went on, "You are also the man Jondrette, the comedian Fabantou, the poet Genflot. And you kept a shabby inn at Montfermeil."

"Never!"

"And I tell you you are Thénardier."

Marius took a banknote from his pocket and threw it in his face.

"Thanks! Pardon! Five hundred francs! Monsieur Baron!"

And with the agility of a monkey, he pulled off his spectacles, brushed back his hair, and, in other words, took off his face as one takes off a hat.

"Monsieur Baron is correct," he said in a clear voice. "I am Thénardier."

Marius spoke.

"Thénardier, I have told you your name. Now your secret—do you want me to tell you that, too? You will see that I know more about it than you do. Jean Valjean, as you have said, is an assassin and a robber. A robber because he robbed a rich manufacturer, M. Madeleine. An assassin because he assassinated the police officer Javert."

"I don't understand, Monsieur Baron," said Thénardier. "You are on the wrong track."

"What?" replied Marius. "Are you denying this? These are facts."

"They are fantasies. It is my duty to tell you so. I do not like to see people accused unjustly. Monsieur Baron, Jean Valjean never robbed Monsieur Madeleine, and Jean Valjean never killed Javert. He did not rob Monsieur Madeleine since it was Jean Valjean himself who was Monsieur Madeleine. And he did not assassinate Javert since Javert killed himself."

"What do you mean?"

"That Javert committed suicide."

"Prove it!" cried Marius.

"I have documents," he said calmly. And he took out some newspaper articles that were yellow, faded, and saturated with tobacco.

Marius read. Here was evidence, dates, unquestionable proof. Marius could not doubt it. Jean Valjean was suddenly elevated. Marius gave a shout of joy.

"Well then, this unhappy person is a wonderful man. That whole fortune was really his own. He is Madeleine! He is Jean Valjean, the saviour of Javert! He is a hero! A saint!"

"He is not a saint, and he is not a hero," said Thénardier. "He is a robber and an assassin. He did not rob Madeleine, but he is a robber. He did not kill Javert, but he is a murderer."

"I could interrupt you here," said Marius, "but go on."

"Monsieur Baron, on the sixth of June, 1832, about a year ago, the day of the revolt, a man was in the Great Sewer of Paris. The man, compelled to conceal himself, had taken the sewer as a dwelling and had a key to it. That night, the man heard a noise. He hid and watched; somebody was coming in his direction. A man was approaching, and that man was carrying something on his back. The man was a former convict, and what he was carrying was a corpse. As for robbery, it hardly needs explaining. Nobody kills a man for nothing. This convict was going to throw his corpse into the river."

"When two men are in a sewer, they must meet each other. This is what happened. The traveler said to the resident, 'You see what I have on my back. I must get it out. You have the key. Let's make a deal.' The one who had the key stalled for time. He examined the dead man and managed to cut and tear off a piece of the victim's coat. A piece of evidence, you understand. Now you understand. The one carrying the corpse was Jean Valjean; the one who had the key is speaking to you, and the piece of coat—"

Thénardier finished the sentence by holding up a strip of ragged black cloth covered with dark stains.

Marius had stood up, pale and hardly breathing, his eye fixed on the scrap of cloth. With his right hand he groped behind him for a key to unlock the closet near the fireplace. He found it, opened the closet, and

reached into it without looking away from the fragment that Thénardier held up.

"The young man was myself, and there is the coat!"
cried Marius, and he threw an old black coat covered
with stains onto the carpet.

Then, snatching the fragment from Thénardier's
hands, he bent down and applied the piece to the hem.
The edges fitted exactly.

Thénardier was petrified.

Marius stood up, desperate and radiant.

He felt in his pocket and walked furiously toward
Thénardier, brandishing a fist full of money.

"You are a liar and a crook. It is you who are the
thief. It is you who are the assassin. I saw you,
Jondrette Thénardier, in your den at the Gorbeau
House. I know enough about you to send you to
prison and further, if I wanted to. Here are a thousand francs, you braggart. Take these and leave this
place!"

Two days after these events, Thénardier left for
America under a false name, with his daughter
Anzelma.

As soon as Thénardier had left the room, Marius
ran to the garden where Cosette was walking.

"Cosette!" he cried. "Come! Come quickly! We must
go. Basque, a carriage! Cosette, come on. Oh! God! It
was he who saved my life. Let us not lose a moment."

Cosette thought he had gone mad.

In a minute the carriage arrived. Marius helped
Cosette in and jumped in himself.

"Driver," he said, "Rue de l'Homme Armé, Number
Seven."

"Oh! What happiness!" cried Cosette. "I did not
dare to speak of it again. We are going to see
Monsieur Jean!"

"Your father! Cosette, your father more than ever. Cosette! He carried me through the frightful sewer. I had fainted. I heard nothing. I saw nothing. He snatched me out of the abyss to be with you. We are going to bring him back, take him with us, whether he wants it or not. He will never leave us again. If only we can find him!"

Night Behind Which Is Dawn

At the knock on his door, Jean Valjean turned his head.

"Come in," he said feebly.

The door opened, and Cosette and Marius appeared.

Cosette rushed in. Marius remained at the threshold, leaning against the door casing.

"Father!" she cried.

Jean Valjean, beside himself, stammered, "Cosette! She? You, madame? Is it you, Cosette? Oh, my!"

Clasped in Cosette's arms, he exclaimed, "You, Cosette? You are here. You forgive me?"

Marius, dropping his eyes so the tears would not fall, stepped forward and murmured, "Father!"

"And you, too, you forgive me!" said Jean Valjean.

Jean Valjean faltered, "How foolish we are! I thought I would never see her again. Only think, Monsieur Pontmercy, that at the moment you came in, I was saying to myself: 'It is all over. There is her little dress. I am a miserable man; I will never see Cosette again.' I was as silly as that! But then the angel comes, and I see my Cosette again!"

"Cosette, do you hear?" said Marius. "That is the way with him. He saved my life, and more. He has given you to me, and what did he do with himself? He sacrificed himself. Every courage, every virtue, every heroism—he has all these, Cosette. The man is an angel!"

"Hush, hush!" said Jean Valjean in a whisper.

"No," replied Marius. "You slander yourself. It is frightful. You did not tell the whole truth. You were Monsieur Madeleine; why have you not said so? You saved Javert, why have you not said so? I owe my life to you; why have you not said so?"

"Because I thought as you did. I felt that you were right. It was necessary for me to go away. If you had known of the business in the sewer, you would have insisted I stay with you. I would have had to keep silent. If I had spoken, it would have embarrassed everyone."

"Embarrassed whom?" replied Marius. "Do you think you are going to stay here? When I think it is only by accident that I discovered it all! We are taking you back. You are a part of us. You are her father and mine. Do not imagine that you will be here tomorrow!"

"Tomorrow," said Jean Valjean, "I will not be here, but I will not be at your house. It is a pity."

Cosette took the old man's hand in hers.

"My God!" she said. "Your hands are still colder. Are you suffering?"

"No," answered Jean Valjean. "It is only—I will die in a little while."

Cosette and Marius shuddered.

"Die?" exclaimed Marius.

"But it is nothing," said Jean Valjean.

He breathed and smiled.

There was a noise at the door. It was the doctor arriving.

Marius approached him and addressed a single word, "Monsieur?" but in his way of pronouncing it, there was a complete question.

The doctor shook his head and said, close to Marius's ear, "Too late."

Jean Valjean seemed to gather strength. Suddenly he stood up. He took a fold of Cosette's sleeve and kissed it.

"He is reviving, Doctor! He is reviving!" cried Marius.

"You are both kind," said Jean Valjean. "I will tell you what has given me pain, Monsieur Pontmercy— was that you would not use that money. It really belongs to your wife. Cosette's fortune is her own."

The concierge had come to see Jean Valjean. "Do you want a priest?" she asked.

"I have one," answered Jean Valjean. And with a finger, he pointed to a spot above his head, where you would say he had seen someone.

It is probable that the bishop was, along with Cosette and Marius, a witness at this death.

Jean Valjean's face grew pale, and his breath died away. He called Cosette, then Marius, to approach. It was the last moment of the last hour, and he began to speak to them in a voice so faint it seemed to come from far away.

"Cosette, the time has come to know the name of your mother. It was Fantine. Remember that name. She suffered a great deal. And she loved you very much. Such are the distributions of God. He is on high. He sees us all. So I am going away, my children. Love each other dearly always. There is scarcely anything else in this world but that: to love one another."

"My children, do not forget that I am a poor man; you will have me buried in the most convenient spot of ground under a stone to mark the spot. That is my wish. No name on the stone. If Cosette will come for a visit sometimes, it will give me pleasure. You, too,

Monsieur Pontmercy. I confess I did not always love you; I ask your pardon. Now she and you are one to me. I am so grateful to you for making Cosette happy."

Cosette and Marius fell on their knees, overwhelmed and choked with tears, each holding one of Jean Valjean's hands. He fell back and looked up to heaven. He was dead.

Grass Conceals and Rain Blots Out

In the Pere Lachaise cemetery there is a stone. The stone is not exempt from the ravages of time, from the mold, from the moss, and from the bird droppings. The air turns it black; the water turns it green. It is near no path, and people do not like to go in that direction because the grass is high and they wet their feet. When there is sunshine, the lizards come out. In spring, the linnets come to sing in the trees.

The stone is entirely blank. The only thought in cutting it was of the essentials of the grave, and there was no care except to make the stone long enough and narrow enough to cover a man.

No name can be read there. Only many years ago a hand wrote on it in pencil these lines, which gradually became illegible under the rain and the dust and are probably gone by now:

> *He sleeps. Although fate was strange to him.*
> *He lived. He died when he lost his angel.*
> *It happened as simply as*
> *the night comes when the day is done.*

REVIEWING

YOUR

READING

BOOK 1: FANTINE

Chapters 1-4

FINDING THE MAIN IDEA

1. Which of the following behaviors did the Bishop demonstrate?

   a) gave money to the needy   b) was not attached to material things   c) respected all living things   d) all of these

REMEMBERING DETAILS

2. Jean Valjean stole a loaf of bread because:

   a) he became a hardened criminal   b) he needed to eat
   c) the baker was stingy   d) his sister's family had no food.

3. Jean Valjean had money when he arrived at Digne because:

   a) he had earned it   b) he had robbed some people
   c) he had hidden it away   d) the bishop gave it to him.

4. One of the special traits that Jean Valjean had was that he:

   a) slept lightly   b) was kind   c) was strong   d) was calm.

5. Fantine had to leave Cosette with the Thénardiers because:

   a) she was going to find work   b) she had no money
   c) she liked the Thénardiers   d) she didn't want her any more.

DRAWING CONCLUSIONS

6. Jean Valjean concluded that "life was a war and that he was defeated." This feeling shows the way he:

   a) thought about his sister   b) tried to escape   c) acted at the bishop's   d) practiced exercises.

USING YOUR REASON

7. Jean Valjean was sentenced to five years on the chain gang. However, he served nineteen years because:

   a) they found additional evidence   b) Javert caught him
   c) he refused to eat   d) he tried to escape.

8. Fantine did not take the affair with Tholomyès as lightly as the other girls because:

   a) she was not a bourgeoise   b) she loved him   c) she was a bourgeoise   d) she did not like surprises.

9. Fantine's leaving her child with the Thénardiers was good luck for them. The benefits they enjoyed included:
a) that she sang like a lark   b) that the girls got to have another playmate   c) that she did work for them.   d) all of these

THINKING IT OVER

10. Victor Hugo makes a distinction between anger and outrage. He says: "a person does not feel outraged unless, in some way, he is fundamentally right." Find evidence from the text to illustrate why Jean Valjean might have felt outraged and not just angry.

Chapters 5-8

FINDING THE MAIN IDEA

1. The reader suspects, then knows, that Monsieur Madeleine is Jean Valjean. Some clues that the author gives include:
a) Jean Valjean had had experience with glass beads
b) M. Madeleine mourned the bishop's death   c) Javert was in the town   d) M. Madeleine saved Fantine's life.

REMEMBERING DETAILS

2. The stranger had arrived in Montreuil-sur-mer and dramatically improved the economy in the town by:
a) building new houses   b) becoming the mayor
c) inventing new techniques for making beads   d) giving money to the workers.

3. M. Madeleine was able to save Father Fauchelevent because:
a) Javert got a jack   b) he knew about wagon construction
c) he was clever   d) he was strong.

4. M. Madeleine saved Fantine from Javert because:
a) she had worked for him   b) she needed help   c) Javert was cruel.   d) all of these

5. Javert wrote to the Prefecture of Police in Paris in order to:
a) resign his post   b) condemn M. Madeleine as a criminal   c) complain about M. Madeleine.   d) none of these

6. During the time that M. Madeleine was away at Arras, something happened.
a) Fantine died.   b) Cosette disappeared.   c) Javert resigned.   d) His hair turned white.

DRAWING CONCLUSIONS

7. When Jean Valjean heard of Champmathieu's arrest, he knew that "all he had to do was leave things alone." In other words, he could:
a) let Champmathieu get convicted   b) stay at Digne
c) forget Fantine   d) let Javert find him.

USING YOUR REASON

8. Sister Simplice lied to protect M. Madeleine. Her motivation could have been that:
a) she did not like Javert   b) she worried about what would happen to Fantine   c) she thought M. Madeleine was a good man   d) she was not subject to the laws of the police.

9. The judge and the prosecuting attorney did not arrest Jean Valjean on the spot probably because:
a) he had confessed   b) they believed that Champmathieu was guilty   c) they knew and respected M. Madeleine
d) they couldn't arrest two people for the same crime.

THINKING IT OVER

10. Jean Valjean whispered to Fantine as she died. What might he have said to her? Find some evidence from the text to support your conclusion.

BOOK 2: COSETTE

Chapters 1-2

FINDING THE MAIN IDEA

1. The reader knows that Jean Valjean left town before he was captured, and that Boulatruelle did see something strange. From these events, we can conclude that Jean Valjean:

   a) was recaptured right away   b) did not outwit Javert
   c) joined the navy   d) buried some money.

2. M. Thénardier asked for Jean Valjean's passport probably so:

   a) he could explain to Fantine   b) he would be able to locate Jean Valjean   c) he could visit Cosette   d) he could write to Cosette.

REMEMBERING DETAILS

3. One reason for concluding that the sailor on the ship was Jean Valjean, even before reading the newspaper report, is that:

   a) the sailor had white hair   b) the sailor was very strong
   c) the sailor was a convict.   d) any of these

4. Which of these was not a way Thénardier thought of Cosette?

   a) useful   b) hard-working   c) ugly   d) deserving

5. Cosette was terrified to go for water, probably because:
   a) she was afraid of the dark   b) it was too hard to do
   c) it was too far to go   d) she had no warm clothes.

6. Thénardier spent a long time making out Jean Valjean's bill so that:

   a) he could be sure the math was right   b) he could be creative in the items he included   c) he could figure out how to overcharge   d) he would be sure not to forget anything.

DRAWING CONCLUSIONS

7. The author says, "There are instincts that operate in all crises of life," to explain why:

   a) the Thénardiers could not help disliking Cosette

b) Cosette hid under the table   c) Jean Valjean knew where
to find Cosette   d) Cosette was not afraid of Jean Valjean.

USING YOUR REASON

8   The reason Jean Valjean bought Cosette the large pink doll
was probably that:
a) it was Christmas   b) she had admired it c) she could
have a friend   d) she would not need to play with Eponine
and Azelma's doll.

9.   Jean Valjean bought Cosette clothes that were all black out
of consideration for:
a) leaving the Thénardiers   b) her mother's death   c) Jean
Valjean's age   d) her escape.

THINKING IT OVER

10.   Jean Valjean tried several times to prevent Cosette from
being abused. Describe the actions he took during the
evening he spent at the tavern. Then summarize the effect
that these actions had on Cosette and Mme. Thénardier.

11.   Cosette was very useful to the Thénardiers. Why do you
think M. Thénardieeir agreed to sell her? Find some evidence from the book to support your opinion.

Chapters 3-5

FINDING THE MAIN IDEA

1.   Jean Valjean's and Cosette's arrival at a convent was very
fortunate because:
a) the police would not search a convent   b) Cosette could
attend school   c) Fauchelevent was gardener there
d) there would be work for Jean Valjean.   e) all of these

REMEMBERING DETAILS

2.   The old Gorbeau house can best be described as:
a) cozy. b) decrepit c) convenient d) well-kept.

3.   Jean Valjean and Cosette spent their time at the Gorbeau
house with Jean Valjean:
a) teaching Cosette to read   b) telling Cosette about her
mother c) teaching Cosette to pray.   d) all of these

4.   Javert was disguised as:
a) a gardener   b) a school teacher   c) a beggar   d) a priest.

5. Jean Valjean and Cosette leave the Gorbeau house after dark after:

   a) they see Javert on the street   b) they cannot pay the rent
   c) they hear someone listening at the door   d) they walk in the park.

6. Fauchelevent was involved with Jean Valjean's life earlier when:

   a) Jean Valjean was mayor of Montreuil   b) Jean Valjean saved his life   c) Jean Valjean was M. Madeleine.   d) all of these

DRAWING CONCLUSIONS

7 Fauchelevent calls Jean Valjean "ungrateful" because Jean Valjean:

   a) forgets the people whose lives he saves   b) does not believe that Fauchelevent will help him   c) does not care for Cosette   d) forgot about the Bishop.

USING YOUR REASON

8. Javert's presence can probably be attributed to:

   a) good police work   b) coincidence   c) Sister Simplice's confession.   d) none of these

9. The prioress agrees to let Jean Valjean and Cosette stay at the convent perhaps because:

   a) she owes Fauchelevent a favor   b) she needs more students at the convent   c) she is innocent   d) she likes Jean Valjean.

IDENTIFYING THE MOOD

10. As Jean Valjean and Cosette flee through the streets, the reader probably feels:

    a) anxious about how they will escape   b) confident that Javert will catch them   c) amused at the chase   d) afraid Cosette will give them away.   e) all of these

THINKING IT OVER

11. Cosette never had any experience in loving someone and being loved back. Victor Hugo says that Cosette "didn't lack the ability, only the opportunity." How is Jean Valjean like or unlike Cosette in this way? Find examples from the story to support your response.

BOOK 3: MARIUS

Chapters 1-5

FINDING THE MAIN IDEA

1. Marius's father's last instructions were for Marius to return the service to Thénardier, who:
a) ran a tavern at Montfermeil b) saved his life at Waterloo c) was sergeant in the army. d) all of these

REMEMBERING DETAILS

2. M. Gillenormand had very clear political beliefs. He could best be described as:
a) loyal to the king b) revolutionary c) fashionable
   religious   wealthy   anti-republican
   republican   fashionable   royalist

3. The emperor who named Pontmercy colonel, baron, and officer of the Legion of Honor was:
a) Napoleon b) Bourbon c) Louis XIV. d) none of these

4. Marius lived with his grandfather instead of his father because:
a) his father died at Waterloo b) his mother died leaving custody to her father c) his grandfather threatened to disown him d) his aunt wanted him.

5. Marius refused to take the money from his grandfather and aunt because:
a) he had a lot of money of his own b) he borrowed from his friends c) he wanted to live economically d) he was too proud to accept it.

6. M. Mabeuf and Marius became friends after they met at:
a) the Luxembourg b) the church Saint-Sulpice c) the bookstore d) the Cafe Musain.

DRAWING CONCLUSIONS

7. Marius was admitted to the bar; in other words, he:
a) could now become a revolutionary b) exercised regularly c) became a legitimate publisher d) was allowed to practice law.

8. Marius changed his mind about his father after he talked to:

   a) his stepmother b) his aunt c) M. Madeleine
   d) M. Mabeuf.

9. Marius probably chose to call himself Baron Pontmercy out of respect for the wishes of:

   a) his aunt b) his grandfather c) his father
   d) Napoleon.

THINKING IT OVER

10. Marius's political beliefs were like those of many students of the time. Rereading the chapters as necessary, as well as the historical background for the novel, list some important parts of Marius's beliefs. Contrast them to those of his grandfather.

Chapters 6-8

FINDING THE MAIN IDEA

1. Marius made a blunder in following Jean Valjean and Cosette home because it made Jean Valjean:

   a) suspicious b) angry c) amused. d) all of these

2. When Marius heard Jondrette tell that his name was really Thénardier, he felt:

   a) thunderstruck b) astounded c) unnerved. d) all of these

REMEMBERING DETAILS

3. When Marius returned to the Luxembourg after a six month absence, the girl had:

   a) moved away b) grown up c) become ill d) fallen in love.

4. Marius began to wear his best clothes when he:

   a) was on his way to work b) had his other suit cleaned
   c) went to the Luxembourg d) went to his father's grave.

5. The Patron-Minette were:

   a) a group of thugs b) a group of revolutionaries
   c) young students d) young boys who lived in the streets.

6. Victor Hugo uses a number of adjectives to describe Jondrette's room at the Gorbeau house, including:
a) filthy, smelly, uncomfortable   b) filthy, smelly, unfurnished   c) smelly, gloomy, cozy   d) smelly, filthy, gloomy.

7. Marius frightened Jondrette by using:
a) Javert's pistols   b) the door bell   c) Eponine's writing   d) a whistle.

DRAWING CONCLUSIONS

8   Thénardier called Jean Valjean the "cause of all my misfortunes." He particularly meant that Jean Valjean:
a) took Cosette away   b) only gave his family clothes   c) was the mayor   d) turned him in to Javert.

USING YOUR REASON

9. Unknowingly, Marius committed the biggest blunder of all. That was:
a) telling Javert about Jondrette's plan   b) going to the Luxembourg   c) keeping the pistols   d) asking Eponine to help him.

10. Jean Valjean and Cosette come to the Jondrettes' room to:
a) bring them warm clothes   b) clean their room   c) give them money   d) to befriend them.

THINKING IT OVER

11. In these chapters, Marius sees his beloved again. Then he hears Jondrette threaten to harm her and her father. Then he hears Jondrette tell his real name. Describe the emotions Marius probably feels as these actions unfold, and explain why his feelings change.

12. When Eponine offers to be useful to Marius, he asks her to do something for him. What is it? Do you think she will be successful? Cite evidence from the story to support your responses.

BOOK 4: SAINT-DENIS

Chapters 1-5

FINDING THE MAIN IDEA

1. Marius moved from the Gorbeau house very quickly. The reason was probably that he felt:
a) sad to have missed Cosette   b) torn in his feelings about Thénardier   c) confused about his political beliefs.

2. The house on the Rue Plumet was perfect for Jean Valjean and perfect for Marius to rendezvous with Cosette because:
a) it looked deserted   b) there were no neighbors   c) it was designed for secret entry.   d) all of these

REMEMBERING DETAILS

3. Javert made his arrests at the Gorbeau house, and the villains were sent to prison. However, by the end of these chapters:
a) everyone has been freed or has escaped   b) all the women are still in prison   c) all the men have escaped.

4. When Marius left the Gorbeau house, he went to live:
a) at the Field of the Lark   b) with Courfeyrac   c) in the Latin Quarter.   d) none of these

5. Marius got the money for Thénardier each month by:
a) working at the publishing house   b) borrowing from Laigle   c) using the money from his aunt   d) borrowing from Courfeyrac.

6. The person who appeared to help Father Mabeuf was:
a) Eponine   b) Madame Jondrette   c) Cosette   d) Azelma.

DRAWING CONCLUSIONS

7. Jean Valjean had a box Cosette called "the inseparable" because:
a) it was impossible for her to open it   b) it was never out of Jean Valjean's sight   c) he always took it with him when they moved.   d) none of these

USING YOUR REASON

8. For Marius to have borrowed money is important because:
a) he could not pay it back   b) he had never borrowed

money before   c) his father asked him to do it.   d) all of these

9. While Jean Valjean was away:
    a) Marius came to the garden   b) Cosette ran away
    c) Javert came to the house.   d) none of these

IDENTIFYING THE MOOD

10. Which word best describes Marius's attitude towards Jean Valjean?
    a) unaware   b) disliking   c) warm   d) respectful

THINKING IT OVER

11. Eponine continues to be important in this story. She makes things happen. Trace Eponine's involvement with Marius's affairs from the time she comes to his room at the Gorbeau house to the time he sees Cosette again. How would you sum up Eponine's role?

12. When Marius falls in love with Cosette, she lives at the Rue de l'Ouest. Although Marius does not know where she has moved, the reader does. Tell where the new house is, why it is so appropriate for Jean Valjean's purpose, and how Marius comes to find it.

Chapters 6-9

FINDING THE MAIN IDEA

1. Marius had one way to be able to stay with Cosette. That was to:
    a) ask Jean Valjean for permission to marry Cosette   b) ask his grandfather's permission to marry Cosette   c) ask Courfeyrac for more money.   d) none of these

REMEMBERING DETAILS

2. Marius went to the garden after ten o'clock because:
    a) Toussaint would be asleep   b) Cosette's "father" would be asleep   c) Marius had to work until then.   d) all of these

3. One evening Marius met someone he knew on the way to see Cosette. That person was:
    a) Jondrette   b) M. Mabeuf   c) Courfeyrac   d) Eponine.

4. Eponine sat by the gate at the Rue Plumet in order to:
   a) meet Marius b) meet Cosette c) meet her sister d) meet her father.
5. The six men came to the house on the Rue Plumet in order to:
   a) meet Eponine b) see the house c) rob the house d) rob Marius.
6. When Marius's grandfather thought about not seeing him again:
   a) the thought cheered him b) the thought chilled him
   c) the thought amused him d) the thought annoyed him.

DRAWING CONCLUSIONS

7. Eponine told her father, "You come near, I'll bark. I told you I'm the dog." She was trying to:
   a) make him laugh b) make him leave the house to her
   c) protect Marius and Cosette d) practice her ventriloquism.
8. When Marius said, "He is not a man who changes his habits," he meant:
   a) his father b) M. Mabeuf c) M. Gillenormand
   d) Jean Valjean.

USING YOUR REASON

9. When Marius saw Eponine, she was awkward, probably because:
   a) her father was going to rob the house b) she was embarrassed to have Marius see her c) Marius didn't speak to her. d) none of these
10. The grandfather disapproved Marius marrying Cosette because:
    a) she had no money b) the courtship was not according to custom c) Marius did not know the father. d) all of these reasons

IDENTIFYING THE MOOD

11. How would you describe the mood of the masses on the day of the General's funeral?
    a) joyful b) agitated c) frightened d) depressed

THINKING IT OVER

12. Marius and his grandfather do not understand each other.
    Describe how the grandfather feels toward Marius. Then
    contrast this with how Marius feels toward the old man.
    Use evidence from the text.

13. Jean Valjean decided to move from the Rue Plumet after
    some strange things happened in the garden. What strange
    things "put him on alert," and why? Why was he afraid?

14. The author says that "Paris was ready for a revolt," and
    the spark was the funeral of General Lamarque. What was
    it about the General that made his funeral touch off the
    revolts? Who are the four people who join the march in
    the last chapter of this group?

Chapters 10-13

FINDING THE MAIN IDEA

1. Eponine finally asked for her reward for helping Marius.
   It was:
   a) a kiss on the forehead   b) thirty francs   c) a promise to
   help her brother. d) all of these

2. Jean Valjean and Cosette have their first conflict over:
   a) what to take to England   b) moving away from the Rue
   Plumet   c) whether or not to bring Toussaint   d) Cosette's
   love for Marius.

REMEMBERING DETAILS

3. Chowder and Souffle were:
   a) dishes served at the Corinth   b) dishes M. Hucheloup
   invented   c) M. Hucheloup's daughters   d) waitresses at
   the Corinth.

4. The leader of the group marching through the streets was:
   a) Marius   b) Grantaire   c) Courfeyrac   d) Enjolras.

5. The barricade was made of:
   a) rubble   b) paving stones   c) vats   d) a wagon.   e) all of
   these

6. The man who had joined the group at Rue des Billettes was:
   a) M. Mabeuf   b) Inspector Javert   c) M. Gillenormand
   d) Eponine.

7. The voice the men heard singing was that of:
   a) Jean Valjean b) Mabeuf c) Gavroche d) Eponine.
8. When the flag fell, the man who put it back up was:
   a) Jean Valjean b) Marius c) Enjolras d) Mabeuf.
9. The person who stopped the bullet intended for Marius was:
   a) Eponine b) Gavroche c) Jean Valjean d) Javert.

DRAWING CONCLUSIONS

10. Marius thought that the voice that called him to the barricade was the "voice of destiny," meaning he was fated to:
    a) die at the barricade b) meet Eponine c) find Cosette's father d) record the events legally.
11. Marius was called the "savior" of the barricade because he repelled the soldiers when he threatened to:
    a) kill himself if the soldiers fired b) blow up the barricade c) kill Javert. d) none of these

USING YOUR REASON

12. The advantage of two barricades was that:
    a) there could be an escape b) that would fool the soldiers c) they could surround the Corinth. d) none of these
13. Marius sent Gavroche to take the letter to Cosette in order to:
    a) save Cosette b) save Father Mabeuf c) save Enjolras d) save Gavroche.

THINKING IT OVER

14. The author tells everything Eponine did to help Marius. Review these actions, and state what you believe her motivation was. Judge Marius's treatment of Eponine. Was it appropriate? Find details from the text to support your opinion.
15. At the end of these chapters, Jean Valjean goes to the barricade with a loaded gun. Do you think he will kill Marius? Recall that when Jean Valjean discovered Cosette had written to Marius he was horribly shaken. Consider what Cosette means to him.

BOOK 5: JEAN VALJEAN

Chapters 1-3

FINDING THE MAIN IDEA

1. Just as he let Javert go, Jean Valjean told him:
   a) they would meet again b) where he lived c) he forgave him d) he would kill him the next time they met.
2. Jean Valjean decided to save Marius rather than let him die, probably because:
   a) he had come to respect Marius b) he knew Cosette loved him c) he is incapable of letting someone die.
   d) all of these reasons
3. Javert ended his life by:
   a) jumping off the train b) jumping out of the carriage c) jumping into the river d) going back to the barricade.

REMEMBERING DETAILS

4. At the barricade in the Rue de la Chanvrerie, there were people numbering:
   a) more than one hundred b) more than three thousand
   c) less than twenty d) less than forty.
5. The soldiers in the Rue Saint-Denis numbered:
   a) in the hundreds b) in the thousands c) about two hundred d) only five.
6. The man who went to get the mattress to protect against the grapeshot was:
   a) Gavroche b) Jean Valjean c) Combeferre
   d) Courfeyrac.
7. Gavroche left the barricade to:
   a) get the mattress b) steal food for the men c) get cartridges from the dead soldiers d) take uniforms from the dead soldiers.
8. Jean Valjean took the injured Marius away. They went:
   a) into the small barricade b) to Marius's grandfather's house c) into the sewers d) into the rivers

DRAWING CONCLUSIONS

9. When Jean Valjean returns to the barricade after taking Javert away, he says, "Done." By that, he means for the men to think:
   a) he has released the man   b) he has killed the man
   c) he has turned the man over to the soldiers   d) his job at the barricade is finished.

10. The author says that Javert was "tormented." His torment was due to:
    a) his situation   b) his health   c) his age   d) his friends.

USING YOUR REASON

11. The tall man in the buttoned-up coat who was tracking the man who disappeared was probably:
    a) Thénardier   b) Gillenormand   c) Gavroche   d) Javert.

12. The five men left the barricade because they:
    a) had families to care for   b) had no money to give to the cause   c) were afraid to stay   d) did not want to die.

13. Jondrette knew that Javert was waiting for him outside the sewer, so he let Jean Valjean go out to be caught.
    a) true   b) false   c) There is no way to know from the story.

IDENTIFYING THE MOOD

14. When Enjolras returned to the barricade after looking around, the mood in the barricade became:
    a) frightened   b) resentful   c) determined   d) amused.

THINKING IT OVER

15. When Enjolras does a reconnaissance and reports that the men at the barricade are abandoned, a voice cries out: "Let's show them that, even if the people abandon the republicans, the republicans do not abandon the people." Who are the republicans, and who are the people. Why might the people have abandoned the republicans?

16. Gavroche taunted the soldiers who fired at him. Do you think he believed he could survive, or do you think he knew he would die? Study the actions of Gavroche, and choose three adjectives to describe him.

17. Why did Javert let Jean Valjean go? Recall the interactions between the two men in these chapters, and form a supported response. Then consider Javert's personality and decide whether, having let Valjean go, Javert had any choice about his fate.

Chapters 4-8

FINDING THE MAIN IDEA

1. Marius made his grandfather very happy by:
   a) calling him "father"   b) bringing Cosette to live in the house   c) being married at the house.   d) all of these

2. Cosette agreed to receive her "father" in the ground floor room because she:
   a) respected his wishes   b) was ashamed of him   c) knew Marius did not want him in the house.   d) none of these

REMEMBERING DETAILS

3. M. Gillenormand made some inquiries while Marius was recovering. The inquiries were about:
   a) Jean Valjean   b) Cosette   c) Théodule   d) the students at the barricade.

4. Jean Valjean gave the money to Cosette so that:
   a) Marius would marry her   b) the grandfather would accept her   c) she could have everything she wanted   d) she would not come to the marriage with nothing.

5. The money had come from:
   a) the jet glass business   b) robbing Lafitte's   c) selling the bishop's silver   d) Fantine's work.

6. Marius continued to try to find:
   a) the man who had saved his life   b) the man who had saved his father's life.   c) both of these people   d) neither of these people

DRAWING CONCLUSIONS

7. The "inseparable" turned out to be:
   a) the candlesticks   b) Cosette's pink doll   c) Cosette's clothes   d) Thénardier's coat.

8. M. Gillenormand gave Cosette away because:
   a) Jean Valjean had hurt his arm   b) Jean Valjean had told
   Marius the truth   c) Jean Valjean asked him to.   d) none of
   these
9. Marius found out the truth about who saved him through:
   a) Eponine   b) Thénardier   c) Basque   d) a letter from
   Javert.

USING YOUR REASON

10. Jean Valjean pretended to hurt his hand so that:
    a) he didn't have to sign his name   b) he didn't have to
    give Cosette away   c) he did not have to have his prints
    taken.
11. Jean Valjean left the wedding dinner because:
    a) his hand was too painful   b) he was not hungry
    c) it was too painful for him to see Cosette with Marius
    d) he had to go home to get the dowry money.
12. Jean Valjean asked to see Cosette every day because:
    a) he loved her   b) he wanted to protect her   c) he brought
    her money   d) he knew she needed to see him.
13. Jean Valjean stopped coming to see Cosette because:
    a) he knew she was too busy   b) he knew Marius didn't
    want him there   c) he knew his visits made her unhappy
    d) the visits made him too unhappy.

THINKING IT OVER

14. Why do you think Jean Valjean told Marius the truth about
    who he was? And why did he not tell Marius who had
    saved him? Consider whether any other action would have
    been consistent with the personality and motivations of
    Jean Valjean. If so, what might it have been?
15. Think carefully about Jean Valjean's decision not to live
    with Cosette and Marius. What were his reasons? Do you
    think he was happy with his decision? Do you think he
    should have made a different decision? Form your
    response, considering the personalities and motivations of
    the three people.
16. Victor Hugo wrote about Cosette and Marius's marriage:
    "It is terrible to be happy! How all-sufficient it is! Being
    in possession of the false aim of life, happiness, we forget

the true aim: duty!" Do you agree that happiness is the false aim of life? Do you agree that duty is the real aim? Do you think Cosette and Marius renounced their duty to Jean Valjean? Do you think Jean Valjean thought so?

17. Do you think that Jean Valjean died a happy man? Support your response with details about that character's personality, actions, and words